Voices for the Future
Volume Three

Voices for the Future
Volume Three

Thomas D. Clareson
Thomas L. Wymer

Bowling Green University Popular Press
Bowling Green, Ohio 43403

Contents

Introduction

This volume of *Voices for the Future* continues the series begun by Bowling Green University Popular Press in 1976. It is, however, the first collection to include studies of major writers of fantasy as well as science fiction, a fact which in itself may say something about the development of the field in recent years. Unfortunately its publication has been somewhat delayed by circumstances that neither Bowling Green Press nor I could control. Hopefully it will be followed in the near future by a group of studies concentrating upon some of the earlier writers of sf and fantasy whom contemporary critics have neglected.

October 1983

Variations and Design:
The Fiction of Gene Wolfe*

Thomas D. Clareson

To say that since Gene Wolfe began publishing in the mid-1960s he has developed into one of the finest writers of science fiction in America states a simple truth but at the same time ignores his versatility. He first established himself in the magazine *Worlds of If*, and, especially, in Damon Knight's *Orbit* anthology series with a number of short stories, many of them no more than five or six pages long. An early novel, *Operation ARES* (1970), perhaps written as early as 1967, gained little critical notice, but in the same year his story "The Island of Dr. Death" narrowly missed receiving a Nebula Award. Critical attention came with the publication of *The Fifth Head of Cerberus* (1972), a trio of inter-related novellas which can be read as a novel and which grew out of the title story, originally published (1972) in *Orbit*. Significantly, Wolfe dedicated that volume "to Damon Knight, who one well-remembered June evening in 1966 grew me from a bean." The following year his third nomination gained him a Nebula for "The Death of Dr. Island" (1973), certainly one of his most "hard core" sf stories.

In sharp contrast to these works, he published *Peace* (1975), which was marketed/blurbed as a mainstream novel and in 1977 won a prize from the Chicago Foundation of Literature. It brings to mind Proust's *Remembrance of Things Past*. Relying upon the first-person point of view, Wolfe probes the imagination of its protagonist, Alden Dennis Weer, an isolated old man apparently recovering from a stroke in a small midwestern town. By necessity something of a recluse, he leads a seemingly uneventful life. Yet especially because he himself is the narrator, he is able to bring together autobiographical incident, disregard rigid time relationships by moving through patterns of association, sketch characters whom he has known, and introduce diverse stories and myths which he has read. As a result *Peace* reveals one of the most

---

*The discusssion of Wolfe's *The Book of the New Sun* appeared in *Extrapolation*, 23 (Fall 1982), 270-274.

1

penetrating studies of character in recent fiction by exposing the richness and complexity of Weer's inner life as he explores his awareness of, and his attempt to understand, himself and his world. Although *Peace* has been judged a mainstream novel, in a recent interview Wolfe has suggested that it is actually a fantasy (or perhaps one should say that its basic technique is that of fantasy so that Wolfe can escape the restrictions of realism); he asserted that the "basic idea is that a man has died and he is haunting his own mind...." The novel opens with the assertion that an elm tree fell the night before. Near the end of the book a woman asks Weer if she may plant an elm tree on his grave after he dies:

...the old legend is—if there's a tree on a grave, when the tree falls, the falling of the tree releases a ghost on the Earth. In *Peace*, that ghost prowls through his memories throughout the book.[1]

Several things about this statement seem important. First, as Wolfe points out, few if any of the critics of *Peace* caught this subtlety, perhaps because the device is not essential to an appreciation of the basic accomplishment of the book or perhaps because the critics were too inured to the conventions of psychological realism. Secondly, it illustrates how slight may be Wolfe's reliance upon fantasy (or the obvious furniture of science fiction) in any given narrative. One thinks, for example, of the brief "Continuing Westward" (1973), which can almost pass as a realistic anecdote of World War One. Most importantly, however, *Peace* remains central to anyone's awareness that for Wolfe what happens is seldom as important as the effect(s) it has. In short, his primary concern has always been with character.

His explanation of what he regards as the central idea of *Peace* helps to explain what otherwise must appear a radical shift in interest, for within a year he published *The Devil in a Forest* (1976), a fantasy vividly evoking life in a medieval forest village, although it does not have a strong sense of specific time or place. In concentrating upon the youthful apprentice Mark, he has created a tale having a universal quality. One associates it with the tradition of *Everyman* and the morality plays as Wolfe probes the unchanging nature of violence and evil, of the real and demonic, as these characteristics impinge upon the consciousness of the youthful protagonist learning of the adult world.

Something of this medieval tone colors *The Book of the New Sun*. The tone is perhaps most noticeable in *The Shadow of the Torturer* (1980), the initial portion of this complex work. The tetralogy is simultaneously the autobiography of Severian, a member of the Guild of the Torturers, whose function is to administer punishment to political prisoners, particularly those of the Autarch, and an account of his odyssey/quest as he travels across Urth to return a religious relic to the order of the Pelerines.

To emphasize these novels by themselves, however, distorts any account of the body of Wolfe's fiction. The bulk of his work is made up of short stories—some, as mentioned, no more than a few pages long—and novellas. The same variety which characterizes the novel marks his shorter fiction. "La Befana" (1973), for example, is cast as a dialogue between an alien and an Earthman about the harshness of life at the very moment when the Nativity may be taking place on their planet. The narrator of "Car Sinister" (1970) tells of an Aston Martin which provides a stud service for automobiles. In "Cues" (1974) aliens resembling bowling balls promise to help a not-so-young Earthman become a successful cartoonist, but this slight tale really exists for its final pun. In both "Slaves of Silver" (1971) and "The Rubber Bend" (1974) Wolfe substitutes the robot bio-mechanic Westing (so named because Westinghouse had gone out of fashion when he was assembled) for the amiable Dr. Watson in two parodies of Sherlock Holmes. Nor should one forget such a Jamesian tale as "Kevin Malone" (1980), in which the narrator tells how he and his wife are hired to care for the country estate of the mysterious Malone. It is a tale concerned with identity and appearances, as well as very existence, instead of the more obvious devices of contemporary sf and fantasy.

Perhaps the true genius of Wolfe lies in the fact that no one narrative mode, no recurrent character, and no single theme or plotline dominates his fiction, as so often occurs in the work of many of his contemporaries. Simple cautionary projections into a dystopian future; quests after exotic adventures, whatever be the world; finding the solution to some problem, however momentous— none of these patterns makes up the principal substance of Wolfe's stories. Even when his narratives move into the realm of fantasy, much of the furniture of science fiction remains visible. But most often it forms part of a richly textured background whose central interest lies elsewhere, be the purpose serious or humorous. Nor is some neat resolution Wolfe's forte (dare one say, intention?); ambiguity, irony, the ending that opens the door of implications— these loom among the objectives he seeks and achieves.

Wolfe's success lies in his ability to manipulate and control his material through narrative technique and style. He seems to have an uncanny ability to discern how a story should be told in order to gain its fullest effect (it does not come easy, however; he has acknowledged rewriting a story several times from several points of view before deciding on an acceptable version). The slight—not more than four pages in print—almost whimsical "Against the Lafayette Escradrillé" (1972), first published in Harlan Ellison's *Again, Dangerous Visions*, provides a case in point. It turns upon one of the most shopworn science fiction devices, the time-warp. Most simply, the first line informs the reader that the plot will focus upon a man who builds "a perfect replica of a Fokker triplane, except for the flammable dope."[2] One spring day while flying it, he encounters a balloon whose passenger is a lovely girl dressed in crinolines and possessing long chestnut curls. He realizes that she is in the balloon made by the women of Richmond from their silks during the last days of the Civil War. She blows him a kiss, but he must leave because his fuel is exhausted. Though he often tries, never again does he meet her.

To begin with, the story must be told from the first-person point of view so that the reader can share the experience, both intellectual and emotional, of the protagonist. Yet it is the matter-of-fact tone of the prose—the understatement—with which the narrator gives his account of the events that sets the tone of the narrative. Wolfe juxtaposes a full account of the building and maintenance of the Fokker against a brief report of the encounter with the balloon. One can recall a number of classic stories in which such a meeting has led to high adventure and pulsating romance. But the quiet manner of Wolfe's narrator disguises the emotional impact of the experience. Only when he explains that "I go up almost every day when the weather makes it possible" and when he wonders whether or not "things would have been different if ... I had used the original, flammable dope"[3] does the reader gain a full sense of the protagonist's anguish and sense of loss. The final reinforcement occurs when he remarks, almost casually, "She was so authentic." Then the reader understands that building the Fokker itself was the escape of a lonely man and that the brief warp in time offered a promise which can never be fulfilled. In short, the prose style and the point of view have given new complexity and vitality to an old storyline by revealing the inner state of the character.

Often the stories appear deceptively simple, a characteristic which makes their impact—their irony—more effective. "Paul's Tree House" (1969) takes the form of a dialogue between suburban neighbors, Russell and Morris, which seems primarily concerned with the fact that Morris' young son has isolated himself in a tree house. Russell in particular argues that Paul should be compelled to come down and then be disciplined. As the two men sip morning whiskey, Russell indicates that he cannot climb the tree because of his heart condition. They do, however, erect a ladder which covers some twenty of the fifty feet to the sanctuary, and Morris does scale the quivering ladder, though he realizes that he cannot climb farther. The reader learns incidentally that Paul has taken pails of rocks up to the tree house. At first glance, then, this narrative has the potential of a realistic portrayal of the inability of children and adults to communicate, for even Paul's father has no inkling of his son's motivation.

To this basic, all-too-familiar frame, Wolfe adds the dimension of science fiction by sketching in the outlines of a dystopian future. His first sentence announces that "It was the day after the governor called out the National Guard...."[4] Yet the two men would go about their normal affairs, just as Morris' wife would go shopping early to escape the heat. Russell refers to rioters and the killing of a policeman in the street, while once Morris is up the ladder he notes that "Something big's burning."[5]

To emphasize the social turmoil, Wolfe inserts the radio announcement that a demonstration by members of the Citizens for Peace has been disrupted by the American Nazi Party. As a gang in a stake-bed truck appears and begins to beat up Morris, Paul tries to defend his father by futilely throwing rocks from his retreat high above the fighting. The sickeningly violent future is upon the reader, but it provides the means by which to criticize a middle class which seems to have become oblivious—perhaps inured—to the wreckage of the twentieth century world. The action of Paul, whose age is never explicitly given, becomes symbolic in that it shows not only his awareness of what is going on but measures the extent to which he vainly tries to escape a world he never made. And yet his gesture—throwing stones—is futile against the forces at work which he does not understand. Again the choice of narrative technique has become an essential factor to the story's success. The scene must be dramatized so that the reader sees (and hears) only surfaces, while the child must be kept off-stage to emphasize the impotence of innocence.

In contrast, "The Recording" (1972) presents the reflections of a first-person narrator, an old man in poor health, who has listened for the first time to a record which was given him some fifty years earlier by a favorite uncle. He explains that in his youth his parents refused to let him use the new phonograph for fear that he would "scratch the delicate wax discs."[6] His uncle promised to buy him a record of his own, but as the two walked to the shop on Main

Street,the older man complained of feeling ill. After demanding the necessary money, the boy left him on a bench, promising to bring back a doctor. His uncle died, and the narrator admits that he actually hid the record because he was afraid it would be his uncle's voice pleading for help. Now, at last, his guilty imagination has realized how silly his superstition has been, for Rudy Vallee sings "My Time Is Your Time." Any angle of narration would have conveyed the narrator's thoughtless cruelty, but the first-person was essential so that the reader understands how oblivious the narrator is to the final irony.

In "Thou Speck of Blood" (1970) Wolfe dramatizes the dilemma of Gibson, one of three astronauts outward bound toward Mars, when he awakens to find that his companion Cappio has had his throat slashed. The third man, Lorenz, accuses him of the murder. Various malfunctions—a dead radio, the breakdown of the deodorizer—have intensified the claustrophobic effects of being confined in the capsule. Gibson kills Lorenz to protect himself and radios a message both explaining his action and expressing his intention to remain on Mars. When the disposer breaks so that he cannot get rid of the bodies, he leaves them in their spacesuits until the stench leads him to discover that Cappio had punctured his and Lorenz's suits and possibly committed suicide. Only after the ship lands does Gibson learn that this has been a similated flight never leaving Moonbase. Although this is an early story, one may fault Wolfe for not allowing Moonbase to know what was happening to the astronauts. There should have been some monitoring system. Yet one may counter by emphasizing that the malfunctions were part of a deliberate experiment and that the personnel at Moonbase, with the ship secure before their eyes, could not imagine the effects of the journey on the three men. The omniscient point of view is essential because this is a plot story with a shock ending; moreover, Gibson's actions and remarks will give an adequate insight into his state of mind.

In "When I Was Ming the Merciless" (1976) Wolfe uses still a different narrative technique to gain much the same effect of shock and horror. The story is presented as the dramatic monologue of a character responding to the questions and remarks of his interrogator. One knows almost at once that he has been the leader of a rebel faction, that at least three groups of rebels have fought among themselves, and that the authorities have finally gained control. Gradually, the reader learns that he is listening to the account (confession seems an inappropriate word because of the attitude of the narrator) of a student revolt which took place at some school, some university. The irony occurs because, as in "Thou Speck of Blood," the revolt was a deliberately staged experiment in behavioral psychology whose results the authorities could not imagine. A second complication in the irony arises from the fact that the students were divided into three factions—the Yellows, Greens and Blues, each individual being identified by a bracelet which could not be removed—who were given the problem of how to deal with highly limited resources and "so many groups of people." (One can only guess the number of actual classes, both high school and college, in which this simulated problem has been played with since the mid-1960s.)

"When I Was Ming the Merciless" demands the narrative technique which Wolfe used, because while the workings of the protagonist's mind are not of primary importance (he undoubtedly is mad), the monologue does focus upon and reveal the state of mind of the young leader, a political science major (the other students, he recalls, were mostly psychology and sociology majors). Moreover, the dramatization of the revolt itself would de-emphasize the effect of and reaction to the abortive experiment; it must be presented as something in the past. The monologue is effective because it allows the student to reveal with pride how efficiently the Yellows conquered the other two groups and established a totalitarian order in which each individual knew exactly how much food, drinking water and bathing water each was allowed. He became the leader of the Empire—first called Mongolia—and refers to the torchlight parades and the strength given the group by its symbol, Ling-Run, two dragons fighting. These details call up other political horrors, but Wolfe perhaps achieves the height of his effectiveness when the leader casually remarks that members of the Yellows often "talked about our lives before the experiment. Each of us would tell the rotten things that happened...."[7] Only through such an allusion can the reader sense both the rottenness of society as it exists and the appeal that an order like the Empire might have. Early in the story the student expresses the desire to discuss the morality of what occurred, and at last he acknowledges that he can "understand" the reactions of the school, the public, and the President to what happened; but on the other hand, those persons cannot realize what the Yellows "went through together"; nor can they know what it was like to be Ming the Merciless. Thus, on several levels at least, society has created this Frankenstein. That the student took as his title the name of the Emperor of Mongo in the Flash Gorden stories of the 1930s represents one device that Wolfe has used repeatedly as he has explored the strange mixture of reality and the unreal in which his characters (and readers) live.

In such stories as this, Wolfe's basic method is to reveal a fixed state of mind in an individual oblivious to, or divorced from, reality. One of his outstanding efforts at this type of story occurs in "An Article on Hunting" (1973), his treatment of the mythic bear hunt running back through American literature from Faulkner through the folktales of the Old Southwest. The objectivity of the first person narrator, a newspaperman, heightens the ironies of his report of the efforts of the "District Commissioner of Ecology" to rid the area of a bear which "has been doing a great deal of damage"[8] by eating apples, many already groundfalls. The reader learns that grizzlies have been exterminated—poisoned—because they killed sheep; the puppies of a hound, Sweet Sue, have been drowned; and a scampering rabbit has its back broken by a thrown stick, though it is allowed to crawl away. When the bear is finally cornered, the supply of anesthetic darts is exhausted on him; yet in case this dose is not adequate, the Commissioner—"always solicitous of the welfare of anyone connected with his department"[9]—insists that one of his colleagues club the unconscious bear with a rock. Such details are incidental to a straightforward account of the hunt, and they provide the backdrop for the newsman's exclamation wondering where else he could find such companionship, such sport. By his use of the pervasive myth, calling up as it does the heroic mode, Wolfe intensifies his condemnation of present/near future society.

Others of his stories, such as "Three Million Square Miles" (1971), concentrate upon the growth of a protagonist's obsession. In this brief tale Richard Marquer reads that some ninety percent of the United States is not employed "in agriculture nor as sites for roads or buildings."[10] He begins to search for this empty land by driving randomly through the countryside. Finally finding an open space between two interstate highways, he loses his bearings and the reader last sees him alone, terrified, on the shoulder of the highway. Similarly, in "How the Whip Came Back" (1970), Wolfe focuses upon a Miss Bushman, an alternate delegate to the United Nations Conference on Human Values; she must decide how to vote on a resolution which would "lease" all persons held in prison, American or otherwise, as laborers to the highest bidders. The American representative pleads for her support because such a procedure would be good business, saving the government and public millions of dollars a year. She is promised that she may lease her husband, now in prison, and in her fantasies she sees him, naked to the waist, in bronze manacles. (The Pope, another alternate, evades the issue by going to the funeral of the last nun so that he will be absent on the day of the vote.)

Most frequently, usually because of the brevity of the early stories, Wolfe focuses upon a single character. One of the major exceptions occurs in "Trip, Trap" (1967), the first of his works published by Damon Knight in the *Orbit* series. The body of the narrative moves back and forth between the reports of a young Earthman, a recent recipient of an advanced degree in Extraterrestrial Archeology, who has been sent to investigate a little known planet, and the consciousness of Garth, a warrior inhabitant of that planet whose society recalls Earth's barbarian hordes. They encounter a troll ("traki") considered an odd curiosity by Finch, the archeologist, and a monster by Garth. Neither narrator comprehends that the troll is a representative of an ancient race which has travelled the stars. Nor, of course, can they understand the actions of one another. Both men perceive themselves and the actions around them very differently, and each acts out his own role according to his cultural training. Thus, Finch acts strictly according to the textbook; Garth, to the customs of the country. The result, particularly because the reader sees Finch through his notebook entries, emphasizes the pedantry and ethnocentricity of the Earthman.

One of the finest of his brief early tales is "Sweet Forest Maid" (1971), strangely neglected in the two recent anthologies of his shorter fiction. In it he concentrates upon the actions of a thirty-three-year-old spinster, Lenor Stacy, as she abandons her humdrum business life to go into the Klamath Forest of Northern California to find "The Adorable Woods Woman." This name has been given the latest sighting of Sasquatch or Big Foot by the man who photographed her "in the hope that this appealing title would dissuade other lovers of the outdoors from shooting her."[11] Wolfe uses Lenor and her actions as a means of attacking society as a whole to show how it has broken its relationship with nature: "At no time did she show interest in hunting, fishing, hiking, camping or any of the other woodsy pastimes that had sprung up like mushrooms on the dead roots of nature."[12]

Lenor is much more than a device for social criticism, however, because Wolfe transforms her into a symbol of the desperate isolation of contemporary mankind. Thus, for the most part he keeps her at a distance, watching her actions. Seldom does she speak for herself (thus emphasizing the lack of communication), and when she does, she speaks *to* herself. Only once does Wolfe allow her more than a single remark. As she responds to the picture of the Woods Woman, she thinks:

> *That thing in your mind is not a gorilla's face. You think words,
> and the things behind the words change until they are no longer
> what they were. That stupid mask in your mind is fantasy, the
> bad, uncaring joke of some Hollywood prop man.*[13]

She goes to the zoo to watch a real gorilla and comes to know its
"wise, sad look." She decides to "do something—just once...." For
the most part Wolfe will tell the reader what must be known to
achieve the symbolic level, as when he explains that Lenor "often
spoke to no one at all from Friday afternoon to Monday morning."[14]
Whatever has caused her to identify with the Woods Woman sends
her up State Route 96 past the little town of Happy Camp. She leaves
her car, plunges into the forest, is lost within days, and develops a
fever. When she finally meets the creature who is the Woods Woman,
she hopes for help, but Wolfe is the one who tells the reader that
Lenor does not know what to say. By keeping her primarily at an
objective distance in the third person (to the extent that no scenes
are dramatized so that he can better condense and speed up the
narration, as well as making Lenor less an individual), Wolfe has
achieved one of his most successful statements regarding the
isolation of mankind in the modern world.

This story also illustrates another of Wolfe's methods.
Parenthetically or not, he will directly intrude his comment or
address the reader. Here, for example, after mentioning the little
town of Happy Camp, he remarks, "(where are you, Bret Harte?)"[15].
At the end of "Melting" (1975), a story in which a wealthy man calls
up assorted beings from time so that they can attend one of his
parties, each guest disappears as the sun rises; when the host
himself vanishes, Wolfe tells the reader, "I was tired of him anyhow.
(I'm getting tired of all of you.")[16] This is another way he has of
reminding his audience that they are dealing with fiction—and
therefore symbol—rather than any literal reality.

On occasion neither the characters nor the action are so
important as the background. Wolfe relies upon this method when
his chief concern is social criticism. An early example occurs in "Of
Relays and Roses" (1970), staged as a Congressional hearing
against a corporation which has brought computerization into the
finding of a marriage partner and provides the service free to its
clients. So successful have they been in bringing about happy
marriages and avoiding both divorces and husbands' early deaths
that the government has brought suit against them because marital
stability threatens the economy.

Wolfe's most notable use of this technique makes a delightful satire of his recent "A Criminal Proceeding" (1980). The first sentence announces the arrest of Stephen Brodie. A straight-faced, first-person narrator—who brings to mind the narrator of "An Article About Hunting," for example—thoroughly details the public reaction and the trial; but the exact nature of Brodie's crime is never specified, although casual details, like the testimony of six chiefs of state, imply that it must be something on a par with Watergate. In this narrative one senses Wolfe's delight as he strikes out in all directions in what must be one of the most hilarious accounts of any American legal action. His targets range from media coverage to the public's reaction to the appointment of Charles Hop Sing to the jury; judged to be a "surrender to demands of the male-grocer-oriental-American community," this selection leads to "renewed violence among the Garment Workers, culminating in the Third Avenue brassiere march...."[17] The narrator reports the necessary year-long refurbishing of the Bronco Stadium Complex to serve as a courtroom (of course members of teams playing there received adequate compensation). Then, too, after appropriate Congressional action, the President and "seventeen simulcra of herself imported from Disneyworld-Havana"[18] sign a mandatory death sentence on certain of the counts brought against Brodie. Still not satisfied, Wolfe builds to an open ending which has religious connotations. (One might note that increasingly in Wolfe's recent fiction, as early as the warden in "The Doctor of Death Island" (1978), many of the persons in authority are women. In "Looking-Glass Castle" (1980) he creates an America in which women dominate and what few men remain are fugitives.)

Perhaps the best way to measure Wolfe's ability to control and manipulate his material is to show how he builds upon a single idea in four very different stories which he did for Roger Elwood's *Continuum* series. In the first of these, "The Dark of June" (1974), Wolfe concentrates upon the reactions of a father whose daughter June has decided to disincarnate—to resign from humanity by passing over into a non-material existence. Although the world of the 1990s does not seem particularly dystopian and although neither wishes to hurt the other, there is some suggestion of a lack of communication between father and daughter. Also since disincarnation is confined primarily to persons under thirty, it seems the latest fashionable thing to do. The story evokes a mild pathos as she leaves him, both acknowledging that in this way neither will see the other dead.

The sequel—"The Death of Hyle" (1974)—again focuses upon

June's father but transforms him to a first-person narrator so that the narrative may make more accessible his emotional reactions and his musings about the insubstantiality of the universe. The action centers on his decision to go to the withdrawal center and pass over. Whether or not he persuades the attendants that he is only twenty-nine, he is administered to and does become one of the N.I.N. ("the not in nature"). Obviously he wants to be reunited with his daughter, but the ending is left ambiguous, open, for June seems to be in hysteria, while a second woman—Laurel—warns him of a creature named Thag.

The principal way in which the third of the series, "From the Notebook of Dr. Stein" (1974), differs radically from the other stories is that it is presented as the dictaphone recording of an interview between the "alienist" Dr. Stein and a young woman identified as DW or Donna, who is possessed by the creature Thag, as well as Laurel Baker, June Nailer, and her father, the protagonist of the other stories. The three patiently explain to Stein that they are trying to rid the young woman of Thag, who is non-human and has seized upon her as a source of energy. They have apparently travelled back in time to the 1920s or 30s from the implications of Dr. Stein's allusions to the work of Cerletti and Bini in Italy and Dr. Huer in the comics. Stein, of course, cannot comprehend their explanations and subjects the girl to shock treatment, thereby killing her. On a very different level, then, Wolfe has explored the problem of communication.

If this handling of the basic idea moves more toward "orthodox" science fiction, then the last tale, "Thag" (1975), moves toward fantasy. Wolfe adopts the framework of the fairy tale, beginning "Once upon a time," as he tells how the boy Eric, with the aid of the spirit Thag—who dwells in a bear's skull when he is present—seizes control of the kingdom and rules for thirty years. One night Laurel, June and her father make their appearance. They are mistaken for Norse gods. When her father asks where they are, June explains that they are in a book—because that is "not more impossible than going backward in time."[19] When Thag appears as a headless, bleeding bear, they refuse to kill him because this time and place is one of low energy and Thag obviously wishes to escape from it. June's father nails Thag's foot to the floor. And Eric rules happily ever after, obeying instructions not to release Thag.

Signficantly, the fourth story does not bring the action to a final end. The potential of at least another tale is there. As a group the stories are important because they indicate how the same idea may be manipulated from a comparatively realistic problem to a fairy tale rich with puns. "Thag" itself has importance on at least two counts. First, Wolfe allows the discussion of its being fiction (a book), during which Laurel explains that "There must be a world that corresponds to each of our fictions, dear, since what never was nor will be is inconceivable."[20] Secondly, this is one of Wolfe's first uses of a medieval setting, a choice that would seem to move deliberately away from science fiction toward fantasy, although here he blends the two of them together very well. The debate as to the nature of fiction, for example, as well as the importance of the energy level of the world prevent the abandonment of the contemporary world which has happened too often when sf writers have permitted characters to travel backward in time.

Wolfe's skill in elaborating a basic idea by changing his perspective toward it is perhaps even more effectively shown in the subtle complexities of *The Fifth Head of Cerberus* (1972). As Peter Nicholls has pointed out, the original novella was finished in 1970 and its expansion to novel length was immmediately contracted for so that the original and the novel (developed by having two new, separate stories added) were published in the same year.[21] Thus, just as Wolfe was able to work on the N.I.N./Thag material in a concentrated period of time, so was he able to explore the implications of "The Fifth Head of Cerberus" even before it saw publication. In the initial phase of the narrative, then, through the memories the first person narrator has of his boyhood and youth, Wolfe creates a richly textured portrait of the town of Port-Mimizon on the planet Sainte Croix. The French flavor results because both Sainte Croix and its sister planet Sainte Anne were initially colonized by the French, who have been pushed into the background by a subsequent wave of colonists. Nicholls has suggested that Port Mimizon is "not unlike" eighteenth century New Orleans: "attractive, sensual, cruel," its culture being hierarchical and based on a slave economy.[22] The central action of the novella involves the narrator's murder of his father when the boy discovers that he is the fifth in a line of clones. Thus, whatever other symbolism one may find especially because of the materialistic nature of the society, the basic issue deals with the problem of identity.

Increasingly, this issue grows into the dominant concern of the book, but because the subsequent stories rely upon/tie into what has gone before, the answer—if one may call it that—becomes increasingly ambiguous. The narrator is helped in discovering that he is a clone by a visiting anthropologist whose interest is with the aborigines ("abos") of Sainte Anne's, a supposedly extinct race thought to have been capable of "shape-changing." The anthropologist, Dr. John V. Marsch, denies that he has come from Sainte Anne; yet he visits the home of the narrator because the boy's Aunt Jeannine—herself a distinguished anthropologist, Dr. Audrey Veil—has advanced the theory ("Veil's Hypothesis") that the aborigines took possession of the original settlers so that now there are few, if any, human beings.

A second novella, " 'A Story' by John V. Marsch," shifts to the ancient past of Sainte Anne and tells of the aborigine, Sandwalker, who journeys across the wastes of the planet to find his brother, Eastwind, long ago kidnapped by marshmen. As he crosses the planet, he meets the so-called "Shadow Children," who may or may not be human; their stories concerning their origins conflict. In their death throes, however, the Shadow Children influence a starship so that it lands. Although the last Shadow child, declaring that his are a "magic people," would cause Sandwalker to be Eastwind and Eastwind, Sandwalker, his action is brought to nothing when Sandwalker drowns Eastwind. As a result he is not certain who he is, but he goes to the shore and meets the men from the starship. Nowhere is there any explanation of the relationship of Marsch to these materials. Is the story a figment of his imagination or, somehow, a documentary drawing upon racial memory?

The third novella, "V.R.T.," provides a possible solution. An army officer reads through the diary of a prisoner, Marsch, who may be a spy and a murderer (he was mistakenly arrested originally for the murder committed by the narrator of "The Fifth Head of Cerberus," but he may have killed an individual, V.R. Trenchard, who claimed abo descent). Marsch is the anthropologist who wanted to study the abos, and he did take young Trenchard on an expedition into the back country. Although the officer reading the diary cannot be fully certain, the implication builds that the prisoner is not Marsch but a duplicate of him. That is to say, he may be a shape-changing abo. The effect of the story is Kafkaesque in many ways, and even frequent rereadings cannot assure the reader that he has caught all the nuances.

In his concern for identity Wolfe may well be asking what it does mean to be human, or he may be suggesting that the primitive abos who had no weapons possessed/possess more humanity than does mankind. *The Fifth Head of Cerberus* marks one of the high points of Wolfe's career—indeed one of the high points of science fiction during the 1970s.

The question of identity, the inability to communicate with another intelligence, the cruelty and violence of man's society: not only are these main concerns of *The Fifth Head of Cerberus*, but they provide some of the central themes of all of Wolfe's fiction. He develops them by returning to certain subject matters; yet any examination of his work shows how thoroughly he has escaped the formulaic patterns.

One notes, for example, how often the societies he portrays are at war. His first novel, *Operation ARES* (1970), already mentioned, projected another conflict in which the United States had been defeated; although a competently written novel, it nevertheless echoed a hundred future wars.

Since then, with several significant exceptions, Wolfe has changed his primary focus from warfare itself, using it primarily for its symbolic value in underscoring the violence of the world. Throughout the first three novels making up *The Book of the New Sun*, the reader learns that armies fight in the north, but as yet there has been no warfare on-stage. In "The Marvellous Chess Playing Automaton" (1977) siege guns bombard Russians trapped in Kostrzyn, but this is incidental to a middle Europe which has been devastated by past warfare and has now been reduced to a kind of medieval state of society. The same medieval quality dominates "Straw" (1975), in which the youthful first-person narrator and his four companions land their fire balloon near "the unfortified country property of a gentleman"[23] and are entertained at a banquet. His group calls itself the "Faithful Five"; they are mercenaries—"free swords"—who travel by balloon all over the unnamed continent looking for whatever fighting may be going on. They need straw for their balloon, they are told that there is none, but the narrator finds a plentiful supply in the stables. When he tries to tell his commander, he is told that he is mistaken; when he insists, his companion shows him smoke on the horizon and informs him that what he sees is thatch burning; "a soldier gets straw only where he isn't welcome."[24] The last line of the story informs the reader that those who are pillaging the countryside attack the villa at moonrise, but no details of any battle are given. Except for the anachronistic balloon, one questions whether or not "Straw" should be read as fantasy instead of science fiction—unless it gives a glimpse of an alternative world.

The same may be said of "Continuing Westward" (1973). Its point of departure is the attempt of the first-person narrator and his observer, Sanderson, to dynamite a Turkish power line during World War One. A premature explosion (did it somehow cast them into an alternative world?) leaves their plane damaged so that they can only lurch across the desert in a ship unable to fly. The principal action of the story occurs after they reach a stone village where the natives entertain them. Indeed, the chief episode involves the narrator's speculations about the young woman making love to Sanderson. When he thinks that she has killed his observer, he seizes her, takes her knife, and sets off with her across the desert in the plane, declaring that somehow they will get back to the British lines. Sanderson comes running after them in his underclothes. Its effect seems more absurdist than science fiction.

The exceptions mentioned occurred relatively early, and one may read them, perhaps, as an expression of Wolfe's reaction to Vietnam and the home front. In "The HORARS of War" (1970) the troops themselves are androids—"Homolog Organisms (Army Replacement Simulations)"—identified only by number. Just the officers are human. Three platoons are pinned down in a nameless jungle and are destroyed during a night attack. The issue of the story turns upon whether or not one of the HORARS, no. 2910, is actually a man, a journalist who underwent training and disguised himself so that he could better report actual battle conditions.He is killed; despite an element of ambiguity his newspaper's announcement of his death implies his humanity.

In "The Blue Mouse" (1971) young Lonnie Daws, a member of a U.N. Peace Force in an unnamed country, finds his camp in danger of being overrun by insurgents. The U.N. force is divided into two groups: the Marksmen, who are the actual combat troops, and the Techs, who operate the highly automated equipment. The groups hate one another, and the implication is that the Techs have been psychologically tested and found to be unable/unwilling to fight. Lonnie, a Tech, acknowledges that when he took the test he was thinking of the mice he experimented on, wondering whether or not his mother would take care of them if he were gone. Now he wants to work with them again; in this wish he finds a motive which sends him into action during a night attack; he holds off the enemy with a flamethrower until armored support arrives.

"Hour of Trust" (1973) turns in on America itself, focusing on a battle at the interchange of I75 and I94 outside of Dearborn. Members of the counterculture who control much of the countryside throughout the United States hold the position against the mercenaries hired by those corporations which have taken up the battle after the Federal government ceased to function. Together with Europeans on whom they are dependent for financial and material aid, the business executives watch the battle on television, communicating directly with their commander who has never seen action before. Their forces are defeated. They are totally out of touch with the reality of the affair; what emerges is that their only commitment is to the surival of big business.

But these stories are not typical of Wolfe's treatment of war. Perhaps because it dealt with the Korean conflict, in which Wolfe served, his most memorable tale is "The Changeling" (1968), although it was one of his earliest and did not directly present the conflict. Its first-person narrator stayed behind in China after the armistice, changed his mind again, and returned to be courtmartialed and serve time in Ft. Leavenworth. Once free, he returns to Cassonsville, his boyhood home. Although individuals remember him, there is no record—not even a school photograph— of his youth, and the newspaper editor insists that no boy from Cassonsville "stayed with the Communists."[25] The enigmatic element of the story enters in the form of an eight-year-old boy whom the narrator remembers as a companion of his childhood. The boy's father explains that he never grew up. The implication that they are one and the same person and that somehow the youngster is a living denial of the narrator's indecisions and frustrations is strengthened by the similarity of their names. The young boy is Pete Palmieri; the narrator has changed his name to Peter Palmer.

In contrast, "How I Lost the Second World War and Helped Turn Back the German Invasion" (1973) must rank with the finest satires in contemporary literature. Presented as a letter dated 1 April 1938 addressed to the editor of a British periodical, the narrative reports "a gamesing adventure which lately befell" the anonymous narrator who has recently taken up residence in Britain.[26] On one level it ostensibly outlines the rules and progress of the "game of World War, as conceived by my friend Lansbury and myself"; on a second level, it gives an account of the great Bath Exhibition, at which Adolph Hitler personally introduces the "People's Car"—intending to take over the British market as he has already taken the eastern European market. Winston Churchill proposes that the People's Car race the British Centurion. The texture of the narrative is too rich with historical allusions and humorous reversals for any summary to do it justice. Suffice to say that the story becomes science fiction only in that Churchill designs the racetrack like a giant transistor, taking advantage of the flow of electrons in one direction, so that the British win. An addendum to the letter identifies the writer as Dwight.

What makes the story memorable, however, is the brilliance with which Wolfe's satire devastates the historical situation of the 1930s, reminds the reader of the actual events of World War Two (as when the narrator points out that coals from Lansbury's pipe "cost us a pair of cities in south Japan" and Churchill warns that the next time they play they must be careful so that they "don't burn up the whole board...."[27]), and anticipates post-war events (as when Churchill warns that the next threat will come from Japanese-made cars, which he understands are already being unloaded at Pearl Harbor). The objectivity gained by the letter form and the irony gained by juxtaposing/reversing game and history give "How I Lost the Second World War..." an unforgettable impact.

Much more serious in tone than any of these stories is one of Wolfe's latest works, "The Woman Who Loved the Centaur Pholus" (1979). Again the narrative turns on a future America, where the classicist Professor Anderson leads a small group of demonstrators against the army in the Wisconsin Dells. This, however, is no struggle involving corporations and counterculture. Instead genetic engineering has made possible the creation of mythological creatures. The army is being used to destroy all such beings, while Professor Anderson carries a sign declaring that "Intelligent Life Is Sacred." The young woman who loves Pholus explains:

> "...We have lost so many of our fellow citizens of this world. All of the larger whales, the gorilla, two kinds of cheetah, all within the last ten years. Now humanity can make real what it has always loved. Now we can see the friends our ancestors dreamed of. The world is big enough for all of us, and some of us don't want to have to live here alone."[28]

However deeply Wolfe may feel on an issue, he is never simplistic. The climax occurs when Anderson and his friends find a faun with a mangled arm; however, Anderson recognizes that this is not the result of a gunshot wound. The faun has been bitten. In short, some one of the genetic engineers has created a mythological monster, be it werewolf, Anubis, or the lion-man of the Vedas. The girl Janet flees with Pholus, but Anderson realizes that "all the relics of the twentieth century except himself would be in the direction opposite the one Pholus had taken."[29] Fear will dominate mankind, and the army will be given freedom to destroy all of the mythological beings.

Genetic engineering has played a role in Wolfe's fiction since "Mountains Like Mice" (1966), in which Homo Gryde had been developed as a lifeform which would be better adapted to colonizing Mars than would Homo Sapiens. His use of the device ranges from "The HORARS of War" to "Sonya, Crane Wesselman, and Kittee" (1970). Although Kittee is incidental to the main concern of the tale, she has been genetically engineered from a cat to act as a servant; however, she reverts to a carnivore when her master dies. The novels making up *The Book of the New Sun* are filled with a variety of creatures half-human, half-animal; many of them have been brought to Urth from other worlds in the distant past, some—the cacogens, even forming colonies—but others have been manipulated to take their present forms.

After aliens have taken possession of the Earth, the protagonist of "The Hero as Werwolf" (1975) believes that he is one of the few humans left alive. He lives by cannibalism; one of his victims asks why he did not change his genes when all the others did. The protagonist insists that his people didn't because they were human. His victim then voices one of Wolfe's basic themes:

> ' . . . Your old breed had worn out the planet; even with much better technology we're still starved for energy and raw materials because of what you did.'[30]

This same anger which Wolfe seems to accept with a kind of resignation toward the inevitable is voiced in "Seven American Nights" (1978) by young Nadan, the Iranian who visits a future Washington, D.C., whose inhabitants no longer know the meaning of the "white house." He finds all of the mutitude on the streets deformed in various ways and remarks upon "the genetic damage that destroyed the old America."[31] One infers that the catastrophe resulted from pollution. He is told that a hundred miles inland lies the "wreck of our entire civilization,"[32] some of whose inhabitants are no longer human.

Except for these outbursts, however, for Wolfe genetic engineering becomes one more method of probing the nature of reality. In this respect robots are equally important. As early as "The Packerhaus Method" (1970), seemingly a routine dialogue between a social worker and an old woman whose father invented a way of keeping the dead alive in a fashion, the reader at last discerns that all of the characters are automatons alive beyond their time. The young narrator of "It's Very Clean" (1972) visits a house of prostitution whose girls are elaborate mannikins controlled by complex computers filling the walls. The climax occurs when he discovers that his partner is a real woman. He flees in anger and disgust as the other mannikins laugh.

Technology itself, however, seldom receives the direct brunt of Wolfe's attack, as it does in the work of so many of his disillusioned contemporaries. An apparent exception is "Eyebem" (1970)—a pun on IBM—the first-person narrative of a robot who has been trained to work with a human companion in the Arctic. Storms trap them; as

he lies dying—his energy seeping away ampere by ampere—
Eyebem thinks how unjust his death is, declaring:

> "We are the advance of the future, not you men. All your stupid
> human history has been just your replacement by us, and there's
> nothing, not one thing, that you can do that we can't do better.
> Why don't you help me?"[33]

"Forlesen" (1974), a satire of life in the corporate-administrative
business world, condenses the life of its protagonist to a single day.
In the morning he awakens knowing only his own name; at the end
of the day, sitting in his coffin, he wonders if life has had any
meaning. This swift passage of life was first sketched in "Loco
Parentis" (1972), published in *Again, Dangerous Visions*.

In "The Death of Dr. Island" (1973), for which he did receive a
Nebula, a young mentally-ill boy is placed aboard a satellite, an
elaborate robot capable of speaking with its human occupants, a
kind of hospital formed in part as an idyllic island. The satellite
itself—it calls itself Dr. Island—elaborates the basic theme when it
explains:

> "...Even among the inner planets space is not a kind
> environment for mankind; and our space, trans-Martian space,
> is worse."[34]

Thus, saving any young person who has a chance of adapting to the
harsh conditions is essential. Dr. Island concludes by suggesting
that for anyone for whom reality is the *unreality* of "metal corridors,
rooms without windows, noise"—in short, space technology—a
return to "an idealized natural setting"[35] is sometimes helpful. (The
story ends with a killing, and the young protagonist is given a new
identity when he falls into something like a catatonic state,
although the hemispheres of his brain had been previously
separated.)

Both genetic engineering and all of technology are the
invention of mankind; he has made his own planet and now must
wallow in it. In a sense Wolfe has employed the furniture of science
fiction and fantasy to symbolize the hostile universe which man has
created.

To phrase it another way, the evil lies in man, as Wolfe indicates
in "Beautyland" (1973), a dialogue between a first-person narrator
and Dives, a wealthy man who explains how he made his money. He
sought to preserve an untouched mountain valley by having people
buy every plant, tree and animal—including perhaps the last six

wild deer in America. From the first, however, "the idea was that we were going to destroy anything that wasn't bought."[36] The objects went unsold. When he confessed that he himself did not have the heart to burn the valley, he found lines of people waiting to do it for him. So he changed his aim; he doubled and tripled prices, and people fought with one another for the privilege of killing a single creature. In addition, because the burning took place at night when it photographed most vividly, he received three million for the TV rights. The clincher comes, so to speak, when the passive, seemingly sympathetic narrator remarks that "I told him I didn't give a damn [how he made his money] as long as it was there."[37]

Wolfe echoes this theme as late as " 'Our Neighbor' by David Copperfield" (1979), in which a phrenologist reports that the quality of pity does not exist in mankind.

On one level, then, because of the hostility of the universe and man's brutality, the recurrent discovery in much of Wolfe's fiction centers upon the terror of actual existence. This leads, as already shown, to the problem of identity, especially as it involves maintaining one's humanity. (One is tempted to count the number of times his protagonists exhibit or find this humanity.)

Since the media form so important a part in the world created by man, Wolfe's use of them in his exploration of identity/reality is most appropriate. In "The Toy Planet" (1971) the narrator visits an isolated planet to meet Stromboli, the master marionettist, in order to learn from him. Only at the end does the reader learn that the narrator is himself a marionette, packed into a box during a spaceflight. In "Three Fingers" (1976) a young man who peddles such icons of popular culture as Pinocchio and Snow White returns to his room to be confronted by Captain Hook, the Big Bad Wolf and The Wicked Queen. Although he identifies them with various figures from history and mythology, they reveal themselves as paunchy persons in business suits before killing him ritually. The ambiguity of the ending, however, raises the question of whether or not they are human or the cartoon characters. One of the most delightful of these pieces, "A Method Bit in 'B' " (1970) provides one of Wolfe's earliest parodies of British fantasy. The constable of Stoke-on-Wold, a man addicted to cinema, tries to sort out reality amid, among other matters, the sighting and killing of a werewolf. He ends by asking the reader whether or not everyone is really in a 'B' film.

"The Island of Dr. Death and Other Stories" (1970) remains one of Wolfe's strongest short stories because his technical skill controls and opens up his several themes more thoroughly perhaps

than any of his work prior to *The Fifth Head of Cerberus*. He uses the
second person point of view not only to gain sympathy for his seven-
year-old protagonist, Tackie Babcock, but also in order to stay out of
the boy's mind. For Wolfe has set as his principal task the objective
evaluation of Tackie's world. The boy lives in isolation with his
mother on an island that is not an island somewhere on the Atlantic
coast. His mother's youthful lover and a few adults, including her
personal physician and friend, Dr. Black, are their only visitors. As
soon as Wolfe suggests that "If you are a boy not wanted in the
house you walk the beach for hours..."[38] he establishes empathy
between the reader and the isolated boy. The adults pay little
attention to him, and with one exception exclude him from their
world.

That one exception is a masterful touch because it provides the
means by which Wolfe evaluates the world in which Tackie lives.
Through his mother's lover he acquires a "wonderful book" whose
story obviously derives from H.G. Wells's *The Island of Dr. Moreau*
and the pulp formulas of the 1930s and 1940s. At once Tackie loses
himself in the adventures and horrors facing Captain Phillip
Ransom. Wolfe alternates scenes between the false island of
Tackie's home and the island near New Guinea where Ransom finds
the fiendish Dr. Death. It is a clever structural device, for each time
Tackie is shunted aside he turns to the book.

By the next morning the imagination of the lonely boy fuses
reality and fiction. Captain Ransom comes ashore from a life raft.
The characters come alive for Tackie—Ransom, Dr. Death, Golo,
Bruno, the beautiful Talar of the Long Eyes, who is a princess of an
ancient, lost city. Immediately the reader begins to compare the
characters from the two worlds, even though Tackie is too
inexperienced to do so. "Thematically, what Wolfe does is juxtapose
the complex horror of Tackie's real life, things from the adult world
which he cannot understand (the reader learns, for example, that
his mother is strung out on drugs), with the sinister yet simplistic
horror of the pulp fiction. The reader must realize that the 'real
world' of Tackie is much more terrible than anything from the make-
believe world of Dr. Death."[39] Wolfe forces the reader to come to this
conclusion for himself, for, as noted, Tackie is too young and
innocent to distinguish morally between the actual and the
fictional. This is the same basic reason Wolfe must handle the story
as he does, for it is, finally, those two worlds rather than the young
boy which are the focal point of Wolfe's theme.

The parallels, ironies and ambiguities are excellent. One of the
finest occurs after Tackie's first conversation with Dr. Death; his

aunt asks him whom he was speaking to. Again, the beast-men ask Ransom to lead them against Dr. Death in order "to cleanse this island which is our home."[40] The final touch occurs when his mother is taken to the hospital after an overdose of amphetamines (Tackie has watched Dr. Black give her an injection); the boy worries because he does not want the book to end, the characters to go away. Dr. Death assures him that they will return if he reads the book again. Thus, the final irony rests with the suggestion of repetition.

Wolfe again blurs what is real and what imaginary in "Seven American Nights." A letter from a private investigator introduces the photocopy of what purports to be young Nadan's diary; yet it is so strange that after reading it, his mother and sweetheart cannot be certain it is his. Secondly, Nadan refers to his purchase of "the greatest creation of the old hallucinatory chemists"[41] who, by implication at least, contributed to America's downfall. After taking the supposed drug, Nadan no longer is certain whether or not what he experiences is real.

As early as "Mountains Like Mice" (1966) Wolfe used a youngster as his protagonist. That story concerns the initiation rituals of pubescent Dirk, who thereby learns that he is descended from persons who came to Mars from Earth. His most horrifying story focusing upon a child— "War Beneath the Tree" (1979)— illustrates again how well Wolfe can adapt a familiar situation to a science fiction framework in order to gain an added effect. On Christmas Eve young Robin—certainly of pre-school age—plays with his fully automated toys which include a Spaceman, a Bear, a Dancing Doll, and Guardsmen; his mother—Ms. Jackson—refers to them as his "transistorized sycophants [who] spoil him."[42] Later Robin sneaks downstairs to see what Santa has left him. He witnesses a struggle between the old toys and the new in which his old playmates are defeated and burned in the fireplace. In the morning after casually remarking that the old toys were programmed to self destruct, his mother explains that just as the new toys appeared as though by magic, the same kind of magic can occur to people. She announces that she is going to have a baby; "the same wonderful thing is going to happen here, in our home."[43] Robin stares at her "with frightened eyes."

Once again Wolfe has shown himself a master of narrative technique. By dramatizing the battle of the toys in a central scene and allowing Robin to be merely an observer, as well as showing that his mother has no understanding of what happened, he does not soften the traumatic experience for the little boy or the reader. In keeping with his central themes, certainly one of the fine touches is the determination of the old toys to survive, as, led by Bear, they attack the new gifts.

No brief survey can do justice to the variety of Gene Wolfe. For example, little mention has been made of his handling of aliens. One such story, "Alien Stones" (1972), measures his uniqueness. Earthmen encounter a seemingly derelict alien ship; eventually, however, through the simulation of a missing man, they reveal themselves. Unlike so many "first contact" stories, in this one the aliens decide that now that they and humans have observed one another, they must separate in order to have time to think.

Impressive as is Wolfe's body of fiction, at this point in time one feels that what has gone before is preliminary to the tetralogy, *The Book of the New Sun*. (It is that reaction to the tremendous impact of what apparently has been seven years' work which makes one especially enjoy his newest short story, "The Last Thrilling Wonder Story,"[44] in which he chats, as author, with his protagonist, Brick, in a manner that parodies the old pulp stories and recalls, at least partly, such earlier works as "The Island of Dr. Death and Other Stories.")

In 1981 Wolfe's *The Shadow of the Torturer* (1980) won both the World Fantasy Award and the British Science Fiction Society award as the best novel of the year. *The Claw of the Conciliator* (1981) won the Nebula Award in 1982, and with the completion of *The Sword of the Lictor* (1981) and *The Citadel of the Autarch* (1982), one would not be surprised if *The Book of the New Sun* won a special award soon for the full series. However that may be, its universe is generating more fine fiction: Wolfe is writing another novel about Urth which does not concern the central character of the tetralogy. And while fandom may continue to debate whether or not the tetralogy should be regarded as sf or fantasy, its recognition as a major work in the field has already been established. Its influence, as noted in an early review in *Extrapolation*, should at least equal that of Asimov's Foundation trilogy.

To begin with, Wolfe has created Urth, an imaginary world which matches in the richness of its detail, those worlds of *The Left Hand of Darkness, Dune,* and *Lord Valentine's Castle*.[45] His accomplishment cannot be too highly praised. The basic texture of the society centering upon Nessus, the City Imperishable, seems to be medieval so that, coupled with a first-person narrator, the world is immediately acceptable. Bit by bit Wolfe includes details that remove Urth from the familiar until one readily accepts its strangeness. One learns that Nessus, the City Imperishable, which provides the background of *The Shadow of the Torturer*, has mushroomed along the banks of the River Gyoll in the southern hemisphere of the planet, but the city is so ancient that its earliest structures have long been abandoned and are now little more than ruins. At some time in the past Urth has known interstellar trade and visitors. Indeed, at present a variety of aliens still inhabit the world. Yet one learns that some of them (past and present) were the products of biological engineering, while in *The Sword of the Lictor* and *The Citadel of the Autarch,* especially, one discovers that some of these beings can travel in time—both past and present; Wolfe refers repeatedly to the "corridors" of time. His ability to mix effectively the familiar and strange is well illustrated in *The Shadow of the Torturer*. His protagonist is an apprentice to the Guild of Torturers, whose function is to administer punishment and justice to political prisoners sent to them, supposedly, by the Autarch. Yet the Matachin Tower in which the Guild dwells in Nessus—one of many towers—is a long-grounded starship.

The sun of Urth has begun to grow cold and, unless some change occurs, a new ice age will come and eventually all life and the planet itself will be destroyed. One result has been the creation of the myth of the New Sun; yet that myth has mystical overtones so that through the early novels, at least, one cannot be certain whether the new sun refers to the second coming of the legendary figure of the Conciliator or to an actual renewal of the solar star. Throughout the four novels Wolfe stresses Urth's decline from greatness; he creates a world caught in a dark, essentially barbaric, yet potentially transitional age.

The effective tension between the familiar and strange which brings the novels alive results in large part because of the success Wolfe achieves in having the reader share the experiences of his protagonist, Severian. *The Book of the New Sun* is the autobiography of this complex man who has total recall. *The Shadow of the Torturer* combines Severian's recollections of his youth and adolescence with central actions following his expulsion from the Guild of Torturers—actions compressed into no more than a day and confined within the walls of Nessus. One learns of Severian's initiation into the Guild; of his love for and murder of the Chatelaine Thecla to save her from torture; the judgment which provides him with the splendid sword, *Terminus Est,* and sends him to far-distant Thrax, the Claw of Windowless Rooms, where he will serve as public executioner. Yet the latter half of the novel focuses upon a series of events which gain him the sacred jewel of the Order of the Pelerines, a wandering order of priestesses; the enmity of the woman Agia; and the love of the woman Dorcas, who has apparently been revived from the dead in the Botanical Gardens. But the novel ends as he approaches the gate of Nessus.

In contrast, both *The Claw of the Conciliator* and *The Sword of the Lictor* record his odyssey northward as he attempts to return the Claw to the Pelerines and as he moves ever closer to the front lines of the warfare between the troops of the Commonwealth and the Ascians. (It seems a perpetual war; in the south it has become almost myth rather than reality.) *The Citadel of the Autarch* moves full circle, bringing Severian again to Nessus. Yet Wolfe escapes the restrictions of the here-and-now, so often a characteristic limiting autobiographical tales. Severian tells the story when he is, comparatively, an old man who has himself become the Autarch, the supreme ruler of the southern Commonwealth. Thus, in addition to his photographic memory which so vividly evokes past scenes and incidents, Severian can make allusions which foreshadow events yet to come and, increasingly in the later novels, especially *The Citadel of the Autarch*, can reflect upon both past and future events, thereby complicating them thematically. (He constantly refers to his ability to remember fully and frequently apologizes for his digressions—that is, his reflections.)

In several conversations Wolfe has acknowledged the resemblance of Severian to Robert Graves' protagonist in *I, Claudius* and *Claudius the God,* stressing that both men are among the most unlikely to become absolute rulers and both are given to reflection. Although Wolfe has created an epic stage and although he permits his protagonist to travel extensively through the world, the emphasis is never upon external action for the sake of action; rather, the four novels become increasingly a study of Severian's reactions and musings. The result is that Gene Wolfe has created one of the richest and most complex characterizations in the field of fantasy and science fiction.

The tone of *The Claw of the Conciliator* differs from the first novel in that its function is to open up the world of Urth for the reader as Severian journeys to Thrax. Against this background individual incidents emphasize the power of the mysterious gem, "The Claw," which is believed to be a relic of the perhaps historical, perhaps mythical Master of Life. Agia's hatred of Severian and her desire to gain vengeance lead him to caves where apelike creatures attack him until they behold the Claw; then the men-apes kneel in awe of the artifact. In the camp of Vodalus, whose life he once saved, he participates in a ritual which brings Thecla back from the dead— or at least seems to—long enough to allow her being to fuse with his. They become a single entity in that henceforth he knows all her thoughts and experiences as well as she. Later he becomes a prisoner in the House Absolute, the domain of the Autarch, where his companion, Jonas, who is something more than human, escapes from Urth down the corridors of time, promising to return. There, too, he is reunited with Dr. Talos, Baldanders, Dorcas and Jolenta—companions with whom he acted in Nessus—so that he may perform in "Dr. Talos's Play: Eschatology and Genesis." In short, the function of *The Claw of the Conciliator* differs from *The Shadow of the Torturer* in that it opens up the mysteries and ambiguities of the planet Urth to Severian and the reader.

This same introduction continues in *The Sword of the Lictor*, the storyline being guided, as in *The Claw of the Conciliator*, by Severian's quest to find the Pelerians and return the Claw to them. However, in this third volume, sickening of his job as public executioner, he rejects his role as torturer, fleeing into the northern mountains to escape the wrath of the governor of Thrax. He and Dorcas, once in love, separate. Again he encounters Dr.Talos and Baldanders, this time on the shores of Lake Diuturna. In a final battle both *Terminus Est* and the Claw are lost to him. Alone, he asserts that this northern outpost was to prove a gateway to the war between the Commonwealth and the Ascians, a war which has since then "engaged my attention almost without cease."

In *The Citadel of the Autarch* he does fight in the war with the Ascians, but that warfare simply provides the background—the narrative thread—through much of the novel. Since the novel is not yet generally available, one hesitates to go into great detail regarding the plot itself or the working out of Wolfe's themes. *The Citadel of the Autarch* completes Severian's odyssey; he comes full circle to the Matachin Tower, but he deliberately cuts the narrative short just before he undertakes the most important action of his life. It is an action which he can undertake only because he is Autarch—and because the thoughts and experiences of the previous Autarch and all of those who went before him—have been fused into the being who was/is Severian. *The Book of the New Sun* is thus open-ended. To explain, or label, the entire work as the "education" of Severian smacks of a foolish understatement; to speak of it as an account of the transcendence, or the transformation, of Severian is equally inadequate. He undertakes that final venture uncertain of its outcome, but filled with the hope of its success.

One interesting aspect of all the novels which has been overlooked is that Wolfe does not completely absent himself from them. Not only does he make use of Dr. Talos's plays and, especially in *The Citadel of the Autarch*, intrude a number of stories which serve as commentaries upon the action, but to each novel he has appended a discussion of some phase of the society of Urth, be it "Social Relationships in the Commonwealth," "Provincial Administration" or "Money, Measures, and Time." This gives him, of course, a chance to introduce expository material, as well as allowing him to guide his readers' reflections. What is more important, however, it permits him to pretend that he is editing an actual manuscript, as when he says in the appendix of *The Citadel of the Autarch* that "Nowhere are the manuscripts of *The Book of the New Sun* more obscure than in their treatment of weapons and military organization." Or, again, in the same appendix, he refers to "my translations . . . ." Through this device he gains a double effect. On the one hand, he adapts—gives a freshness to—a convention as old as fantasy and science fiction in order to gain an aura of authority/authenticity. On the other, however, like such contemporary writers as Barth and Coover, he reminds the reader that these narratives are fictional constructs and should be read as fiction—that is, as entertainment, as metaphor and symbol.

Although Timescape announces that the fourth volume concludes Severian's narrative, Wolfe himself has said that there will be a fifth, independent novel, *The Urth of the New Sun*.

For now, however, the voice to listen to is that of Severian as he pronounces judgment upon his narrative: "Perhaps I have contrived for someone *The Book of Gold*. Indeed, it may be that all my wanderings have been no more than a contrivance of the librarians to recruit their numbers; but perhaps that is too much to hope." He has done that and more, for Severian, who began as an apprentice to the Guild of Torturers, has provided his readers with a complex insight into the condition of Urth/Earth. His voice will echo through the finest science fiction/fantasy of the rest of the century.

Notes

[1] Melissa Mia Hall, "An Interview with Gene Wolfe," *Amazing/Fantastic*, 29 (September 1981), 129.

[2] Gene Wolfe, "Against the Lafayette Escadrille," *Gene Wolfe's Book of Days* (Garden City: Doubleday, 1981), p. 161.

[3] Wolfe, "Against the Lafayette Escadrille," p. 164.

[4] Wolfe, "Paul's Tree House," *Gene Wolfe's Book of Days,* p. 28.

[5] Wolfe, "Paul's Tree House," p. 34.

[6] Wolfe, "The Recording," *The Magazine of Fantasy and Science Fiction*, 42 (April 1972), 98.

[7] Wolfe, "When I Was Ming the Merciless", in Terry Carr, ed., *The Ides of Tomorrow* (Boston: Little Brown, 1976), pp. 127-136.

[8] Wolfe, "An Article on Hunting," *Gene Wolfe's Book of Days*, p. 130.

[9] Wolfe, "An Article on Hunting," p. 138.

[10] Wolfe, "Three Million Square Miles," *Gene Wolfe's Book of Days,* p. 165.

[11]Wolfe, "Sweet Forest Maid," *F&SF*, 41 (July 1971), 61.

[12]Wolfe, "Sweet Forest Maid," *F&SF*, 41:60.

[13]Wolfe, "Sweet Forest Maid," *F&SF*, 41:61.

[14]Wolfe, "Sweet Forest Maid," *F&SF*, 41:60.

[15]Wolfe, "Sweet Forest Maid," *F&SF*, 41:62.

[16]Wolfe, "Melting," *Gene Wolfe's Book of Days*, p. 182.

[17]Wolfe, "A Criminal Proceeding," in Ursula K. Le Guin and Virginia Kidd, eds. *Interfaces* (New York: Ace, 1980), p. 209.

[18]Wolfe, "A Criminal Proceeding," p. 212.

[19]Wolfe, "Thag," in Roger Elwood, ed. *Continuum 4* (New York: Berkley, 1975), p. 135.

[20]Wolfe, "Thag," p. 136.

[21]Peter Nicholls, "The Fifth Head of Cerberus," in Frank N. Magill, ed. *Survey of Science Fiction Literature* (Englewood Cliffs, N.J.: Salem Press, 1979), 2:770.

[22]Nicholls, "The Fifth Head of Cerberus," 2:771; Thomas D. Clareson, "Gene Wolfe," *Dictionary of Literary Biography: American Science Fiction Writers, Part Two, M-Z* (Detroit: Gale Research Co., 1981), 8:207.

[23]Wolfe, "Straw," *Galaxy*, 36 (January 1975), 12.

[24]Wolfe, "Straw," *Galaxy*, 36:13.

[25]Wolfe, "The Changeling," *Gene Wolfe's Book of Days*, p. 149.

[26]Wolfe, "How I Lost the Second World War and Helped Turn Back the German Invasion," *Gene Wolfe's Book of Days*, p. 61.

[27]Wolfe, "How I Lost the Second World War...," pp. 74-75.

[28]Wolfe, "The Woman Who Loved the Centaur Pholus," *Isaac Asimov's Science Fiction Magazine*, 3 (December 1979), 115.

[29]Wolfe, "The Woman Who Loved the Centaur Pholus," *Isaac Asimov's Science Fiction Magazine*, 3:118.

[30]Wolfe, "The Hero as Werwolf," *The Island of Dr. Death and Other Stories and Other Stories* (New York: Pocket Books, 1980), pp. 60-61.

[31]Wolfe, "Seven American Nights," *The Island of Dr. Death*, p. 361.

[32]Wolfe, "Seven American Nights," *The Island of Dr. Death*, p. 405.

[33]Wolfe, "Eyebem," in Damon Knight, ed. *Orbit 7* (New York: G.P. Putnam's Sons, 1970), p. 77.

[34]Wolfe, "The Death of Dr. Island," *The Island of Dr. Death*, p. 106.

[35]Wolfe, "The Death of Dr. Island," *The Island of Dr. Death*, p. 94.

[36]Wolfe, "Beautyland," *Gene Wolfe's Book of Days*, p. 42.

[37]Wolfe, "Beautyland," p. 42.

[38]Wolfe, "The Island of Dr. Death," *The Island of Dr. Death*, p. 1.

[39]Thomas D. Clareson, "Gene Wolfe," *DLB* 8:208.

[40]Wolfe, "The Island of Dr. Death," p. 13.

[41]Wolfe, "Seven American Nights," *The Island of Dr. Death*, p. 373.

[42]Wolfe, "The War Beneath the Tree," p. 173. *Geene Wolfe's Book of Days,* p. 169.

[43]Wolfe, "The War Beneath the Tree," p. 173.

[44]Wolfe, "The Last Thrilling Wonder Story," *Isaac Asimov's Science Fiction Magazine* 6 (June 1982), 144-169.

[45]Thomas D. Clareson, "Books," *Extrapolation,* 21 (Winter 1980), 389.

Uncertain Futures:
Damon Knight's Science Fiction

Douglas Robillard

Most of Damon Knight's fiction was produced during the 1950s and 1960s, and, sadly for his readers, he has published very little fiction since. Instead, he has been engaged prominently as an anthologist and editor, assembling a number of worthwhile collections of published sf and carefully exercising his editorial judgment on unpublished stories for his long series of *Orbit* anthologies to bring the work of innovative and interesting writers before the public. His work with the Science Fiction Writers of America and fiction workshops has been of great significance.[1]

But then it might be said of Knight's career that it has often taken strange turns. His engaging autobiographical account, "Knight's Piece," places him as illustrator, short story writer, critic, reader in a literary agency, and sometime magazine editor.[2] His first book, *In Search of Wonder*, was not fiction but science fiction criticism, "an informal record of ... the Boom of 1950-1955." In his author's note to that volume, he calls it "a period that produced some of the best science fiction ever to appear in hard covers, along with a fascinating flood of the worst science fiction ever conceived by the mind of man."[3] We find Knight commenting often upon the changing aims and accomplishments of sf during this period. Reviewing a novel by Poul Anderson in 1959, for example, he observed that Anderson's book does not always transcend its pulp fiction origins and, by way of generalization, adds:

> The American pulp tradition is a tradition of form: a Western novelet, in the pulps' heyday, was as rigidly structured as a fugue. A writer in the pulp tradition takes his form whole and embellishes it as best he can.[4]

Twenty years later, speaking of his own fiction, Knight surveys the subjects and techniques of the stories and says, "I think it worth noting that all these unconventional stories managed to get published in science fiction magazines in the 50s."[5] These are virtually the notes for a history of sf that Knight has not written; a

30

leading element in it is his positing of an important transition in the 1950s from the predominantly pulpish adventure sf to a more sophisticated, literary, richer and varied fiction whose authors go beyond the rigidities of past forms. The view is implicit in Knight's comments on stories by older writers, and it seems to place a "Golden Age" of sf about a decade later than many readers place it.

A survey of Knight's own fiction shows him dealing with the best-known and most-used sf subjects—time travel, dangerous inventions, encounters with aliens, space explorations—turning them inside out to see what more they can yield. His fiction bears up extremely well under rereading; construction is careful, characters come to life and display individuality and feelings, style is never less than adequate and often exceptional. It would seem that most of the attention he has received has been reserved for his short stories; a received opinion is that the short fiction represents his best work.[6] And, in fact, there is something to that view, though, like most views, it is subject to some moderation and disagreement.

I

In 1973 Robin Scott Wilson edited the anthology, *Those Who Can: A Science Fiction Reader*, whose premise was that a number of writers should choose one of their own stories that they felt was characteristic of their work and write about "its genesis, development or aims in a brief essay."[7] Knight chose "Masks," a story he had published in *Playboy* in 1968, wrote the required short essay, and then produced "An Annotated 'Masks'," which printed the text of his story and, on facing pages, offered his observations at strategic places. In this way, he was able to do more than generalize; he could present the story as though it were a musical score, calling attention to the workings of the beginning, the introduction of various elements and patterns, the attitudes and states of mind of the characters, and even discussing the plain advantages of excluding certain kinds of material from the text. This is an excellent method, for writer and reader, where the score, or the story, or the chessboard is in plain sight and can be referred to as explanations go forward. Knight's annotation is a formidable exhibition of a writer's calling attention to the subtleties of performance that have a way of half getting past the reader; and it shows the well worked out artistic decisions about how and how much to offer, how much to reduce, what to exclude. It is a demonstration of the story as poem, a unitary and artistically rendered whole, all of whose parts must be kept in mind simultaneously and dynamically.

The story that Knight chose to discuss is one of his latest and one of his best. It has an illustrious precursor in C.L. Moore's "No Woman Born" (*Astounding,* December 1944). In Moore's story, Deirdre, an entertainer of exceptional talent, is burned so badly that her body is beyond curing or recovery; but, by a marvel of inventive technology, craftsmanship, even art, she is revived and restored in essence and personality to a mechanical, metallic body, a robot body motivated by a human mind. The fabricators have artfully captured her form, movement, personality, her very wholeness of spirit, and have succeeded in giving her a body that is both functional and aesthetically satisfying:

> She had, Harris realized as the first shock quieted, a very beautifully shaped head—a bare golden skull. She turned it a little, gracefully upon her neck of metal, and he saw that the artist who shaped it had given her the most delicate suggestion of cheekbones, narrowing in the blankness below the mask to the hint of a human face.... Brancusi himself had never made anything more simple or more subtle than the modeling of Deirdre's head.[8]

Everything in Moore's story is designed to add to the double illusion of strangeness and beauty. Deirdre is as good as new, better than new in some ways, for she is restored with powers she could never possess as a flesh-and-blood person.

In his commentary on "Masks," Knight calls attention to Moore's story:

> As I got deeper into the story, I became more and more convinced that the psychic effect of losing the whole body and having it replaced by a prosthetic system had been too casually shrugged off by previous writers, even C.L. Moore in her beautiful "No Woman Born."[9]

Knight's version, characterized by him as "a costive, difficult story written over a period of three years,"[10] is very different from Moore's. It is harsh and unremittingly dark. The character is a man instead of a woman. He has been injured so seriously that he is only recovered to life in a metallic body by miracles of prosthesis. But as a metallic man, he really doesn't work all that well. He is an expensive government project, kept going by a large force of technicians and scientists at huge cost, and, even so, he does not seem to be a very successful project. In the earlier days of sf, scientists built space ships or time machines in their garages. The facts of life have demonstrated the government's role in space ship building, and Wilson Tucker, in *The Year of the Quiet Sun* (1970), showed how governments will finance and control the building of time-travel devices. Knight applies the same grim thesis to prosthesis and life-saving arts, and with similar results. Jim is not C.L. Moore's graceful and pleasing machine—not quite masking a warm, attractive, artistic human. Instead, he is a more or less ordinary citizen, dourly boxed in metal, feeling cut off from everything. His looks are appalling:

> Opposite her sat someone tall, in gray shirt and slacks, leaning back, legs out, arms on the arms of his chair, motionless. Something was wrong with his face.... The tall figure turned its head and Sinescu saw with an icy shock that its face was silver, a mask of metal with oblong slits for eyes, no nose or mouth, only curves that were faired into each other (p. 255).

This is one of the masks. Below it is another, a futile cosmetic attempt of his fabricators at human characteristics. It is "good-looking, normal-looking. Only the eyes wrong, pupils too big. And the lips that did not open or move when it spoke" (p. 257). And below the fake cosmetic mask is more metal, another mask for the human part. As often as possible, Knight finds excuse to say *it* rather than *he* or *him*.

The metal figure here is a parody of the human, as Knight's story is a parody of Moore's. Unlike Deirdre, Jim derives no pleasure from his resurrection and his new body; he is simply encased and suffering. He has been responsible for putting the metal mask atop the fleshly mask to mock the sentimentality of his keepers. Cut off from the human, he thinks of himself as a complex tool, and proposes that foolish humanizing attempts be stopped and that he be placed in a functional metal body for surveying and prospecting on the moon. In this way he can cease being a project, earn his keep, get away from humanity, and take pride in "running clean and cool" (p. 259). Here is an essential difference in the treatments of Moore and Knight. Moore does not get into Deirdre's consciousness in any significant way but allows her to explain herself in a long monologue. Knight works close to his character, slipping into Jim's point of view to demonstrate just how circumstances have changed him. The matter of running clean and cool is the pride of machinery, of valves and relays. In this mental state, human matters—such as organisms, offal, grease, tears and wet eyes—earn Jim's loathing. He kills and disposes of a pet pup that represents the nightmarish vision of the flesh, the innards and slimy, bulging softness. In the ironic conclusion of the story, he obsessively envisions himself on the moon in an environment of clear, sharp, sterile apartness, observing the home planet: "Earth hung overhead like a rotten fruit, blue with mold, crawling, wrinkling, purulent and alive" (p. 261).

A story like "Masks" represents what we might call "late" Damon Knight. But even early in his career, he achieved the skills that make his stories resonant and insightful. The popular and often reprinted "To Serve Man" (*Galaxy*, November 1950) is an elegant and sardonic little fable about the encounter with aliens that does not necessarily come off well. Here Knight is writing out of a long and rich tradition of alien-human encounter stories. H.G. Wells's Martians in *The War of the Worlds* (1898) are entirely alien in physiology and outlook and have nothing in mind but conquest. On the other hand, Stanley G. Weinbaum's Tweel, in "A Martian Odyssey" (1934), is far too appealing to seem monstrous, though the story contains other alien monstrosities. The Martian of Raymond Z. Gallun's "Old Faithful" (1934) is appealing to his terrestrial friends by long distance communication but monstrous to their sight until reason and recollection make them accept him. In Murray Leinster's "First Contact" (1945) the aliens are near-human, reasonable and compassionate, and they can win through to a sensible compromise with humankind.

Among the many stories offering variants on the subject of alien-human contact, Knight's tale of the Kanamit is a neat object lesson. The Earth will be more easily invaded by attractive aliens than by horrible ones; and if they are attractive enough, Earth may submit willingly. But Knight's Kanamit are hardly attractive:

> The Kanamit were not very pretty, it's true. They looked something like pigs and something like people and that is not an attractive combination. Seeing them for the first time shocked you; that was their handicap. When a thing with the countenance of a fiend comes from the stars and offers a gift, you are disinclined to accept.[11]

Yet the Kanamit can pass lie-detector tests and their mission seems perfectly altruistic—to bring peace and plenty, to rid the world of war, hunger and suffering—and all without reward. We have been told often enough to beware the bearers of gifts, but who is to beware gifts like a free power source, increased soil fertility and a machine that will suppress explosive detonations and end war and violence? The succinct question of a doubter, "how can anybody trust a thing that looks as if it ate the baby?" gives the clue that is ignored, till even the doubter is not sure his doubts are well grounded. The

Kanamit seem likely to be able to offer cures for heart disease and cancer, improve the general health of humanity, and carry out the injunction of their own handbook, *How to Serve Man*. But their title is wittier than humans know.

What is new and distinctive in this early story is its stylistic assurance. The establishment of two magazines, *Fantasy and Science Fiction* in 1949 and *Galaxy* in 1950, did offer markets for this kind of writing. Knight's mature development as a writer coincided with the publication of these new magazines, and he contributed stories to both. "To Serve Man" appears in the second issue of *Galaxy*, in company with other stories that continue to be vital: part of Simak's serial, *Time Quarry*; Asimov's "Misbegotten Missionary"; and Fritz Leiber's "Coming Attraction."

A more serious and darker presentation of the alien-human encounter is to be found in "Stranger Station" *(F & SF,* December 1955). Knight has offered a curious remark about the story: "I once tried to write a series of stories with titles derived from the running heads of Donald Day's *Index to the Science Fiction Magazines*. 'Stranger Station' was one of them."[12] The ambiguous *them* is typical of the author. One of the stories written? One of the running heads? In Day we find a running head that reads "Stranger-Station," and other running heads in the volume should have piqued Knight to write a great deal more, for here and there we see "Indigestible-Invaders," "Prescience-Problem," "Pygmalion's-Rain" and "No-Omega."

But Knight has nevertheless created a story of high excellence. Plot and exposition unfold in "Stranger Station" in such a way as to make the story a mystery whose solution must be found. Exposition is sparse; we learn that humanity was in the infancy of interplanetary travel when, in 1987, an expedition to Titan discovered an alien, an interstellar traveller. There had been a feeling of distress on both sides; human and alien seemed to set up mutually painful vibrations, and the result, in the case of the alien, was the exuding of a golden fluid. By a neat touch of irony, the fluid is virtually an elixir of life, for a drop of it will arrest human aging for twenty years. Here, then, is the beast who gives off a necessary beauty. The stranger station is an uneasy accommodation, a satellite to be visited every other decade by human and alien, in a painful though minimal relationship for the valuable reward of life. Humans come to depend upon this unusual, stand-off accommodation, though the mystery asserts itself: why? Nobody gives away something for nothing. The Kanamit, of "To Serve Man," brings gifts but eats people. The aliens freely and painfully give life to humans in the stranger station but appear to expect no return.

When Paul Wesson takes on his stint of service at the station, he is charged to solve the riddle if he can. He approaches the solution in a sociological equation: "When two alien cultures meet, the stronger must transform the weaker with love or hate." The alien culture is the stronger, the more advanced, the one capable of interstellar travel. But the aliens have not invaded or even approached the Earth. They see the progress of human culture as a threat; humans will eventually move out into the space between the stars. What the aliens have been quick to discover is that, once an initial distress has worn off, the two races can tolerate each other. They have learned that they can transform the human element into something better, more loving and, therefore, inhuman. This is what humans keep learning, too late to avoid the transformation.

But the story is more complex than an account of it can be, and its artistic ordering is different from a reasoned account. The characterization of Wesson and of Aunt Jane, the alpha network system that runs the station, is full and effective. The network may be a machine, but it is human all the same, careful, pleasant, protective, capable of feeling both pain and love. Knight has successfully reversed the standard motifs of sf: the alien, a monster in appearance, to the human view at least, hardly ever appears in the story. The aliens, as a species, are not inferior to, or on a level with, their human counterparts, but superior, better and more clever. The conflict between aliens and humans does not have to be resolved with space ships and marvelous weapons, for it is essentially a psychological, sociological and perhaps moral and spiritual conflict.

As in Knight's best stories, the writing rises easily to its highest occasions. The closer Paul comes to solving the mystery, the further he moves from the human, the more he becomes transformed, till, at the end, he cannot communicate with humanity. Students find the text of the story dense, not easily unraveled. It is a tribute, Knight's tribute, to *Fantasy and Science Fiction*, that he makes no concessions to easing the burden for the reader, and that the editors would publish the story in a popular magazine.

Knight always views with deep misgivings whatever will seem, at first look, to advance humanity materially or otherwise. Gifts from well-meaning or not so well-meaning aliens are cause enough for suspicions. Inventions fare no better. In "Semper Fi" (*Analog*, August 1964, under the title "Satisfaction") a device called a mentigraph can reproduce sensations, improve them, and even, it seems, create them. It is better than real life, and so its characteristic side effect is indifference to the real, which is likely to be more a burden than the machine-induced satisfactions. In "Ask Me Anything"(*Galaxy*, May 1951) a gift of knowledge is left to humanity by an alien race they have destroyed. Unable to be destructive themselves, the aliens nevertheless possess a sense of ironic humor and know that the great human failing of humanity is to pervert what it uses. A great new source of knowledge is less likely to lead to transcendence than to self-destruction.

But one of Knight's short stories does offer humanity a chance and introduces his most appealing alien, the indescribable one in the pages of "Four in One" (*Galaxy*, February 1953). George Meister, and the other members of his exploration team on a strange planet, quite literally "stumble into the most interesting organism" there, by falling into a native life form, a fairly simple and unprepossessing hunk of protoplasm. It absorbs the food that falls onto its body and sinks slowly into it; whatever is indigestible, whatever it does not want, it excretes easily by letting it fall through and out. When George and his companions fall in, their bodies are dissolved for nourishment and their brains and nervous systems worked into the creature's fabric, as being far too interesting to be done away with. They learn slowly of their predicament and opportunity. The story, with its knowledge, comes to us through George's point of view, for he is the quickest witted of the four and the quickest to adjust. He is enchanted by the various possibilities of his discovery; he believes that it should be named, in best scientific style, after him, as "something *meisterii*." The fact is that what at first seems a disaster, destruction of the human vision of itself, is really a great though not easily perceived gift. The creature that these humans have become is capable of repairing almost any injury and is probably immortal. Here is the great gift itself, offered in an unusual vessel; as usual in Knight's stories, the gifts that humans dream of possessing come along in peculiar packages.

Transcendence is a subject that has a powerful grip upon the science fiction imagination. Man is imagined as a limited being. There are bounds to his intelligence, his abilities, his potential and his mortality. To reach beyond the limits seems a wistful dream, often accompanied by the injunction that the human must shed humanity to achieve his aim. In Clifford Simak's "Desertion" (1944), mankind is attempting to survey Jupiter by transforming men into a Jovian life form, the Lopers. But those sent out do not return, for they have discovered that, as Lopers, they transcend human limitations and become something better, more desirable and, at the same time, something inhuman, perhaps inhumane. In *Downward to the Earth* (1969), Robert Silverberg demonstrates convincingly the transcendental virtues of sapient life forms other than human, for immortality is involved. There often seems to be a feeling, expressed or acquiesced in silently, that mankind, as a kind, is far from the perfection of creation. Another step is needed to insure its advancement and, at times, even its survival. Most of the humans in Simak's story choose to become Jovian Lopers and leave Earth to robots, dogs and ants. By the end of Arthur C. Clarke's novel *Childhood's End* (1953), humankind, with the aid of extraterrestrials, evolves to the point where it throws aside the husks of bodies and joins all the single units of spirit or essence into a communal entity—a single mind, an intelligence, perhaps an Oversoul. Mankind's aspirations go beyond the gross fleshly condition. There is no regret in the loss of the human, and the turn to the inhuman is accepted eagerly.

Stories about such transformations are usually very serious, but in "Four in One," Knight manages to handle his subject with some engaging humor and irony. His humans are badly fitted for extraterrestrial exploration. Scarcely knowing each other, they form badly matched teams; in the group that Knight surveys, one otherwise useless member is nothing more than a security officer assigned to make sure that there will be thoughtless and unwavering obedience. If they cannot operate as a team, they certainly cannot operate agreeably as parts of a more intimate unit. George and Vivian can manage sympathetic thought and action, but the others, discordant elements, must be eliminated from the organism.

Then, fleeing from mankind on the planet, for they are likely to be shot on sight, George and Vivian experiment with their new body and even reshape themselves into something resembling human form. They busy themselves learning their potential and readying themselves to use it, realizing that, as George asserts, "We're the future." His new understanding of his destiny, and what is likely to be human destiny, is underlined by the last words of the story: "He had completed the name of his discovery—not, as it turned out, anything *meisterii* at all. *Spes hominis*: Man's hope."[13]

II

In his autobiographical account in *Hell's Cartographers*, Knight talks at some length of his experience with the writing of novels. His first two novels deal, as he says, with the effects of dangerous inventions, and he is persuasive in his conviction that some advances in technology are going to bring about radical changes for the worse. His first novel, *Hell's Pavement* (1955; republished as *Analogue Men*, 1962) has its origins in "The Analogues" (*Astounding*, January 1952), a short story that has not been reprinted, for, with a few changes, it is essentially the first section of the novel. A machine has been invented which curbs people from committing criminal acts by causing them to experience the vision of whatever would prevent them. To the question, what would someone see, Dr. Martyn answers:

> Nobody knows except himself. A policeman, maybe, or his mother as she looked when he was a child. Someone whom he fears, and whose authority he acknowledges. The subconscious has its own mechanism for creating these images; all we do is stimulate it—it does the rest.[14]

Martyn has been able to foresee the possible dangers of such an invention, and the short story tells of his attempts to thwart it. The body of the story is his careful account, to a sympathetic listener, of the dangers inherent in the device: tyranny, for example, if the machine is used to treat anyone who might oppose a government. Martyn's story is plausible, his appeal is powerful, and the listener promises help. But Knight's conclusion is sharp with the irony of the situation. It is already too late; Martyn has himself been treated and is unburdening himself to an analogue, a figure that he wants to be able to tell. He has been ordering drinks for an imaginary confessor. Only a waiter in the bar notices: "If a well-dressed, smart-looking guy like that wanted to sit by himself all evening, talking and buying drinks for somebody who wasn't there, was there any harm in it?"[15] No harm at all, the waiter thinks, but the harm is greater than anyone, even Martyn, might imagine.

A few changes alter the magazine story effectively into the opening of the novel. A new character is created, Kusko, the head of the institute developing and controlling the analogue machine. After Martyn leaves the bar, happy to have been able to put a stop to the possible menace, Kusko encounters the waiter who is puzzled about the customer ordering extra drinks and talking to himself. Is he crazy, the waiter demands. "Not crazy," Kusko answers. "Some would call him 'disturbed,' but he's harmless—now."[16] As indeed he is, and as newsmen are when Kusko can reveal to them the power of the machine; they have been treated so that they will not reveal what he tells them.

These events occur in the year 1990. By 2134, when most of the story takes place, the results of the analogue machine can be clearly seen. People have been treated so that they possess "angels" which guide them along inflexible behavioral paths. For the most part, they are consumers in a society where obsolescence is planned and the production of the easily ruined and disposable is the norm. Consumption is a religion; salesmen belong to a religious order; an appropriately reverent person is "store-fearing"; a "money-saver" is an object of social scorn. The world lives by startling slogans: "The customer is always wrong"; "Parsimony is the root of all evil"; "Wear it out/Trade it in/Use it up/Buy again" (p. 36). The novel takes the reader through this world by taking a young man, Arthur Bass, through it too. Arthur is one of the very few who are immune to the treatment of the analogue machine, and so he possesses no angel and has to fake his reactions. He is singled out, given special training, and becomes a member of an underground movement that is trying to change the system.

But changes do not come easily; the system is deeply embedded in the social fabric:

> The analogue treatment was originally developed as a control for dangerously unstable persons; but it worked so well that in the last century and a half, mental instability has become the norm .... we can't get adequate figures, but we have a good reason to think that three people out of ten would be hopelessly insane without their "angels." (p. 207)

It is not possible to pull down even a subversive system without causing chaos. It is only just possible to try to delay the inevitable crash till its effects might be lessened.

The chief pleasures of the novel come from Knight's inventiveness. The society he portrays is vividly exhibited. When Arthur is sent to college, presumably to educate him to be a salesman, there is a chance for a neat exercise in satire. The ostensible curriculum includes "Sacred Physics, Mercantile Philosophy I, Mercantile History, Sacred Mathematics and Consumer Psychology" (p. 127). But the College is the underground's most effective instrument for change, and its hidden agenda includes a curriculum that the present masters of the world would not approve.

In discussing his second novel, *A for Anything* (1959), Knight says, "I thought I would try this again with another gadget, and this time I chose the matter duplicator, because I thought previous writers had handled it badly."[17] The statement reveals something of Knight's method: he has carefully surveyed the field, taken note of subjects and treatments, and then made the subjects his own by changing them, introducing new elements, making them more logical. Sometimes he has seemed to turn them inside out to see what new motives they can reveal. In an article "What is Science Fiction?" Knight attempts definitions, drawing from a variety of sources. He concludes that a story is perceived as science fiction when it contains the right mix of the following elements: science, technology and invention; the future and the remote past, including all time travel stories; extrapolation; scientific method; other places, such as planets and dimensions, and the visitors from them; and catastrophes, natural or manmade.[18] The list is a thorough one, and it would be difficult to find a science fiction story whose themes did not fit somewhere in it. Knight, who has treated most of the subjects, is wry about some of them. In introductory remarks to "Anachron," one of his short stories, he says, "This is the first of a series of stories that God sent me as a punishment for having said that the time-travel story was dead."[19]

A matter duplicator is just about as possible as a time machine, and Knight offers about as much detail in working out its conception. Here again he is developing a novel from a previously published short story, "A for Anything" (*F&SF*, November 1957), and, again, it is worthwhile to see how he brings in changes as the story develops. The matter duplicator is a version of the legends of fabulous providers of something from nothing, the cornucopia, the magic lantern, or the miraculous purse that never empties. In Knight's story, the device is, appropriately enough, a cross, Constantine's sign for conquering. In the magazine story, but not in the novel, Knight offers some theory to explain the invention. If there are parallel worlds, each containing possible versions of people and lives, there ought to be such manifolds of all other objects as well:

> everything—dogs, trees, chewing gum. Stars. Movie theaters. One of everything, out of a possible infinity. So when you ask me where the extra ring came from, or whatever, I can say to you that maybe we rotated it in from one of these other space-times. We caused one little speck of matter to move from one line to the other.[20]

In the novel Knight dispenses with explanations of where the machine comes from and how it works. It is a Gismo that works, and that is enough. A gismo, after all, is nothing more than a whatsit, a manifestation of the inexplicable, a miracle. So the novel begins when a character receives a package containing simple operating instructions and two of the machines. The reasons for the unknown inventor-genius to send two machines are straightforward and self-evident. Everything can now be duplicated, including the duplicating machine itself. The effort is minimal, the power source is minimal; but the effects are enormous and far-reaching. What Knight has done is to take sf as a version of "science beyond science" and ask the proper questions about it. If a device can exist—never mind that we do not think it can—then we must ask, what are the expected results. Before the end of the original short story, Knight demonstrates that one of the results will be a society where slavery becomes the norm.

Then, as he has done before, Knight takes the reader into a distant enough future to see how widespread the effects of his cause have become. In the fourth chapter of the novel, we are in the world of the year 2149, and the society we know of—production, interdependence and economic liberalism—has been displaced by a society of a wealthy minority borne up by slavery. It is a world of feudal estates, or Keeps, such as Buckhill, where Dick Jones, a young man who has been born into a position of wealth and rank, is ready to be sent to Eagles, another Keep where he will receive further education and training to enable him to succeed his father as leader in his own community. Knight is able to draw upon a useful and well-known novelistic technique, the story of education; as Dick learns how the world works, the reader learns with him. It is a world of preferment and power. The usual possessions mean little because they can be easily duplicated. Slaves, or slobs, can be duplicated as easily as jewelry, clothing, food. There is a rare virtue in possessing something which will not be duplicated, a private possession, or one's own self. And while food can easily be duplicated and come before the diner fresh and hot, it is a sign of lower status to eat duplicated food; better to eat freshly produced food, freshly prepared by slaves, at great labor and expense. The slaves, duplicated in large numbers, are, in one of Knight's bits of wordplay, "dupes," or duplicates, made from a single "prote," a prototype. The novel is, in large part, about being duped or deceived. At Eagles, Dick learns that his own picture of the world is inaccurate. Ruell, who has planned to act for him as friend and counselor, explains:

> At Eagles, everything is power; orbits and spheres of power, tides of power. As you have none yourself, you must take a protector: the question is, which? Now nothing is ever given for nothing, at Eagles; what have you to offer? Let's see; no particular talents nor skills, no connections at Eagles except myself—and nothing to expect from me but good advice,

incidentally—no supporters, no special information, in short, nothing but your person. . . We shall have to make a ladies' man of you.[21]

The freemen, at the top of society, dupe themselves into believing that the slaves are less than human because they are duplicated, that to be duped is to be a slave. When Dick is asked if it would make a difference if he learned that he, himself, had been duplicated, he reasons:

What difference would it make? Why, all the difference. Between freedom and slobbery—between all the good, decent, proud things and all the abased, slovenly, subhuman things. (p. 185)

But slaves are not subhuman because they are duplicated. The choice of a prototype that is not especially bright, a deliberate act of the masters, has contributed to their inferiority. And they have even overcome this defect to a degree, demonstrating that they are not subhuman by setting up a subculture below ground and successfully, at least for a time, overturning the system in a carefully planned revolt. Their wise leader offers Dick a chance at leadership when Eagles falls into the hands of the slaves; they recognize that he could mediate between them and other vengeful Keeps. But he cannot put off his freeman prejudices and sides with his kinsmen who put down the insurrection. He is ready to continue the cycle rather than break it and begin to change the world for the better; or, as he puts it, "he knew he was a Man at last, and had his work ahead of him" (p. 208).

A crushing form of slavery and life without choice are some of the effects of technological discovery. But another powerful side effect of the Gismo is that it has brought scientific progress to a halt. Space travel, a promising development, has not been continued because the dominant society, seeing the far-ranging effects of one invention, fears that another such could rip open the fragile stability of the social fabric and ruin civilization. Population is down sharply, cities have been abandoned in favor of the Keeps— each an independent fiefdom—and much of the world has reverted to forests. Consideration of possible alternatives, of action and changes, is restricted to club meetings and discussions that go nowhere.

Careful extrapolation in these two novels builds a vivid picture of possible futures resulting from man's unbridled inventiveness. A third novel, *Beyond the Barrier* (1963), is very different. There is nothing better than Knight's own description of it:

> I turned for relaxation to another novel which I made up as I went along; I called it *The Tree of Time*. It was a wild van Vogtian adventure involving an amnesiac superman from the future and a search for a monster which turned out to be the hero in disguise, etc. I enjoyed writing it . . . . All my friends and well-wishers hated it, but I sold it everywhere—F&FS, Doubleday, book club, paperback.[22]

The title, *The Tree of Time*, was given to the magazine serial version (*F&SF*, December 1963, January 1964), and the story is as wild as Knight hints. He had criticized A.E. van Vogt devastatingly in the past, and perhaps God was punishing him again by sending him a van Vogt plot to work out. It features mysterious murders, odd aliens, a monster called a Zug, a time machine and a rather confusing plot. It is interesting to see Knight turning, somewhat uncharacteristically, in this direction. The novel reads well and is fast-paced. It does seem lighter in weight than Knight's other books; perhaps it is more a story for relaxation, an adventure rather than a book of serious thematic import. But it is attentive to detail and is well thought out in its motivation.

Although Knight barely mentions *The Other Foot* (1966) in his autobiographical account, he does call it his favorite among his books.[23] This short novel has also been published under an alternative title, *Mind Switch*, possibly because that title gives it more a flavor of science fiction. At any rate, the titles complement one another in revealing Knight's themes. At one level, the story is about a familiar subject in science fiction and fantasy, the switch of identities between Martin Naumchik, a male human, and "Fritz," an extraterrestrial biped. But, at once, Knight begins to offer variations on the theme. The bipeds from Brecht's Planet, some eighteen light years from Earth, are hardly monstrous or terrifying; instead, they are smaller, milder and rather more likeable than their human counterparts. Here Knight takes the opportunity to demonstrate sympathetically the difficulties of being imprisoned in a new identity, a different body, a different set of feelings, as Martin, in Fritz's body, becomes a zoo animal. Meanwhile, Fritz, in Martin's body, has all the problems of coping in a confusing and threatening alien society.

But the alternative title is there as well, to remind the reader that Knight is also talking about "the shoe being on the other foot." An extraterrestrial biped is handled with an odd mix of courtesy and casual cruelty; the Herr Doktor Gruck, director of the zoo, shakes hands with Fritz and is careful not to show distaste. But he is happy to acquire a new animal for display and handles him as one might a dog, opening the biped's jaw to show his "dentition," or probing his groin with a hand to show the audience his "sexual maturity." Martin quickly becomes aware, in Fritz's body, of the degradation of being a zoo species.

Knight is also concerned with human myopia in sexual matters. The sexual shoe is on the other foot. Because Fritz is provided with inguinal glands resembling a human male's, it seems natural to assume that the little biped is also male. But it is learned that the organ has nothing to do with reproduction, and that "Fritz" is a female rather than a male. This is a neat turnabout; a creature with a stronger, male-appearing body is female, and the real male has a slighter, female-appearing body. The female, "in rut" as the humans express it, assumes the aggressive role in courting and lovemaking (pp. 132-133). The male seed is not fired into the female, but is carried on the forehead in a colorful egglike knob, which the female aggressively bites off and ingests. All of this material is sketched in lightly by Knight. Martin never learns what it is like to be a man in a woman's body, for he is generally too preoccupied with learning what it is like to be a human in an alien's body and with trying to make his predicament known. The inversion of sexual roles is meant to come as a surprise at the very end of the novel and so it requires a retrospective survey of the various complexities of the story to get at Knight's motifs.[24]

The mind switch itself is the result of a faulty experiment in time travel which is being conducted in another location. The experiment leads to "a zone of turbulence in the spacetime continuum" (p. 19), a pleasingly unexplained device that causes more than the unfortunate switching of identities between Martin and Fritz. The dislocations in time and space are widely variable. The present time of the novel is the year 2002, but the dislocations reach back in time to 1950, when a flower blooms, inexplicably, on the moon; to 1970, when an Omaha apartment building disappears, to turn up, months later, in the Atlantic Ocean as a catastrophe of destruction and drownings. The dislocations move forward, to the year 2369; backwards, to the writing on the wall in Babylon, and to the freezing of mammoths in Siberia. Knight shows a prodigality of invention in his tale, capable of sustaining a much longer novel, or even another book.

III

A form of fiction that seems to suit Knight's talents and gifts particularly is the short novel. Like a number of other writers, he has been able to take advantage of its virtues and peculiarities. A short story, a splendid mold, is sometimes just too compact; a novel can lose some of its force through its range, diversity and length. But the novella, or short novel, allows the writer to work beyond the restrictions of the short story and still retain much of its unity. A recent collection, *Rule Golden and Other Stories* (1979) offers five of Knight's short novels and exhibits his range effectively.

In *The Dying Man* (*Infinity*, September 1957, under the title "Dio"), he treats, poetically, the subject of immortality by opposing a world of immortals to a single aberrant case of mortality, aging, and death, and is thus able to describe, in detail, the kind of social fabric achieved by a single technological discovery. We have seen that immortality has been an attractive motif in science fiction when it is accompanied by transcendence, a change from the human. It seems to be a curse when it remains shackled to the human form. Jonathan Swift's Gulliver had praised the immortality of the struldbrugs, enlarging upon the magnificent advantages of longevity, till he learned the terrible truth that immortality was accompanied by aging, senility, loss of economic stability and isolation from the younger generations. An earlier story by Knight, "World Without Children" (1951), takes hold of some of the problems of immortality. Side effects include sterility, ennui, a halt to progress; having achieved interstellar travel, people are disinclined to do much about it. A resistance movement fails, and the men involved are imprisoned and left skeptical about the future:

> We're here, and we're the last, and that's all. After that, nothing but the big dark and the big cold. Besides, it isn't going to be very pleasant later on, and people will begin to see that, too. There's a bottom limit to the size of population that can support an industrial economy. They'll pass it, going down .... Wars. Plagues. Natural catastrophes. Crop failures. Looters and bandits. Every man for himself.[25]

Fortunately for humanity, women have taken the matter into their hands and secretly provided new births for new generations to succeed the older ones in the world.

In *The Dying Man*, a central condition to the techniques that provide immortality has been an arrest to the process of maturation;

the immortals are youthful, exuberant, eternal adolescents. When Dio, the mortal man, begins to mature, grow and age, he learns that the price of immortality has been a hollowness, a detachment from reality and, inevitably, boredom. The art of sculpture, for example, is too easy when the granite can be cut and treated like a piece of cheese; for it to be worthwhile, the stone must fight back. The eternal adolescents are a sad lot, wandering restlessly, seeking games, entertainment, change. There is nothing for them to do; and in a mortal life, however limited it is, there is something to do. Work and art are barricades against the attack of mortality. The changing perspectives of one's ages are vital, and there is an orderliness and inevitability to the process that lend it dignity and significance. Dio comes to understand this, and his attitude to it is the usual mortal one, fear of the inevitable, but a respectful attention to its part in the whole process of existence:

> Here I am, going to die, and I wouldn't go back. You see, I want to be myself; yes, I want to go on being myself. Those other men were not me, only someone on the way to be me. (p. 186).

Knight has been able to make the best possible case for immortality by giving his immortals health, eternal youth, companionship, economic freedom. In such a circumstance, Gulliver and other wishers for longevity should be satisfied. But the worm gnaws. The process is not natural and therefore not satisfactory.

In important ways, Knight is again showing the effects of invention upon entire civilizations. In *Natural State*, the subject is the slow collapse of the cities, the remnants of a civilization based upon the machine. Few cities are left by the year 2064; they are short of metals, they have reached a crisis stage where they will have to plunder one another, and though their citizens will not admit it or do not understand, they are doomed as socio-economic units. To the citizens of the cities, it is civilization and refinement which they represent, as against the Muckfeet, barbarians and objects of scorn who inhabit the outside world, eating disgusting natural foods, smelling bad and remaining unaware of the great virtues of a mechanical civilization.

The story is cast in a comic and ironic vein, in which Knight adopts the device of sending a city-bred man out among the natives, charged with the task of changing their ways and converting them into consumers of the city's products. He has the conditioning of his own background and a built-in disgust to overcome, as well as all the prejudices that favor his own way of doing things. What is borne upon him slowly is that the outworld way is the sensible and progressive way, and the way of his cities is ruinous. Biological engineering has been perfected to the extent that the outsiders can live more efficiently than their citified counterparts, at lower outlays in time, labor and wealth, and with a more sensible adjustment to the environment. Here Knight dips grandly into fantasy as his characters, growing everything they can possibly need, breed animals and plants with special talents and capacities. Talking birds become libraries, remembering and reciting. There are houseplants which grow complete houses, eggs which produce weaving insects that will create whole garments, salamanders for heating, knife bushes, glovebeasts. A racing animal is "part horse, part lynx, part camel, and part pure horror."[26] It is a charming and fascinating collection of monstrosities, all presented with straightforward humor and all nearly entirely convincing.

The Muckfeet have art and drama. Alvah, the city man, who has been a promising "realie actor" before taking on his mission, joins a theatrical company that is doing *Hamlet*, a play he didn't know:

> [It] turned out to be an archaic version of *The Manager of Copenhagen*. The text was nothing like the modernized abridgement he was used to, or the Muckfeet's slovenly speech either. It was full of words like *down-gyved* and *unkennel*. It was three-quarters incomprehensible until he began to get the hang of it, but it had a curious power. *For who would bear the whips and scorns of time, the oppressor's wrong, the proud man's contumely, the pangs of despised love,* and so on and so on. It rumbled, but it rumbled well (pp. 139-140).

Alvah is shocked, then relieved, to learn that he has the makings of a promising stage actor. The story records his slow and reluctant acceptance of a way of life he had been taught to hate, a sensible coming to terms with what he had denied, and the gaining of love and affection from a people he had learned to disdain. By the end of the novel, he is allied with the Muckfeet and acts as their intermediary in negotiating the surrender of his own city.

Rule Golden (Science Fiction Adventures, June 1954) represents a somewhat startling reversal for Knight. An alien comes to Earth and is captured by a worried United States government. As it turns out, he is inflicting the gift of peacefulness upon our violent citizenry. Before Earth can break out into the community of powerful extraterrestrials, its inhabitants must learn, once and for all, the golden rule they have mouthed and hardly ever practiced.

With a considerable amount of disorientation, they do learn and are made better. The story takes a view like that of "Stranger Station," though, here, the alien's problem is more easily solved, humankind is changed without being wholly transformed, and the gift exacts no terrible price. In *The Earth Quarter* (*If*, January 1955), there is more of the ironic sharpness we have come to expect of Knight, with humans out in the community of extraterrestrials, but this time as remnants of a broken civilization and as ghettoized immigrants in the shabby quarter of an alien city upon a strange planet.

Double Meaning is another novella which hinges on the reversal of attitudes, as people come slowly to the understanding that their accepted, lived-with version of life is probably all wrong. This is Knight's tale of galactic empire, a concept he believes to be "a practical impossibility."[27] In the year 2518, the Earth Empire is powerful and confident. It has a policy toward non-human cultures that includes surveillance, or war, or subversion and sabotage. But, faced with crisis, it demonstrates that it has become a decaying artifact, suffering from rigidity, "excessive reliance on prescribed methods and regulations, and inadequate emphasis on original thinking." The excuse of its officials is size; the empire contains two hundred and sixty inhabited planets and a population of more than eight hundred billion. Pembun, an outworlder from a planet that has won its independence from the empire, is independent in his thinking and, in a report, can diagnose and report the ills of an ossified state:

> The tendency of Empire executive personnel to interpret regulations and directives in a rigid and literal manner is in my opinion clearly related to the increasing tendency toward standardization in Home World art, manners, customs and language. In the final category, I would cite the obsolescence of all Earth languages except Standard, and in Standard the gradual elimination of homonyms and synonyms, as well as the increasing tendency to restrict words to a single meaning... (p. 220).

The failure of the Earth Empire to deal with the alien Rithian campaign of terror hinges upon this defect of language. The Rithians are flexible physically, mentally and linguistically. Their plot against Earth works on the basis of humor and puns which offer considerable leeway in interpretations. Faced with the probable locations where bombs have been placed, security officials cannot penetrate the clues offered them because the clues can be interpreted according to a wide variance of language and meanings.

Mankind is victimized by its own tendency to slough off originality, clear thought and cranky individualism.

It is often a dark future that Knight posits for mankind. Its ingenuity can be its ruination; inventiveness can lead to stagnation; ambitions and needs can place it in untenable positions. Humanity seems to possess only the most limited possibilities for success. But Knight himself says it well:

> who are we? where have we come from? where are we going? what is man? and how should he live? If we are to survive as a culture, which at this hour is not certain, these are the problems we are going to have to solve, and they are as exciting now as the problems of space travel were fifty years ago.[28]

Notes

[1]Among Knight's anthologies are *A Century of Great Short Science Fiction Novels* (1964), *Science Fiction of the Thirties* (1975), *A Science Fiction Argosy* (1972) and *A Pocketful of Stars* (1971).

[2]Damon Knight, "Knight Piece," in *Hell's Cartographers: Some Personal Histories of Science Fiction Writers*, ed. Brian W. Aldiss and Harry Harrison (New York: Harper & Row, 1975), pp. 96-143, 225-227.

[3]Damon Knight, *In Search of Wonder: Essays on Modern Science Fiction* (Chicago: Advent Publishers, 1967), p. xii.

[4]Damon Knight, "Wine With Your Bottle, Sir?" *F&SF* (May 1959), 76. Reprinted in *In Search of Wonder*, p. 136.

[5]Damon Knight, "Introduction," *Rule Golden and Other Stories* (New York: Avon, 1979), p. 3.

[6]See, for example, the article on Knight in *The Science Fiction Encyclopedia*, ed. Peter Nicholls (New York: Doubleday, 1979), pp. 334-335. Knight's short story collections include *Far Out* (1961), *In Deep* (1963), *Off Center* (1965), and *Turning On* (1966). A number of stories have not been collected from original magazine publication. *The Best of Damon Knight* (New York: Pocket Books, 1976) contains twenty stories but leaves out some of the best, an unfortunate omission since some of the earlier collections are not easily available. A useful bibliography and an article by Theodore Sturgeon on Knight's writings can be found in the November 1976 issue of *F&SF*, a "Damon Knight Issue."

[7]*Those Who Can: A Science Fiction Reader*, ed. Robin Scott Wilson (New York: New American Library, 1973), p. xi.

[8]"No Woman Born," in *The Best of C.L. Moore*, ed. Lester del Rey (New York: Doubleday, 1975), pp. 206-207.

[9]*Those Who Can*, p. 210.

[10]*A Pocketful of Stars*, ed. Damon Knight (New York: Doubleday, 1971), p. 250.

[11]*The Best of Damon Knight*, p. 9.

[12]*Hell's Cartographers*, p. 227.

[13]Damon Knight, *In Deep* (New York: Manor Books, 1972), p. 40.

[14]Damon Knight, *Hell's Pavement* (Greenwood, Ct: Fawcett, 1971), p. 12.

[15]"The Analogues," *Astounding* (January 1952), p. 45.

[16]*Hell's Pavement*, p. 19.

[17]*Hell's Cartographers*, p. 135.

[18]*Turning Points: Essays on the Art of Science Fiction*, ed. Damon Knight (New York: Harper & Row, 1977), p. 63.

[19]*The Best of Damon Knight*, p. 145.

[20]"A for Anything," *F&SF* (November 1957), p. 9.

[21]Damon Knight, *A for Anything* (New York: Avon, 1980), p. 89.

[22]*Hell's Cartographers*, pp. 140-141.

[23]*Hell's Cartographers*, p. 140. Damon Knight, *The Other Foot* (New York: Macfadden; Barthell Corp., 1971).

[24]I am especially indebted, at this point, to Professor Thomas L. Wymer for his perceptive and suggestive comments about the sexual themes in the book, and I have gratefully made use of his suggestions.

[25]"World Without Children," *Galaxy* (December 1951), p. 49. The story is reprinted in *Five Galaxy Short Novels*, ed. H.L. Gold (New York: Doubleday, 1958).

[26]"Natural State," *Galaxy* (January 1954), p. 30. The magazine illustrations by Emsh offer a vivid addition to the story that is lost in the book reprint.

[27]*Rule Golden and Other Stories*, pp. 2-3. The story, published in *Startling Stories*, January 1953, appears in book form as *The Rithian Terror* (New York: Ace Books, 1965), part of an Ace Double volume which also printed Knight's short story collection *Off Center*.

[28]Damon Knight, "Goodbye, Henry J. Kostkos, Goodbye," in *Clarion II: An Anthology of Speculative Fiction and Criticism*, ed. Robin Scott Wilson (New York: New American Library, 1972), p. 84.

The Majesty of Kindness:
The Dialectic of Cordwainer Smith

Gary K. Wolfe & Carol T. Williams

"There's a special sort of majesty to kindness. It's the best part there is to being people."

C'mell, in "The Ballad of Lost C'mell"

Paul Myron Anthony Linebarger, who wrote science fiction under the unlikely name "Cordwainer Smith," was a man of many careers and a writer of striking constrasts. As the above quotation suggests, he was supremely concerned about what is most important about being human—yet his most memorable heroines are apt to be not human at all, but rather cats and dogs. He was a writer whose stories, written mostly during the fifties and sixties, seem remarkably prescient about our own age's concerns involving sex and love, romance and nationalism—yet he set most of these stories in a distant future bizarre even by science fiction standards. As a professor of political science and an authority on propaganda and psychological warfare, he was acutely sensitive to the dangers of self-delusion and romantic idealism—yet as a science fiction writer he gave the genre some of its grandest and most delicate romantic myths. His best stories—"The Ballad of Lost C'mell," "The Dead Lady of Clown Town," "The Game of Rat and Dragon," "Scanners Live in Vain"—repeatedly seek to find some unifying principle between romantic dreams and mundane reality, between personal stories and vast political movements, between tender human emotions and fierce, threatening environments that can be conquered only through technology. He was among the first modern science fiction writers to recognize the visionary potential of the technological imagination—and his visions were technologically sound enough that already today one of them—the notion of photonic sail-ships—is being seriously discussed as a possible means of propulsion in deep space.

Even the name under which he published his science fiction stories might be taken as symbolic of the dual concerns that consistently characterize his work—"cordwainer," the shoemaker, worker in leather, shaper of animal skins into something resembling human form; and "smith," the worker in metals, maker of tools, technologist. The organic and the technological—these are the contrasts that lie at the heart of the first story published under the name Cordwainer Smith, and they would remain important throughout the remainder of his too-brief career as a science fiction writer. The first story was "Scanners Live in Vain," and though written in 1945, it was rejected by every major science fiction publication before finally being accepted by an obscure oversized pulp called *Fantasy Book* in 1950.[1]

"Scanners" are human beings surgically restructured to survive in the hostile environment of space, variously called "the Up-and-Out" or "the Great Pain of Space." Part human and part machine, the Scanners have had their brains severed from all sensory input and must take periodic readings of the instruments attached to their bodies even to discover if they have themselves been injured. Although the scanners perceive themselves as heroic, there is nothing transcendent about this union of man and machine, and the scanner is one of the most memorable images in science fiction of the literal dehumanization of man in the service of technology and the appropriation of the cosmos. The protagonist of the story, Martel, is a Scanner married to a human woman, and thus caught between the worlds of technology and human relations. In order to experience human sensations when he is with his wife, he must "cranch" (a process never clearly explained). Cranching makes a Scanner human, but it makes him ineffectual as a Scanner; thus the Scanners must choose between being human and being mechanical (or between being alive and being dead, as Martel thinks of it): they cannot be both at once.

This, then, is the central dilemma of the story. Humans cannot travel safely in space without the protection of the Scanners, and Scanners cannot function without sacrificing a part of their humanity. Space is the realm of technology, earth of the organic. The title of the story refers to the discovery of a new scientific process that would render the Scanners unnecessary. At first, the Scanners respond to this threat to their profession like a powerful labor union: they decide that the scientist who discovered the new process, Adam Stone, must be killed. Martel, realizing the full value of Stone's discovery, thwarts the murder attempt and, like other Scanners, is surgically restored as a human.

And what is this great discovery of Stone's that enables humans to survive in the "great pain of space" without Scanners, this new synthesis that permits man to leave earth without suffering the dehumanization that the Scanners represent? It is a synthesis of the organic and the technological that is idiosyncratically Cordwainer Smith's. " 'I have loaded the ships with life'," Stone explains to Martel. By insulating the passengers with masses of living things, Stone found, they would remain unhurt by the pains of space. " 'I tried many kinds, and finally found a sort of life which lives in the waters. Oysters. Oyster-beds. The outermost oysters died in the great pain. The inner ones lived. The passengers were unhurt' " p. 35. Through this discovery, man is able to retain his humanness without sacrificing his technology, but only if that techology is based on a model of life (the oysters) rather than machines (the Scanners).

So Cordwainer Smith became the only science fiction writer to give us an image of humans soaring through space in spaceships full of oysters. It is a bizarrely comic image and a strangely poetic one, but primarily it is an image of the kind of dialectical synthesis that Smith constantly strove for in all his writings. He would later give us even stranger images of space travel—men battling out-space dragons with the aid of telepathic cats, enormous photonic sails with pods of passengers trailing along behind, golden warships ninety million miles long, passenger ships in which travel seemed like spending an afternoon on the lawns of Mt. Vernon. And yet none of these images is quite as frivolous as it might at first seem. For all his wild imaginings, Cordwainer Smith was a writer deeply concerned with the most fundamental human issues—how to achieve sexual and social identity, how to use power, how to reconcile romantic dreams with mundane reality, how to gain both protection and freedom, how to remain human in the face of technology—even how to *become* human, and what it is that defines "being people." At times, he addresses these questions in ways that may seem to some simplistically Christian; at other times, he introduces ambiguities and complexities of meaning that invite and reward even the skeptic rereading his best stories several times.

Obviously, so complex a writer as Cordwainer Smith was not born full-blown in the pages of *Fantasy Book* in 1950. Nor were the stories of Cordwainer Smith the first works of fiction to come from the pen of P.M.A. Linebarger, Professor of Asiatic Politics at Johns Hopkins, godson of Sun Yat Sen, military intelligence officer in China, author of a classic text on psychological warfare. Linebarger had published a science fiction story as early as 1928, when he was only fifteen, but for most of his diplomatic and academic career the ideas that would later make up the stories of Cordwainer Smith were confined to private notebooks. During this time, Linebarger published his *Psychological Warfare* text, several studies of Asian politics, a spy novel called *Atomsk* (written under the name of Carmichael Smith), and two remarkable non-science fiction novels called *Ria* and *Carola*, both written as Felix C. Forrest—a name, according to J.J. Pierce, adopted as a pun on the name given to Linebarger as Sun Yat Sen's godson, meaning "forest of incandescent bliss."

Both *Ria* and *Carola* are worth looking at briefly, not only for the ways in which they foreshadow the science fiction of Cordwainer Smith, but also for the perspective they offer on why Linebarger may have finally turned to science fiction, and why he found his greatest success there. Linebarger published *Ria* in 1947. Both it and *Carola* were written while he was in China and mailed to the United States in installments. On its surface the 1947 novel is the story of Ria, a thirty-six year old American war widow troubled with a psychosomatically crippled hand. The burden of the plot is a kind of psychological detective story concerning Ria's quest through memory for the source of her problem and specifically her memories of a period spent in 1922 at a German spa named Bad Christi. Though the novel is interesting for its feminine perspective and for the issues of political philosophy raised by the characters at Bad Christi—issues that seem to be the entire *raison d'etre* of the novel's middle section, which moves away from Ria's quest to concentrate on these other characters—it also offers numerous insights into the central ideas that were to occupy Linebarger in his later fiction. Among the characters of the novel and their concerns, we can already see Linebarger's imagination straining at the limiting conventions of "realistic" fiction and trying to explore ideas and even characters that would be better suited to a science fiction milieu. One character, for example, is a German named Baerenschlaeger who moves to America in search of an heroic new world and changes his name to Charles Bearslay. But Bearslay finds the new world rewarding only in its technology; he feels alive only on the highways driving his powerful LaSalle, which in a moment of insight into the relation of man and technology he sees as, " 'Good God and Jesus!...Better than I am!' "[2]

> Everything was perfect except living. That was bad. American life was poor, nervous, wild, dreary. He had this machine, this satiny green perfection of articulate steel; but he had nowhere to go.... As long as he, Karl Baerenschlaeger, could be the soul of a green LaSalle coupe, he was something worth being; but when he had to be the man, Charles Bearslay—ah, then, he was not so much! (p. 133)

Bearslay's identification with his heroic machine, in its mundane way, gives us a hint of the power that comes from identifying with technology—power that would later be expressed in more mythic form in Cordwainer Smith's fantastic stories of scanners, pinlighters, and go-captains.

Other characters as well foreshadow the world of Cordwainer Smith. Among the visitors to Bad Christi is a character who personally almost verges on science fiction—a seven foot tall, ninety year old Russian *emigre* named Prince Todschonotschidsche, who seems to be something of a mouthpiece for political and philosophical ideas that Linebarger wants to explore, but cannot work easily into his narrative. The Prince explains to Ria that we are not to be explained by any "materialistic philosophy" such as Bolshevism, but that our everyday selves are " 'the masque for some creature of an unknown order.' " This unknown creature within is the source of all our vital power, of the energies which make us human, and it does not yield to simple formulations, not even to "good" and "evil" (194).

The Prince's observations are prompted by Ria's involvement with an older German named Carlo Brautigam, a Faustian figure who at once seems hero and villain. Brautigam's philosophies and actions are wrong, the Prince explains, but wrong " 'because he is himself, because there is something in him that is not in the formula of his life. He is doomed because he is strong, because he does have real force' " (197). Brautigam's attempt to break out of the "formula of his life" is an early version of the pattern-breaking that characterizes Smith's science fiction heroes, and his good-evil, "vital force" aspect makes him a clear precursor of the powerful Vomacts in the future world of the Instrumentality of Mankind.

Ria's mother, too, is an early version of a character type who would play a significant role in the Instrumentality stories. She will endure and prevail, says the Prince, by " 'doing the actual work, curing the actual diseases, solving the soluble problems. As to the insoluble...they [these characters] leave such things alone' " (199). This could as well be a description of the solid, simple heroes and heroines of the Cordwainer Smith stories—Dita in "The Burning of the Brain," Commander Suzdal of "The Crime and Glory of Commander Suzdal," the cow-man B'dikkat of "A Planet Named Shayol." Smith has his glamorous, romantic heroes and heroines as well, of course, those who do go after the "insoluble," such as Underhill and Lady May in "The Game of Rat and Dragon" or C'mell and Jestocost in "The Ballad of Lost C'mell"—but the real world, he seems to feel, will always be run by the mundane heroes, as we shall see later.

Ria herself comes off rather weakly against these more firmly drawn characters, rather like a screen against which Linebarger projects his more clearly defined figures. At times she seems like a precursor of feminism, wondering aloud to her father if she will be able to count on anything more from life than "marrying the boys" (237); at other times she seems merely a passive participant in events. Perhaps this is intentional; her passivity seems important to the book's mystical climax. Never having found a full explanation for her psychosomatic symptom, Ria stands looking at the night sky over the North Carolina coast and sees approaching "something which came nearer and nearer in enormous, down-looping spirals" (239). This "unseen and indefinable power" is not explained further, but from it Ria learns the deceptively simple lesson that is the "message" of the book, and a lesson that would later be learned, in different fictional contexts, by C'mell and others: "Everything you ever do, everything you ever think, becomes you.... That's all there is of you. There is no more; you are your life, and the things within that life go on resounding forever" (238).

At the very end of the novel, Ria experiences this force again in a dream:

> ...her body and head began to grow. They grew to immense heights.... To the illusion of height, there came an illusion of sound. A deep resonance, unlike any sound which she had heard before, came to her. Just as she had looked with her eyes at the unseen, so now she strained with her ears for the unheard. She listened, and this time there was no tension, fear, no hypnotized passiveness. She felt that she stood somewhere in the lower part of her own tremendous skull, and that she listened to the fluent deep roar of a resounding bronze instrument of some kind—something metallic, something which sounded like the instrumentality of man, not like the unplanned noises of nature and the sea (241).

Apart from the fantastic imagery of this passage, Linberger here first introduces a phrase that is to become perhaps the single key concept in his science fiction stories—"the instrumentality of man." In the Cordwainer Smith stories, of course, the Instrumentality of Mankind is the all-powerful, ultimately sufficient universal government that serves as the agency of man in the universe. But as this pasage from *Ria* suggests, "instrumentality" becomes a kind of pun, meaning not only agency, but also instrumentation—the works of man as opposed to the works of nature. The antinomy becomes crucial to Linebarger's later fiction.

Carola, published in 1948, also offers insights into Smith's work, but less through a variety of characters than through the attempts of Carola to establish her own identity, through its acute portrayal of psychological relationships, and through its portrayal of cultures in conflict. *Carola* seems to handle the woman's viewpoint more successfully than *Ria*, but its story is even more complex. It is told in flashbacks from the point of view of a woman who seems at first inordinately fond of the paraphernalia of American life and femininity:girdles, stockings, high-heeled shoes, and the world of order and cleanliness these things represent:

> She liked the highness of this American world, and the cleanliness, and the good sterile deadness. Nothing lived but man, save for an occasional bewildered bird. Carola liked it that way. She hated to see green things grow. She hated the lush, brainless hostility of plants which sat rooted and defiant in the earth to which they maintained a mute but willful claim. Carola liked and admired the human beings who had set the mark of their control upon the natural world.

Carola would be a model citizen for the Instrumentality of Mankind in its decadent phase, but the earlier events of her life explain well how she came to this attitude. Episodes from her childhood reveal how she felt rejected by her parents in favor of a brother who had died, and how in her earliest search for identity she began to androgynously identify with "little dead brother." Later, perhaps in an outgrowth of this, she becomes so closely involved with a female friend that there is talk of lesbianism. These rumors cause her first lover, a radical named Ugo, to spurn her, and she eventually marries a Chinese student visiting the United States, Carson Ding, and returns to live with him in China. But Carson's mother is insanely jealous: she has Carola drugged, her clothes stolen, and even her baby killed. Furthermore, Carson's brother, who calls himself Tarzon, clearly has designs on Carola. Desperate, Carola has an affair with a Nazi while on a vacation with Carson in 1931. Gradually, Carson comes to feel she has alienated him from his family and culture, and expresses a wish to die. Carola obligingly smothers him and then allows herself to be raped by Tarzon, taking her vengeance on him by informing him that she has just killed his brother. She makes her way to Shanghai, but is denounced by Americans there as a spy, and turns to the Japanese. A Japanese helps her to get to Lisbon, where she apparently betrays him in order to gain passage to America, where she sets out to build a new life for herself and becomes engaged to a simple, unglamorous man with the unglamorous name E.E. Spoot.

Despite the incredible, Gothic complications of this plot, Linebarger's psychological astuteness shows up again and again— in the love-hate relationship between Carson and Tarzon, in the relationship between Carson and his mother, in Carola's relationships with her parents, with her friend Pauline with whom she is accused of lesbianism, with the radical Ugo, and with Carson himself. Also, the parts of the novel set in China shine with their descriptions of the landscape and culture, and the alienation Carola feels therein. But there are also foreshadowings of Cordwainer Smith, not only in Carola's eventual love for the artificial over the vegetative, for the "instrumentality of man" over the instrumentality of nature, but also in details. Carola's pet cat, Pete, for example, suggests vaguely the telepathic human-cat relationship that is later to play a central role in "The Game of Rat and Dragon": "...sometimes she had the superstitious feeling that Pete was indeed talking to her through telepathy and that his little cat-thoughts were echoing into English as they beat against the sounding board of her own mind" (pp. 217-218). And the teaching of Carola's Chinese mentor Ouyang (a name reflected in the Douglas-Ouyang planets of "Under Old Earth") espouses advice that is no more or less important to Carola's quest for identity than it would be to the scanners and underpeople of the Instumentality. " 'Man has form,' " Ouyang tells Carola. " 'He must stay within that form' " (p. 229).

Many of Carola's problems, Linebarger seems to be saying, arise from her trying to break out of her given form, and Carola's own meditations on this matter are the sheerest science fiction:

> If she were God, herself, and had the power to make of the human individual anything she wished, would she retain two eyes—or instead give the new Adam and Eve multicellular vision? Would she keep the terrible voracity of people, or give them an eating system needing less nearly incessant replenishment? Would she have them have two sexes? If sex was good, why shouldn't there be more of them, so that it would require just the right combination, piquant to discover and induce, to make a team—say, eight or ten, all of them as different, each from the other, as men and women now were? But in the interest of the will, knowledge, curiosity, should people be people at all? What would be the best thing to be? Carola remembered that she had ended up saying:

> *Self-aware omniscient triangles contemplating the universe from outside of time* (p. 212).

Perhaps more than any other passages in his early works, this shows Linebarger straining at the bonds of the traditional genre in which he was working. Even as an interior monologue, such a vision makes Carola seem near-psychopathic: what is clearly needed is a genre in which such imaginings can be accepted for the light they shed on the ideas that underlie them, and where they do not need to be fully subsumed in the mind of a character. In his science fiction stories, Linebarger would indeed experiment with the forms of humanity: first with the Scanners, later with the underpeople and the hideous experiments inflicted upon prisoners in "A Planet Named Shayol." And in the science fiction stories, too, Linebarger would be able to make his romances more romantic, his heroes and heroines more heroic, his politics more elemental. There is much in *Ria* and *Carola* that makes them worth reading, but their overall effect is to demonstrate how much more at home in science fiction Linebarger's imagination was, and how much more successful he was in shorter forms (a judgment that seems borne out even by his one science fiction novel, *Norstrilia,* which, though not lacking in inventiveness, seems something of a diminution and dilution of the powerful themes of his short stories).

Perhaps one reason the Instrumentality stories succeed more than the non-science fiction novels, more even than *Norstrilia,* is that Linebarger's strengths seem to lie less in plotting than in the presentation of individual scenes and the implication of a tantalizing imagined universe. Like many other science fiction writers, Cordwainer Smith makes use of an elaborate scheme of future history that seems far more fully developed than any single story reveals.

Exactly how precisely he intended to establish a chronology for this future history is uncertain; J.J. Pierce's timeline in *The Best of Cordwainer Smith* gives the Instrumentality stories a range of some 12,000 years, from the advent of the Vomacts (daughters of a World War II German scientist who had placed them in suspended animation in orbiting space capsules at the end of the war, and whose descendants play a key role in the Instrumentality) to the "Casher O'Neill" stories (published in book form as *Quest of the Three Worlds*, 1966). Pierce calculates that the Vomacts return to Earth between 4,000 and 5,000 A.D., but in "Mark Elf" (1957), Smith has the first one of the vom Acht sisters, Carlotta, return to earth "about sixteen-thousand years after she left Hitler's Reich."[4] The second sister, Juli, returns some two hundred years later in "The Queen of the Afternoon" (published posthumously in 1978), a story which describes the birth of the Instrumentality. Thus it is possible that all the Instrumentality stories take place sometime after 18,000 A.D.

But the dates are really not important, since the key to Smith's use of future history is not to establish an extrapolative chronology, but to impart to his tales the distancing necesary to give them the quality of true myth, or to convey, in Franz Rottensteiner's terms, "an outlook, a world-view, colored and distorted as if transmitted by oral tradition."[5] His narrators frequently speak as if the reader were aware of the body of legends and myths that make up the history of the Instrumentality, and allude to the ways in which the narratives entered these legends through word-of-mouth. If a more purely extrapolative writer such as Asimov uses the Roman historians as models for his future history, Smith is closer to medieval historians and romancers such as Chretien de Troyes or Geoffrey of Monmouth, or to the ancient Chinese historians and storytellers with which he was so familiar.

And most of the Instrumentality stories are romances in every sense of the word: not only do they portray larger than life figures engaged in epic actions, they also address the romantic dreams of ideal relationships that so affect our notions of sex, love and power. There are certainly political aspects to Smith's ambiguous utopia; the "underpeople" (animals remade in human form) become, as Arthur Burns notes, "a sort of social allegory for the American Negro"[6]; there is evidence of corruption in high places, and the elimination of pain for the upper classes leads to decadence. Linebarger is certainly critical of the rigidly class-structured society such as he saw in China, and is concerned that science might make life too comfortable and predictable. But like other lasting utopians, his imaginary world exists for the sake of this one—to present, through art, his ideas on how to live better this life in this world. And in this the science fiction stories have much in common with *Ria* and *Carola*: romantic dreams may be glorious, but they are not the answer. The mundane and the real are what we must learn to live with and to value. Even Smith's style reflects this deliberate counterbalancing of the romantic with the real; witness this passage from *Norstrilia* describing the realization through a telepathic "linked dream" of the impossible romance between the hero Rod McBan and the cat-girl C'mell. The god-like "Catmaster," E'telekeli, who arranges the linked dream, tells McBan:

> "You want C'mell.... You shall have her, in a linked dream, her mind to yours, for a happy subjective time of about a thousand years. You will live through all the happy things that you might have done together if you had stayed here and become a c'man. You will see your kitten-children flourish, grow old and die. That will take about one half-hour.[7]

The final, jarring sentence brings us abruptly out of the reverie created by the preceding sentences and reminds us that the real world is, after all, what we are living in. Eventually, Rod must return to his human wife, Lavinia, on Earth. He keeps "a special kind of tenderness" for C'mell, and comes to realize, "It was not marriage which they had, but it was pure romance." Lavinia, on the other hand, represents "home itself, and love. Lavinia was in it, dear Lavinia ..."(p. 262). The Lavinias, Smith repeatedly seems to say, are what we must value.

In story after story, mundane reality regularly gives way to sudden, blazing heroism and transcendent romance—only to have the mundane reassert itself in the end. In "The Lady Who Sailed the *Soul*" (1960; co-authored with Linebarger's wife Genevieve), Smith drills us on the drudgery and menial discomfort of captaining a starship through some eighty years of space to "New Earth" and back. The captain is Helen America, Smith's only human woman heroine. At one point when she is being instructed, Helen waxes heroic, reciting to "the technician" all she will do under each trying circumstance, and ending, rather grandiosely, " 'And if the sail fails, I wait as long as I live' " (p. 55). The technician, sounding very much like Linebarger himself, deflates her high-blown ideas of romantic adventure and potential tragedy with a speech that celebrates the mundane. " 'Tragedy is not the hard part'," he says.

> The hard part is when you don't quite succeed and you have to keep on fighting. When you must keep going on and on in the face of really hopeless odds, of real temptations to despair.

> *   *   *

> "You've got to remember what your job is. You're going because a sailor take a lot less weight than a machine.... You go simply because you are expendable.... So remember that the tragedy and the trouble you face is mostly work. Work, and that's all it is. That is your big job" (p. 57).

But despite the anti-romantic aspects of space travel as described by the technician, and despite the tedious training Helen undergoes in preparing for her voyage, it is romance which after all seems to save the day. When mechanical failures endanger her mission, it is saved in the nick of time by the mystical appearance to Helen of her old and only lover, Mr. Grey-no-more, who "stood clear and handsome, the way she had seen him in New Madrid" (p. 63). Helen follows his advice, and miraculously the "forever-unidentifiable obstruction" vanishes and the ship sails on to safety.

Yet lest we be tempted to treat the story as a fable of romance triumphant (or worse, as a sexist parable of the dependent woman saved by the competent man), Smith distances the story by presenting it as told by a mother to her daughter, and then by providing an epilog in which the daughter, now grown, rejects the romantic dream represented both by the toy she had been playing with when her mother told her the story, and by the story itself. As a little girl, she had been playing with a "spieltier," a fantastic combination of doll and animal that at once suggests the manipulation of lower life forms that came to fruition in the underpeople and the traditional sex-role modeling of little girls playing with dolls. As a child, the girl is fascinated by the spieltier and enchanted by the tale of Helen America, but years later, as an adult, she becomes the representative of a new generation, and rejects both the toy and the story. " 'Mom, you ought to get rid of that thing'," she says of her childhood toy. " 'It's all used up and it looks horrible with your nice period furniture' " (p. 65). As for Helen America and Mr. Grey-no-more, the daughter says, " 'it was awful. Those messy people, and the horrible way sailors live. I don't see how you idealized it and called it a romance—' " (p. 66). The mother clings to the romantic ideal, but the daughter warns her not to be " 'a sentimental old slob'," and this ambiguous message comes through to the reader as well. The common-sense, unromantic daughter, the new generation, is what asserts itself in the end.

As names such as "Helen America" and "New Earth" suggest, many of the Instrumentality stories meld this concern with romance versus the mundane with an awareness of our own nationalistic myths. Though Linebarger's politics may be masked by allusion and indirection, his romances often involve the quest for national dreams as well as personal fulfillment—particularly the American dream. In "The Lady Who Sailed the *Soul*," the chief figures of romance are Helen America (who perhaps suggests Helen of Troy as well as America) and the explorer-hero-Columbus figure Mr. Grey-no-more. Helen's passengers, significantly, are pilgrims seeking a new world to settle, "religious fanatics" in the words of a lord of the Instrumentality (p. 54). Mr. Grey-no-more longs to leave "New Madrid" for "New Earth" because, he tells Helen, " 'it's like Earth must have been in the old days, I guess. There's something fresh about it...' " (p. 53). And it is the lure of this new world, this romantic political dream, that causes him to give up the prospect of marriage to Helen (though they are eventually reunited).

"The Burning of the Brain" is another curious romance about love, marriage, and nationalism, but here the parallels with America are made even more explicit. This story takes place at a later period than "The Lady Who Sailed the *Soul*," and the sailing ships have been replaced by "planoforming" ships—Smith's version of the common enough convention of hyperspace. Yet space travel in such a ship is presented in a series of sea and water images that suggest the early explorers of America: space is "rough like the wildest of storm-driven waters"; "The art of getting past all the complications of space was far more like the piloting of turbulent waters in ancient days than like the smooth seas which legendary men once traversed with sails alone" (p. 85). The narrator speaks of "whirlpools" in space, and at takeoff of "the tissue of space" shooting up around the ship "like boiling water" (pp. 87, 89). If this is not enough to suggest sea travel, the captain of the ship is "Magno Taliano," whose name easily translates as "the great Italian," suggesting that he is another Columbus-figure. The American theme is reinforced by the design of the interior of the ship, which "was built to resemble an ancient, prehistoric estate named Mt. Vernon" (87). And Magno's niece and eventual successor as captain is implied to be one of America's first citizens: "she was called 'Dita from the Great South House' " (p. 86).

Amid all these allusions to America, Smith constructs another classic romance, this time about Magno and his wife, Dolores Oh. Dolores was "once so beautiful that she took men's breath away, made wise men fools" (p. 85), and so on. Like Helen America and Mr. Grey-no-more, these lovers are presented as archetypal figures; their story is compared to that of Heloise and Abelard as well as that of Helen America.

They are described as more powerful, more beautiful, braver, and in all ways better than ordinary human beings; their legendary romance had "left forty planets talking and half the ship lines stunned" (p. 85). But Dolores, "proud beyond all common limits of pride," has refused the rejuvenescence process that enables Instrumentality citizens to live four hundred years without aging; she wants it proved that someone likes her for herself and not just for her great beauty (p. 85). And indeed Magno does; for him the "ghastly witch" is still "somehow the beautiful girl he had wooed and had married one hundred sixty-four years before" (p. 87). But Dita, who is telepathic, sees something else in her aunt's mind: a fear "forever and without limit that there was really nothing to herself...without Magno Taliano" (p. 87). This breeds a curious resentment in Dolores: she secretly longs for her husband to be ruined in his profession as her beauty was ruined, and she craves this ruin "as some people crave love and others crave death" (p. 91).

Dolores gets her wish. An inexplicable, "never before committed" error in preparing the planoforming mechanism leaves the ship stranded in space, and Magno must guide it to safety on the unaided power of his brain alone. Doing so, he "burns out" his paleocortex and becomes a gentle, infantile idiot. At the end, led from the room by Dolores, "his face for the first time in more than a hundred years trembled with shy and silly love" (p. 94). When Magno destroys his brain, Dolores bursts into tears, but Smith does not say what those tears mean.

Were it not for Dita, this story, too, might appear sexist, although to make such a charge would be to ignore Smith's compassion for Dolores's fear that "there was really nothing to herself." But the presence of Dita—beautiful, simple, gifted, quietly capable—suggests that it is not women who are castrating, but rather the schism that our conventional ideas of romance enforce between extraordinary beauty and extraordinary talent, between the qualities of male and female. Dita has some of the beauty of Dolores, and in the end, through her telepathic connection with Magno, she acquires as well his remarkable skills as a planoforming captain. Thus, in Smith's dialectic, she becomes an image of the synthesis of the oppositions represented by the two lovers. Dita is not ordinary, but she is not a gloriously romantic figure either, and in some ways she is the noblest expression in Smith's stories of the triumph of the real over the romantic.

Not always is the contrast between the romantic and the mundane carried out in terms of sexual relationships. In "Golden the Ship Was—Oh! Oh! Oh!" (1959)—perhaps the most romantic title in all of Smith's work—a ninety million mile long ship of gold serves as a Trojan horse in the war against Raumsog, a Hitler-like figure whose propaganda was as outrageous as his violations of galactic law, and who "expected Earth to fall before the threat itself" (p. 118). The golden ship is concocted as a dummy to distract the Raumdogians while the real, ugly bombs fall, the work of bureaucrats, epitomes of the mundane. The bombs that are finally used against Raumsog have little of the glamor that the golden ship suggests: they discharge a "combination of organic and inorganic poisons with a high dispersion rate" and kill some seventeen million people in a single night. "The weapons were not noble," Smith tells us (p. 121):

> The Lords of the Instrumentality played at being chivalrous and did love money, but when life and death were at stake, they no longer cared much about money, or credit, or even about honor. They fought like the animals of Earth's ancient past—they fought to kill (p. 121).

These ignoble weapons are sent forth from a ship that in every way is the epitome of the mundane, the unglamorous. The ship is unregistered and bears the "very simple and threatening name: *Anybody*" (p. 119), and it is named by the not particularly heroic

Prince Lovaduck (whose name suggests a proletarian expression of surprise), accompanied by a "chronopathic idiot" capable of moving the ship back and forward in time and a "poor little crazy girl" whose "psionic radiations" create bad luck everywhere on the enemy planet at the moment Lovaduck's ship drops into its atmosphere (p. 119-120). We should not be misled by Smith's unflagging inventiveness in creating such characters, for this is inventiveness used against romance (we shall see it again in "A Planet Named Shayol"): Smith's message is that poor fools, idiots, and second-level bureaucrats will win wars with ugly weapons while golden illusions mesmerize us. And to preserve the illusion, the Lords erase Lovaduck's memory of his mission; the history of wars such as this can be made to seem glamorous only if we suppress the reality. The mundane reality is wiped from memory, the grand illusion kept intact, and the Raumsog war enters the romantic legendry of the Instrumentality as something noble. As the narrator says at the outset of the story, "The Raumsog war was never known to the general public except for the revival of wild old legends about golden ships" (p. 115).

Thus, in stories of war as well as of love, Smith keeps telling us that life is a work of ordinary wonder. When Commander Suzdal in "The Crime and Glory of Commander Suzdal" (1964) rejects the Instrumentality's offer of the company of illusory "dancing girls" for his space mission, his reason is that " 'Getting back to a real Alice [his wife] is going to be one of my biggest reality factors' " (97). As it happens, Suzdal does not get home; he is banished to a prison planet for a crime that threatens one of the fundamental oppositions in Smith's universe: the opposition of male and female.

"The Crime and Glory of Commander Suzdal" is more parable than story. On the planet Arachosia, for no known reason, "feminity became carcinogenic" (p. 103), resulting in the death of all women and the invention of an artificial womb enabling men to be bisexual. Unlike other science fiction portrayals of monosexual societies (Sturgeon's *Venus Plus X* or Le Guin's *The Left Hand of Darkness* for example), Smith's Arachosians turn into an ugly, uncreative, warring homosexual world, lacking the "fundamentals in the human personality itself, the balance of male and female, the family, the operations of love, of hope, of reproduction. They survived, but they themselves had become monsters and did not know it" (p. 106). For Smith, the balance between male and female is essential to the quality of human life, and it is perhaps a mark of Suzdal's heroism that he recognizes this and answers a message to his ship from the Arachosians. This later becomes one of his crimes ("what business was it of his to relieve a distress ages old?" [p. 112]); the other is his inability, once on the planet, to destroy the "monstrous" Arachosians. As a result of his crimes, Suzdal is banished to the Instrumentality's version of Hell, the planet Shayol (from the Hebrew *Sheol*). If Arachosia threatens to break down the opposition between men and women, Shayol threatens an even more fundamental opposition: that between men and animals.

"A Planet Named Shayol" (1961) was published before "The Crime and Glory of Commander Suzdal"—though Suzdal is briefly mentioned in it—and is worth noting for the appearance of another of Smith's "ordinary" heroes, the "cow-man" B'dikkat. B'dikkat is the overseer of the prisoners on the desert planet, where the Instrumentality's mad scientists (including a Dr. Vomact) experiment on them by growing extra limbs and organs in their bodies, aided by painful, parasitic "dromozoa." When "four beautiful children," their brains removed, are sent to the planet for experimentation, B'dikkat revolts. He roars at the convicts:

> "You're people, or you were. You understand people; I only obey them. But this I will not obey.... His face was illuminated by a determination which, even beyond the edges of the drug which made the convicts love him, made him seem like the father of this world—responsible, honorable, unselfish (pp. 367-368).

B'dikkat makes known to the Lords of the Instrumentality the horrors of Shayol and saves the day: not a great hero, but an honorable, ordinary "underperson" pushed to heroic behavior. Like Dita in "The Burning of the Brain," he is a character whom Smith treats with special affection, and like Dita, he is a synthesis of the opposition at the heart of his story, in this case the opposition between man and animal. In other stories as well, we will see how Smith seems to regard the underpeople as symbols of hope, of possible synthesis and resolution.

B'dikkat's simple act of conscience might seem to imply a moral system that is deceptively simple, but when viewed in the context of the overall story of the underpeople, its complexity and importance show clearly. Essentially, it is a reiteration of the message of *Ria* that "everything you ever do...becomes you...you are your life, and the things within that life go on resounding forever." The form of underpeople, as well as of people, is less important than their actions. When in "Alpha Ralpha Boulevard" (1961), the protagonist Paul (one of Smith's few non-heroic human protagonists) is saved from death by C'mell because, she explains, he once saved some young birds, he asks, "Is that all there is to *good* and *bad?*" (p. 313). And Smith's answer seems to be yes: what we do is more important than what we are.

Many of these themes come together in one of Smith's longest tales, "The Dead Lady of Clown Town" (1964), at once an epic romance and a comical anti-romance about ordinary people and underpeople. Of its romantic heroines—Mary, Elaine and D'joan—D'joan is central, but Elaine is the viewpoint character, the reader's point of identification; her life and feelings are described in detail whereas D'joan's are not, and we are let inside her mind.[8]

D'joan is Joan of Arc in dog form, and Smith dwells on Elaine's unromantic, chance begetting by a computer tender who would rather plunk his guitar (pp. 126-129), and on Elaine's humanness. She was born a misfit: an old-fashioned healer-witch who is "doomed" to want to help the sick in an age of hospitals (p. 129). She enters the old "forgotten" door to the world of the underpeople, including D'joan, only, Smith insists, as "the tired caprice of a thoroughly frustrated and mildly unhappy woman. Nothing more. All the other descriptions of it have been improvements, embellishments, falsifications." Yet he himself—typicall of his style—just before these demythifying, realistic words, has written the grand heroic line: "The opening of a door changed her own world and changed life on thousands of planets for generations to come" (p.133). It is his habit to debunk the myths and miracles—and also to report them in the style of simple facts.

When Elaine and the mysterious "Hunter" make love, D'joan becomes Joan, who leads the underpeople out of "life and life-with" and the anti-romance message, "don't possess. Just *be*" (p. 167). In the revolution that follows, the robots join the underpeople. Cruel murder of women and babies (the pretty little blonde" rats with "pink or blue bonnets") is described graphically (pp. 195-196), and signalled as important by the uniqueness of this style in Smith's stories. And the final heroines are two women who are sent to judge the beaten revolutionaries, and who innocently determine the revolution an historic victory by demanding a trial for the underpeople, because "perhaps they are people" (p. 188).

Finally, of course, the underpeople are put to death, but not before Smith has made his point through them: Utopia demands the rediscovery of humanness—hate, pain, fear and all. That is, it demands *acht*: the double meaning of "Take care." *No* feeling is Cordwainer Smith's hell (and here we see reflected Linebarger's work in psychological warfare, particularly brainwashing and debrainwashing). It is a hell greater—and more human—than the nightmarish aberration, the planet Shayol. The one underperson-animal who does not follow Joan out of the sewer is Crawlie, the "beautiful, bison-girl," who because of her "pride" cannot "love people," not even her fellow underpeople (pp. 181, 199). With what country do you associate the bison? And why is it a girl?

"Norstrilia" is also Smith's America. It controls the drug "stroon" that deadens feeling and leads to a world paid on credit cards, discoursed in codes, and peopled with double agents. It is depicted in "Mother Hitton's Littul Kittons" (1961), a tale worth a paper in itself, a meld of Vonnegut at his most mordant and intimations of Watergate (see footnote 16). It has a Bogart anti-hero (named "Bozart") and, on the front line, a defense minister, or "ministress" (p. 257), who is Bella Abzug Mother. Mother Hitton

> was a ruddy-faced, cheerful blonde of indeterminate age. Her eyes were blue, her bosum heavy, her arms strong. She looked like a mother, but the only child she had ever had died many generations ago. Now she acted as mother to a planet, not to a person; the Norstrilians slept well because they knew she was watching. The weapons slept their long, sick sleep (pp. 257-258).

"Sick" is the key word.

Mother Hitton's weapons are the sexual animal, the mink, who "destroy the amoral hero Bozart in his space-ship with his all-powerful lust and the self-devour[ing]" it engenders in him (pp. 280-281). The women judges in "Clown Town" are Lady Goroke, mother of the first Lord Jestocost, who with his sons will "bring justice back into the world" (p. 207) (C'mell's Lord is the lucky seventh Jestocost), and Lady Joanna Gnade, who later will come to Shayol to rescue the babies, the unromantic, humanly imperfect, compassionate Commander Suzdaland the other prisoners, and the cow-man B'dikkat, who put an end to soulless murders. They are good and they are bad, these mothers.

Thus it all comes together in a conplex weave of the human, the animal and the divine; the heroic and the ordinary; politics and the soul; romance and anti-romance. And Smith goes beyond simple sexists or feminists because he *keeps* the romance: the mysterious moment when Mr. Grey-no-more's spirit infuses Helen America to save her ship of pilgrims; the spirit of E'telekeli, which magically intervenes in human and underpeople affairs at critical moments; the mystical fornication of Elaine and the Hunter, which creates Joan of the Light from the Dog Joan. But there is always the distancing; we are always told that this is a story, a ballad, a film, a legend, that it is not quite real. The reality, instead, lies with the heroism of B'dikkat, the quiet competence of Dita, the technical

warfare of Lovaduck, Paul saving the small birds. Perhaps it is
Paul's saving the birds in "Alpha Ralpha Boulevard" that is
Smith's view of real heroism; it is a simple act of kindness, and yet it
has majesty, as do all such simple acts. The Rediscovery of Man,
after all—that great historical movement that finally saves the
Instrumentality from decadence—is in essence the rediscovery of
simplicity when

> ... the Instrumentality dug deep in the treasury, reconstructing
> the old cultures, the old languages, and even the old troubles.
> The nightmare of perfection had taken our forefathers to the
> edge of suicide. Now under the leadership of the Lord Jestocost
> and the Lady Alice More, the ancient civilizations were rising
> like great land masses out of the sea of the past.
>   I myself was the first man to put a postage stamp on a letter,
> after fourteen thousand years ... ("Alpha Ralpha Boulevard,"
> p. 283)

It is this world of the ordinary, symbolized by postage stamps
(which also play a central role in *Norstrilia*), that will save us. This
is also the theme of the stories in *The Quest of Three Worlds* (1966),
in which the hero Casher O'Neill has to be told that his greatest
victory is achieved almost without his knowing it. " 'The best way to
find freedom is not to look for it'," his lover Celalta explains, " 'just
as you obtained your utter revenge on Wedder [an enemy of
Casher's] by doing him a little bit of good.... You have won at last
the immense victory that makes all battles seem vain. There is food
around us....' "9

But there is little doubt that Smith values the romance as well.
In "The Ballad of the Lost C'mell" (1962), one of his finest stories,
the two lovers are indeed legendary, a supreme man, the seventh
Lord Jestocost, and the supreme cat-girl, C'mell. Jestocost

> was a man who had little love, no fear, freedom from ambition
> and a dedication to his job: but there are passions of government
> as deep and challenging as the emotions of love. Two hundred
> years of thinking himself right and of being outvoted had
> instilled in Jestocost a furious desire to get things done his own
> way.
>   Jestocost was one of the few true men who believed in the
> rights of the underpeople. He did not think that mankind would
> ever get around to correcting ancient wrongs unless the
> underpeople themselves had some of the tools of power—
> weapons, conspiracy, wealth and (above all) organization with
> which to challenge man. He was not afraid of revolt, but he
> thirsted for justice with an obsessive yearning which overrode

all other considerations (pp. 318-319).

C'mell is a "girlygirl," like a Japanese geisha, "not a bad girl but a professionally flirtatious hostess" (p. 321). She is also the daughter of an underhero, the greatest athlete the underpeople had produced, C'mackintosh, whose death, it seems to Jestocost, leaves a void in underpeople leadership. He picks C'mell. At first, she can't believe that the great, official man is *that* type.

> She started to give him smile No. 3 (extremely adhesive) which she had learned in the girlygirl school. Realizing it was wrong, she tried to give him an ordinary smile. She felt she had made a face at him.
> "Look at me," he said, "and see if you can trust me. I am going to take both our lives in my hands" (p. 322).

They make a compact. The synthesis of cat and human woman, she plots with him to free the underpeople and it is hard work: "She was so tired that she sat down into the chair with an innocent voluptuousness .... 'I must ask you to pull your clothing together a little,' said Jestocost in a clinical turn of voice. 'I am a man, even if I am an official ....' She was a little frightened by his tone ...": the old romantic convention of him as boss, her as tease.

More romantic conventions: she sees him as a father figure: her hero father merged with E'telekeli, the cat-god. Lost in their conspiratorial telepathy (" 'Daddy!' she sighed happily"), she kisses him: for him, "it was pleasant ...." She, when she realizes, vomits (pp. 325-326).

She realizes she loves him. But love between "people and underpeople" is unlawful, *acht*. She dreams of her father ("Between them there was an aching void of forever-unspoken words.... They were so close to each other that they could get no closer...."[p.329]). And then she dreams of Jestocost, the older powerful man: " 'That's it,' she whispered to herself, 'with all the kindness that one of these passing men have ever really shown .... There's a special sort of majesty to kindness. It's the best part there is to being people' " (p. 330).

Jestocost "did know, and yet he didn't" of her love. " 'We're born in the wrong age,' he thought" (p. 330). He chooses the cause, justice for the underpeople. " 'We've got to keep personalities out of it.' " Smith interposes (unusually): "So he thought. Perhaps he was right."

Their conspiracy works. The spirit of E'telekeli, working through her and through him, communicates knowledge of the escape routes from Earthport to the underpeople. The lovers' usual triumph over the dragons is won.

But here the story changes from Smith's common pattern. Its last section begins not unusually. C'mell is described unromantically as growing fat running a restaurant, and Jestocost's visit to the restaurant is recounted. But, unusually, the romantic tension builds rather than diminishes; and Smith does what he does nowhere else: uses the gossip, the legends, the ballad about C'mell and Jestocost not to distance the love story and extol the mundane, but to give it unique fulfillment. Smith has a striking habit—perhaps his greatest artistic gift—of mirroring his romances in the world's reaction to them, merging art—films, ballads, tales, plays—with ordinary gossip (the ambiguous term "legend" conveys both his meanings), thus being able both to distance—and hence elevate—the romance, and at the same time, humanize and demythify it. At the beginning of "The Lady Who Sailed the *Soul*," the laconic Smith narrator notes that "It was lucky that people lost their pictures" of their romantic hero[es]" Helen America and Mr. Grey-no-more, because in reality he was "a very young-looking man, prematurely old," and "sick" at the time of the romance, and she was thoroughly ordinary: "a freak but a nice one: a grim, solemn, sad little brunette who had been born amid the laughter of humanity [echoes of Elaine's birth in "Clown Town"]. She was not the tall, confident heroine of the actresses who later played her" (p. 41).

But in "Lost C'mell," it is different. During his visit to her restaurant, Jestocost asks C'mell about the "rhyme" the under-people sing about her, which refers to a human lover. She denies one, while underneath, "her heart cried out": "*It was you, it was you, it was you...Darling, will you never, never know...*? He never knew that when he left she went back to the kitchen and cried for a while" (p. 336).

C'mell dies; Jestocost sees her numerous look-alike great-granddaughters around "the corridors and shafts" of Earthport, not "half-slaves," but now "citizens (reserved grade)" with "photopasses which protected their property, their identity and their rights" (p. 336). At last "his own time came" and "in the ending he wanted to know something": he thinks to E'telekeli, "...*I must know. Did she love me?*"

The cat-god tells Jestocost's mind that C'mell loved him so much she let him go, loved him " 'more than death. More than life. More than time. You will never be apart.' "

"*Never apart?*"

" 'No, not in the memory of man,' said the voice, and was then still."

And the story ends: "Jestocost lay back on his pillow and waited for the day to end."

In the art fused with ordinary life of ballads and other popular art—that is, in the "memory of man"—lies the fulfillment of C'mell and Jestocost's love, and somehow it works, becoming the one happy ending in Smith's romances, the one full synthesis of the mundane and heroic, of life and art. And in that one line in "The Ballad of Lost C'mell"—that unusual comment on Jestocost's decision not to love C'mell: "So he thought. Perhaps he was right"— Smith reveals himself to be not quite certain himself of the "rightness" of the denial of romance in so many of his tales. Perhaps the real synthesis that he seeks—between human and animal, man and woman, romantic and mundane—is not to be fully achieved even in his imagined universe of the Instrumentality. In the end of *The Quest of Three Worlds,* the very latest moment in the chronology of the Instrumentality that Smith was to write about during his life, Casher O'Neill finally finds "peace and happiness" settling down in a large communal family, his days of heroism over, his quest ended. "They had no obligation but to live and to be happy," Smith writes. "The threat and the promise of victory were far, far behind" (p. 174). But there is a wistfulness in this happy ending, too: not only is the threat lost, so is the promise. There is, after all, a great longing for the romance, a need for the legends and the heroes. In the end, we are left like Ria of Linebarger's first novel, standing on the North Carolina coast, her problem not fully resolved by the details of real life, aware of some vast "instrumentality" that perhaps *cannot* be fully resolved or explained by looking for answers among the mundane. Like all living dialectics, that of Cordwainer Smith never fully abandons the antinomies with which it starts. Smith's stories seem somehow more real because they *are* bizarre and romantic, and they seem more romantic, perhaps, because of the kernel of reality that lies at the heart of his work.

Notes

[1] J.J. Pierce, "Cordwainer Smith: The Shaper of Myths," in *The Best of Cordwainer Smith*, ed. J.J. Pierce (New York: Ballantine, 1975), p. xiv. This volume is the closest thing we have to a definitive collection of Smith, and unless otherwise indicated, page references in the text to the science fiction stories will be to this edition. Most of the details on Linebarger's life are also taken from Pierce's introductory essay to this volume.

[2] *Ria* (New York: Duell, Sloan, and Pearce, 1947), p. 134. Future page references will be made in the text.

[3] *Carola* (New York: Duell, Sloane, and Pearce, 1948), p. 4. Future page references will be made in the text.

[4] "Mark Elf" is included in *You Will Never Be The Same* (Evanston, IL.: Regency Books, 1963); the quotation is from p. 144.

[5] *The Science Fiction Book: An Illustrated History* (New York: New American Library, 1975), p. 150.

[6] "John Foyster Talks with Arthur Burns," in *Exploring Cordwainer Smith* (New York: Algol Press, 1975), p. 19.

[7] *Norstrilia* (New York: Ballantine Books, 1975), p. 250. Future references to *Norstrilia* will be by page number in the text.

[8] As Sandra Miesel points out in "I Am Joan & I Love You," this distancing from D'Joan serves to make her more romantic and magnify her "heroic experience" (*Exploring Cordwainer Smith,* p. 27).

[9] *Quest of the Three Worlds* (New York: Ace, 1966), p. 148. Future page references to *Quest* will be made in the text.

"The Passions in the Clay": Mervyn Peake's Titus Stories

Joseph L. Sanders

During Mervyn Peake's life, his writing received just enough critical and financial encouragement to keep him trying, never enough to give him any assurance that a substantial number of people cared about what he wrote. That has changed. Today Peake's fiction, especially the works concerned with Titus Groan, have been republished, widely distributed in paperback, and, most importantly, admired by an increasing number of serious readers. We do care, and we are now trying sympathetically to understand what about Peake impresses us.

One problem Peake faced is the still-persistent prejudice against fantasy as mere escapism. This is the attitude that Emyr Humphrys expresses in an early review dismissing Peake's novel *Gormenghast* as "an over-grown fairy tale, without any discernible moral, having no more connection with the reality of living than the Hunting of the Snark."[1] Actually, the reverse is true in the Titus stories. Through his depiction of fantastic forces that emerge out of the stories' settings—and the characters' development as they react to that setting—Peake presents a realistic picture of human life. The best way to appreciate this is through a detailed survey of setting and character development in the three novels and one novella Peake wrote about Titus Groan. Seeing Peake's intent and accomplishment more clearly should help us make a fairer evaluation of the Titus stories.[2]

First, however, we should get clear what manner of fantasy Peake's stories *are*. At first glance the Titus stories appear to have little kinship with a fantasy novel like Tolkien's *The Lord of the Rings*, filled with monsters, wizards and magic rings. Yet the real purpose of fantastic elements in Tolkien's story is to extend human desires and fears far beyond their normal range. Magic and monsters objectify human passions that disrupt the natural order. In Tolkien's fantasy, fears take physical shape and desires become supernaturally achievable. In *The Lord of the Rings*, the Ring represents a common wish, the craving to master all knowledge and power, while the creatures and wizards show alternative ways to achieve that goal by brute force or study. Tolkien views life as a terrible struggle between desires and moral impulses, which one cannot understand let alone direct but in the midst of which he must trust in divine benevolence and hope for final victory. By accepting healthy tradition and trying to submit to the purposes that tradition offers, one can at least haltingly participate in satisfying action.

Peake's type of fantasy also moves outside normal setting and familiar devices to present his conception of the human condition. It works, however, from a quite different viewpoint in a quite different manner. Peake does not accept the orthodox religious tradition that undergirds Tolkien's fiction. Furthermore, he does not believe that true power can be trapped in a ring, diagrammed by a sage, or seized by violence. In fact the systematic study of supernatural power, in religion or magic, is impossible; Peake not only rejects any particular religion but denies that man can gain any benefit from using a religious/ethical tradition as an aid to understanding. Thus, though forces beyond human comprehension sometimes are at work in Peake's stories, they resist easy labeling. The supernatural empathy between Titus and Keda's child, in *Titus Groan* and *Gormenghast*, is one such fantastic element. The mysterious certainty that guides Keda through the last month of her life may be another. However, clairvoyance or other violations of familiar natural order are very rare in these first two books; the major fantastic element is found not in the action's foreground but in its background. The action in these first two books takes place in or near Gormenghast—an immense castle, self-sufficient and completely cut off from contact with any outside society. One character, Dr. Prunesquallor who is familiar with astronomy, observes the "evening star" in the night sky, suggesting that Gormenghast is located on this Earth.[3] Elsewhere, however, it is revealed that Gormenghast must have been totally isolated in its wilderness for at least 368 years (*TG*, p. 255). Gormenghast appears to have no real counterpart in past or present, and it is difficult to imagine the castle as part of a future that would leave it so undisturbed. It exists in its own world, one similar to the real world but not part of it.

Gormenghast's unnatural existence allows Peake to examine the human condition from a fresh perspective. At the same time, the lack of overtly fantastic forces in Gormenghast reflects Peake's attitude toward the basis of responsible action. In *Titus Groan* and *Gormenghast*, there are no easy magical tools by which one can manipulate Gormenghast's power, but on the other hand the characters actually need not fear such a power's violent intervention in their lives. In a completely different setting, "Boy in Darkness" uses many more elements that are overtly fantastic: *Titus Alone*, set in still another part of Peake's special world, uses others. However, in these works, too, characters lack full control over themselves and cannot pledge allegiance to some superhuman source of control; at the same time, still, they need not be controlled by tradition or ritual. Although most characters are not aware of it, because the human passions that went into their society's creation are hidden by the aura of revered mystery, they are free. No "god" appears directly or indirectly in the Titus stories. Instead, men worship a set of physical objects and the tradition associated with them. Peake believes that man's desires and fears created the setting and the tradition that envelopes it. He pictures man as the source of all meaning and all delusion, and shows one particular young man, Titus, becoming aware of himself in those terms and rousing himself to fight free of tradition and the settings that enforce it.

Peake's few direct comments about his practice of writing show his concern with a tradition-bound setting and the people living in it. In his description of the writing of *Titus Groan*, called "How a Romantic Novel Was Evolved," Peake states that his book grew randomly from some idle jottings, "a page of nonsensical conversation between two pompous half-wits."[4] Peake's remarks stress the importance of characters in the story's evolution, and printed with his essay are several pen and ink sketches of important characters that Peake says he drew to help "visualize the characters and to imagine what sort of things they would say" ("Romantic Novel," p. 80). But Peake's essay is only about 300 words long; the rest of "How a Romantic Novel Was Evolved" consists of five excerpts from *Titus Groan*. One is the conversation between Titus' aunts, the Twins, that roughly fits Peake's description of the doodlings with which it began. Three other excerpts, however, show characters acting instead of talking—and acting, always, in close relation to Gormenghast, an indication of how the castle, not the characters, dominates the stories.

It seems appropriate though to examine some of Peake's descriptions of Gormenghast and its surroundings, to see how characters are able to react to that setting.

At first, like the characters, the reader is likely to be overwhelmed by the castle's physical presence. The castle can be seen from as many angles, in as many ways as any real place. It is a mass of stones, a heap of walls and towers above an eruption of hovels: "mean dwellings that swarmed like an epidemic around its outer walls .... Over their irregular roofs would fall throughout the seasons, the shadows of time-eaten buttresses, of broken and lofty turrets, and, most enormous of all, the shadow of the Tower of Flints. This tower, patched unevenly with black ivy, arose like a mutilated finger from among the fists of knuckled masonry and pointed blasphemously at heaven. At night the owls made it an echoing throat; by day it stood voiceless and cast its long shadow" (*TG*, p. 9). Again, seen from a distance in summer, Gormenghast is a sprawled bulk in the dust: "It lay inert, like a sick thing. Its limbs spread. It took the shape of what it smothered. The masonry sweated and was horribly silent. The chestnuts whitened with dust and hung their myriads of great hands with every wrist broken" (*TG*, p. 358).

Peake's vivid descriptions convince the reader of Gormenghast's physical existence. The stories swim in such descriptions, all useful in the story and striking in themselves. Early in *Titus Groan*, for example, Steerpike escapes from a locked room to the castle roof and climbs about, trying to find a way back inside to safety; the episode lets Peake show the terrific size of Gormenghast, but it also gives him a chance to present vivid, fascinating sights like the following: "He had seen a tower with a stone hollow in its summit. This shallow basin sloped down from the copestones that surrounded the tower and was half filled with rainwater. In the circle of water whose glittering had caught his eye, for to him it appeared about the size of a coin, he could see that something white was swimming. As far as he could guess it was a horse. As he watched he noticed that there was something swimming by its side, something smaller, which must have been the foal, white like its parent" (*TG*, p. 116).

These passages are not only vivid descriptions; they are integral parts of the story's argument. In its first appearance before the reader Gormenghast seems to challenge "heaven" and thus the natural order of life, making an obscene gesture of defiance. But its proud egotism is countered by details that suggest failure. In the second description, the castle is presented in terms developing the earlier description's suggestion of sickness, mutilation and defeat underlying Gormenghast's pretensions. The third quotation also shows that things are happening at Gormenghast outside the inhabitants' knowledge or control. This time the disruption actually looks healthy and vital—but Steerpike's own response shows the meagerness of his vision, and this is important to the story because the way a man uses his senses reveals his potential for development. One sign of Steerpike's failure to become more fully human is his desire to force all the marvelous things he sees from atop

Gormenghast to work towards his personal profit. Although he sees clearly, Steerpike sees everything either as a useful tool or as worthless trash. Since the scene he views cannot benefit him, he dismisses it from his mind. On the other hand, one sign of Titus' potential for human growth is his sudden ability to see objects as themselves, as he sits in the castle schoolroom:

> it had been the colour of the ink, the peculiar dark and musty blue of the ink in its sunken bowl in the corner of his desk, which had induced his eyes to wander over the few objects grouped below him. The ink was blue, dark, musty, dirtyish, deep as cruel water at night: what were the other colours? Titus was surprised at the richness, the variety. He had only seen his thumb-marked books as things to read or to avoid reading: as things that got lost: things full of figures or maps. Now he saw them as coloured rectangles of pale, washedout blue or laurel green, with small windows cut in them where, on the naked whiteness of the first page, he had scripted his name....
>
> He even saw his own hand as a coloured thing before he realized it was a part of him: the ochre colour of his wrist, the black of his sleeve....[5]

In still another way Peake's descriptions express his attitude toward man's predicament. Though concrete, they are extremely incomplete. Peake concentrates on rendering flashes of vision or parts of a scene thrown suddenly into dramatic highlight. Here, for example, is a panorama of Gormenghast and the surrounding country:

> Three shafts of the rising sun, splintering through the murk, appeared to set fire to the earth where they struck it. The bright impact of the nearest beam exposed a tangle of branches which clawed in a craze of radiance, microscopically perfect and adrift in darkness.
>
> The second of these floodlit islands appeared to float immediately *above* the first, for the sky and earth were a single curtain of darkness. In reality it was as far away again, but hanging as it did gave no sense of distance.
>
> At its northern extremity there grew from the waspgold earth certain forms like eruptions of masonry rather than spires and buttresses of natural rock. The sunshaft had uncovered a mere finger of some habitation which, widening as it entered the surrounding darkness to the North, became a fist of stones, which in its turn, heaving through wrist and forearm to an elbow like a smashed honeycomb, climbed through darkness to a gaunt, time-eaten shoulder only to expand again and again

into a mountainous body of timeless towers.

But of all this nothing was visible but the bright and splintered tip of a stone finger.

The third "island" was the shape of a heart. A coruscating heart of tares on fire.

To the dark edge of this third light a horse was moving. It appeared no bigger than a fly. Astride its back was Titus. (*G*, p. 88).

This fragmentary vividness works directly to Peake's advantage, since it permits him to suggest that the things he describes so vividly are parts of a vast and shadowy whole; the many objects left undescribed are thus attached to particular things that dazzle a reader's senses. This corresponds to the way one normally sees things. Naturally Titus cannot see every object in the schoolroom, simultaneously, with the same rich vividness. Intense vision cannot register whole scenes; it must focus on a few objects, to explore them in detail. At its keenest, sight perceives fragments of the whole.

This recognition amplifies something we noticed earlier. Fragmentary description is appropriate because so many of the things described *are* fragments. In the passages quoted above, Gormenghast is described in adjectives like "broken," "mutilated," "smashed," "time-eaten" and "splintered." *Titus Groan* opens with a description of the Tower of Flints, "patched" only by ivy and inhabited by owls. It is a visual symbol of defiance, self-will—and defeat. Furthermore, in *Titus Groan*, Peake thus describes in detail one wing of the castle:

> Most of these buildings had about them the rough-hewn and oppressive weights of masonry that characterized the main volume of Gormenghast, although they varied considerably in every other way, one having at its summit an enormous stone carving of a lion's head, which held between its jaws the limp corpse of a man on whose body was chiselled the words: *"He was an enemy of Groan";* alongside this structure was a rectangular area of some length entirely filled with pillars set so closely together that it was difficult for a man to squeeze between them. Over them, at the height of about forty feet, was a perfectly flat roof of stone slabs blanketed with ivy. This structure could never have served any practical purpose . . . .
>
> There were many examples of an eccentric notion translated into architecture in the spine of buildings that spread eastwards over the undulating ground between the heavy walls of conifer, but for the most part they were built for some specific purpose, as a pavilion for entertainments, or as an observatory, or a

museum. Some in the forms of halls with galleries round three sides had been intended for concerts or dancing. One had obviously been an aviary for though derelict, the branches that had long ago been fastened across the high central hall of the building were still hanging by rusty chains, and about the floor were strewn the broken remains of drinking cups for the birds; wire netting, red with rust, straggled across the floor among rank weeds that had taken root. (*TG*, pp. 174-175).

Much of Gormenghast now is deserted and falling into ruin. Even as it was built, however, the castle was designed piecemeal, conceived in fragments. Just as the eye can see only parts of any scene fully, the mind also can comprehend any project only partially, and, when it tries to grasp too much, is defeated eventually by nature, time, and its own vanity—the desire to believe that it has triumphed. The House of Groan proclaims its victory in the midst of confusion and decay. Most of the inhabitants of Gormenghast register the presence of the Tower and the other structures without really perceiving their import. Though they use what they see in different ways, Steerpike and Titus are apart from this general blindness. And their clear sight permits them to shape the story's action because they can act in ways inconceivable to the other people in Gormenghast.

Clearly, the other characters are only hazily conscious of reality, and thus largely are unable to act effectively. For example, the Countess avoids the most pleasant and attractive room in the castle precisely *because* "there were no shadows lurking in the corners"; she prefers "those parts of the castle where the lights and the shadows were on the move and where there was no such clarity" (*TG*, p. 82). This craving for indistinctness is analogous to the Countess' mental retreat from the world around her, which separates her from husband, daughter and son, and from which she rouses only when Gormenghast's gloomy tradition is threatened.

The Countess is not alone in such willful semi-blindness; most of the other characters also are grotesquely incomplete in their understanding of themselves and their world. But where Gormenghast's physical incompleteness suggests Peake's understanding of human limitations, man's inability to see objects as wholes, the onesideness of the characters shows not simply their natural limitations but also the way Gormenghast has narrowed and warped them. The pretentions associated with the place have produced an immense body of ritual whose effects almost invariably are negative. Peake believes that ethical religious tradition is based not on some supernatural manifestation but on one man's own desire to evade consciousness of his lack of ultimate knowledge and control by *claiming* allegiance with supernatural intelligence and power. Responding to the tendency of thought to meander in unforeseeable ways and to collapse into chaos, the rulers of Gormenghast have accumulated a body of ritual to hold their own fragments of meaning together. By labeling certain actions significant, ritual occupies and secures the minds of its adherents. But the process is circular. Ritual depends upon ritual for significance. No modifications, no freshly relevant meanings can be permitted. And the people who are most formed by ritual lack even the knowledge that there is any other way to see life; they have no way even to become conscious that they have been distorted.

For Peake, tradition embodies the most stultifying of human impulses—the will to dominate, to see the world remade in terms of self—its failure hidden only by its own self-sanctified mysteriousness. Tradition promises a share in the delight of dominating nature. In return a man must surrender his individual self to the greater self. The worshiper feels himself a part of a power that fits his deepest urges (though he is not created in *its* image, as the tradition states), within which he can follow any desire as long as he consciously frames his actions in traditional images. But the worshiper is thus prevented from developing his individual self. Such tradition can show a man only a distorted, deadening image of himself. Yet, as in Gormenghast, most people accept a role determined by tradition in preference to developing themselves freely. They are willing to imagine no other existence.

Most of the people who live in Gormenghast cling firmly to the castle's tradition. Lord Sepulchrave, Titus' father, holds off his chronic melancholia by complete absorption in ritual: "The many duties, which to another might have become irksome and appeared fatuous, were to his Lordship a relief and a relative escape from himself" (*TG*, p. 177). Even when the day's routine is over, he secludes himself in the castle library, escaping into his books. He encounters his wife only on ceremonial occasions (*TG*, p. 176). In short, his intellect, crouched under the sheltering ritual, does him no good.

By the same token, it is because of ritual that his wife's vitality is able to express itself only with inarticulate creatures. She accepts all the physical demands of ritual by divorcing her mind from the human life of the castle. In a reverie, she plans to teach Titus the same survival technique when he is older: "I [will] tell him about the skies' birds and how he can keep his head quite clear of the duties he must perform day after day until he dies here as his fathers have done and be buried in the sepulchre of the Groans and he must learn the secret of silence and go his own way among the birds and the white cats and all the animals so that he is not aware of men " (*TG*, p. 346).

Titus' older sister, Fuchsia, is less successful at finding a "safe" outlet for her energy. Early in the novel she is seen dreaming vaguely of a friend from outside her world and its ritual (*TG*, pp. 124-125). Yet Fuchsia *is* part of Gormenghast, too, as she perceives when Steerpike approaches her: "behind him she saw something which by contrast with the alien, incalculable figure before her, was close and real. It was something which she understood, something which she could never do without, or be without, for it seemed as though it were her own self, her own body, at which she gazed and which lay so intimately upon the skyline. Gormenghast, the long, notched outline of her home" (*TG*, p. 236). And after her father's disappearance, Fuchsia recognizes "that she was no longer free, no longer just Fuchsia, but of the blood" (*TG*, p. 398). Her character is not transformed, her role as Lady Fuchsia only adding to the tangle of purposes and feelings that ensnares her, but she is at last firmly caught within the trap of Gormenghast. Her instincts still pull her toward freedom, but the only thing Gormenghast offers her is the coldblooded artificer, Steerpike, who recognizes Fuchsia's imaginative nature and plays on it to gain her trust (*TG*, p. 237).

Some other main characters' accommodations to Gormenghast reveal why Fuchsia, and Titus, in his turn, are repelled by a life guided by ritual. Flay has devoted his life to the castle's oppressive tradition, denying his emotions any spontaneous expression. After he is banished from the castle, when the Countess sees him throw one of her cats into Steerpike's face, he discovers that he can enjoy another kind of life: "his love of this woodland glade he had selected grew with the development of a woodland instinct which must have been latent in his blood" (*TG*, pp. 383-384); despite this, however, he keeps as close to Gormenghast as possible, worshiping the *idea* of the ritual going on within the walls.

Dr. Prunesquallor, on the other hand, impresses the reader by his spontaneous sympathy for Fuchsia, as much as by his bizarre mannerisms. He is the only character who can be depended upon to respond generously and effectively to the needs of people around him. His sound impulses are further shown as he muses over whether or not to ask Steerpike's aid in caring for the deranged Sepulchrave: "I will bear him in mind and dispense with him if I can but a brain is a brain and he has one and it may be necessary to borrow it at short notice but no no I will not by all that's instinctive I will not and that settles it" (*TG*, p. 342). Yet, Prunesquallor is trapped too: "although the Doctor, with a mind of his own, had positively heterodox opinion regarding certain aspects of the castle's life ... yet it was *of* the place and was a freak only in that his mind worked in a wide way, relating and correlating his thoughts so that his conclusions were often clear and accurate and nothing short of heresy" (*TG,* p. 407).

The Twins share a mindless devotion to order that is symbolized in their dearest possession—the Room of Roots. Steerpike, having flattered his way into their confidence, is astonished at the Room, which is filled with the dead, carefully handpainted roots of a tree that still clings to the wall outside the Twins' apartment; they imagine that birds will flock to "those roots whose colours most nearly approximated to their own plumage, or if they preferred it to nest among roots whose hue was complimentary to their own" (*TG*, p. 217). But in addition to reflecting the system's foolishness, the Twins show its viciousness as they dream of the power that tradition owes them so that they would be able to "make people do things" (*TG*, p, 93). Even after Steerpike has made them his dupes by promising them power, each of the Twins muses, "one day perhaps I will banish Steerpike when he's done everything for us ... because he isn't really of good stock like us and ought to be a servant" (*TG*, p. 340).

All these characters see life in terms of tradition and let their lives be ruled by ritual. Gorgmenghast's ritual does nothing positive for them. At best, it gives them a neutral refuge from personal difficulties, but more often it encourages weakness, by overwhelming individual needs with its oppressive, indecipherable "values." For that very reason, however, the characters find it more comfortable to cling to the dead framework of ritual than to fight free. They neglect the problems whose solution might cost them real effort, and thus real pain, in favor of playing safe, mind-numbing games. And so they see everything in terms of Gormenghast. They cannot question its importance, because to do so would be to doubt the way they have spent their lives, the way they *see* life. Instead they cling to their duties and the wisps of power associated with those duties.

Steerpike is the only character in *Titus Groan* who realizes that power might be seized despite ritualistic prohibitions. At first glance, Steerpike appears to be the most sympathetic character in the book; he seems to be simply a young man who wants to escape from the brutal life of a kitchen servant. Steerpike displays intelligence and courage, for example, as he climbs from the room in which Flay had locked him to the roof of Gormenghast. But, as already noted, Steerpike uses his abilities chiefly to stock his mind with knowledge about immediately useful information: "a passion to accumulate knowledge of any and every kind consumed him; but only as a means to an end. He must know all things, for only so might he have, when situations arose in the future, a full pack of cards to play from" (*TG*, pp. 193-194). Significantly, what he studies while Dr. Prunesquallor's servant is the concoction of poisons.

In fact, Steerpike tries to exert too much control over the incomprehensible forces of life—as a result of which he ultimately loses all control. Steerpike is sympathetic only to a point. He sacrifices vision and understanding as he pursues his goal. When necessary Steerpike can simulate emotion, but his real passions are held in check by cunning (*TG*, p. 134). His ruling passion is a desire for power. Like the Twins, he understands that power is the ability to compel a person to do something; unlike the Twins, he understands how to gain power in Gormenghast. But he does not realize the personal effects of that effort. Because he keeps his true self so much enslaved, he may actually be the character *most* enthralled by the proud, ultimately self-destructive spirit of Gormenghast.

Above all, Steerpike realizes that the power of his personal influence is not enough. He needs to command the power of ritual. After the castle ritualist dies in the library fire set by the Twins at Steerpike's command, Steerpike attaches himself to Barquentine, the new ritualist. Again he files for his future use the knowledge he gains: "it was in his mind to find himself on Barquentine's decease the leading if not the sole authority in matters of ritual and observance. In any event, the subject fascinated him. It was potential" (*TG*, p. 420).

For the baby boy Titus Groan, too, the future appears to be utterly determined by ritual. Lord Sepulchrave charges Titus' nurse "to instill into his veins, from the very first, a love for his birthplace and his heritage, and a respect for all the written and unwritten laws of the place of his fathers" (*TG*, p. 197). As we have seen, the best life the Countess can imagine for Titus is one of mechanical obedience to ritual, with his real concern elsewhere. Later, at the Earling ceremony, Barquentine tries to seal Titus' future by intoning the formula stating that Titus "will forever hold in sacred trust the castle of his fathers and the domain adhering thereto .... That he will observe its sacred rites, honour its crest, and in due time instill into the first male of his loins, reverence for its every stone until among his fathers he has added, in the tomb, his link to the unending chain of Groans" (*TG*, p. 427).

Even as a baby, however, Titus does not fit the role intended for him. As he looks up at Keda, his wet nurse, Titus' face shows that he is part of an older tradition than Gormenghast's: "there was the history of man in his face. A fragment from the enormous rock of mankind. A leaf from the forest of man's passion and man's knowledge and man's pain" (*TG*, p. 97). During the Earling, Titus instinctively rebels against ritual, refusing to hold the symbolic objects (*TG*, p. 429). At the end of the ceremony, Titus further violates Barquentine's commands: "while the concluding words were being cried in a black anger ... Titus had sunk to his knees and had begun to crawl to the raft's edge with a stone in one hand and ivy branch in the other. And then, to the horror of all, had dropped the sacrosanct symbols into the depths of the lake" (*TG*, p. 430).

It could be said that Titus simply is behaving like a normal baby. However, Peake takes the opportunity to link Titus to uncontrolled, illogical, nonverbal forces of which the other characters repress awareness. In the midst of Titus' spontaneous rebellion, he utters a cry that is answered by Keda's baby (*TG*, pp. 430-431). For some time Peake has suggested a supernatural sympathy existing between the Thing and Titus (cf. *TG*, p. 357). The link thus symbolized will be very important in Titus' development, since in *Titus Groan*, Keda performs the only complete act of rebellion, representing the overwhelming but unreasoning power of instinct. Wandering purposelessly, after her lovers kill each other, Keda feels a baby growing within her. But as she listens to a bird's cry, she realizes there is a way to find freedom from pain: " 'It is over!' screamed the beaked voice. 'It is only for the child that you are waiting. All else fulfilled, and then there is no longer any need' " (*TG*, p. 308). She lives only to deliver her child; then she is free to die. Keda's child, thus, represents pure, vital freedom, in conception and development. Yet it is clear that this freedom is of a particular kind—impulsive and heedless, echoing the cry of a bird rather than answering a human communication. Titus is instinctively drawn toward the Thing's freedom; later, he will have to see whether it can satisfy his whole self. We should note, however, that in *Titus Groan* the only other person who gives himself up to such a mood is the insane Lord Sepulchrave who, after his library is burned, seeks to submerge himself in another kind of life by imagining himself one of the owls in the Tower of Flints. They eat him alive (*TG*, p. 382).

Titus Groan ends as Steerpike wriggles his way toward the center of power and as Titus shows signs of possessing an individual will. The story obviously is unfinished; rather a sense of impending change disturbs the inhabitants of the castle: "through honeycombs of stone would now be wandering the passions in their clay. There would be tears and there would be strange laughter. Fierce births and deaths beneath umbrageous ceiling. And dreams, and violence, and disenchantment. And there shall be flame-green daybreak soon. And love itself shall cry for insurrection!" (*TG*, p. 438).

At the beginning of *Gormenghast*, seven years have passed. Relatively little has changed. The Twins have fled from their official apartment, at Steerpike's command, and are concealed in a deserted wing of the castle, still hungering for power. Outside the castle walls, Flay has adapted thoroughly to life in the woods but still identifies with the House of Groan (*G*, p. 256). The Countess and Dr. Prunesquallor are only beginning to be troubled by still unfocused suspicions of Steerpike; she is awakening to the hint of Gormenghast's ritual (*G*, p. 27), and he is beginning to concentrate his considerable intellect because of a feeling that the people he loves are in danger (*G*, pp. 40-41). Fuchsia is still not quite a mature woman, though no longer a child. She feels drawn to both Titus and Steerpike—to Titus because of his rebellious attitude, to Steerpike because of his "vitality and air of secrecy" (*G*, p. 25). Titus is seven years older, still torn by conflicting demands of blood and ritual (*G*, p. 9). Steerpike is stronger.

Most of *Gormenghast* is taken up with the development of these two young men—and the castle's response.

Steerpike appears quite secure at first. He has concealed his viciousness and is entrenched as Barquentine's assistant. Yet Steerpike cannot be content with the power that comes from administering ritual. He must keep the Twins to perform for him and must indulge himself in random exercise of power. As several teachers cross one of the courtyards, for example, an object hurtles downward and strikes one of them on the wrist; high above, "Steerpike ... raised his eyebrows at the sound of the cry so far below him, and piously closing his eyes he kissed his catapult" (*G*, p. 191). Power is satisfying only when it can be used at will, and Steerpike is growing tired of waiting to display his power.

He is also tired of concealing his true self; the desire to scream his personal defiance of Gormenghast is eroding his rigid self-control. The combination of fatigue and impatience undoes him. In planning Barquentine's murder, Steerpike is so eager to show Barquentine his superiority that he underestimates the ritualist. Set afire, Barquentine still manages to seize Steerpike, and the two burn together. As they struggle, Steerpike forces himself to act purposefully despite the pain. He succeeds. Yet he is changed. Besides the burns that scar his face, Steerpike has suffered injury to his self-confidence: "His poise had been so shattered that a change had come about—a change that he knew nothing of, for his logical mind was able to reassure him" (*G*, p 252). He is unaware of any alteration as he continues with the same plans for his future, while entrenching himself in the job of ritualist: "His miscalculation over Barquentine's murder had been unforgivable and he did not forgive himself. It was not so much what had happened to his body that galled him, but that he should ever have blundered. His mind, always compassionless, was now an icicle—sharp, lucent and frigid. From now onward he had no other purpose than to hold the castle even more tightly in the scalded palm of his hand" (*G*, p. 271). Before murdering Barquentine, Steerpike was anxious for power; now, holding practical power over Gormenthast, he cannot understand that his hold on himself has been dangerously weakened even as he resolves to control himself even more tightly.

Steerpike soon commits more serious mistakes. As interpreter of the ritual, he plans to dispose of Titus by sending him on ceremonial missions via crumbling stairs or deliberately weakened catwalks (*G*, p. 311). At the same time, he decides to woo Fuchsia, to seal his power by marrying the only other heir to Gormenghast. By playing on her sympathy for his injury and her admiration for his courage, Steerpike leads Fuchsia to accept him as a closer—and ever more secret—friend. Fuchsia is unable to analyze Steerpike: "unlike this new companion, this man of the dusk, whose every sentence, every thought, every action was ulterior, she lived in the moment of excitement, savouring the taste of an experience that was enough in itself. She had no instinct of self-preservation" (*G*, p. 306). Steerpike carefully imitates love, even painstakingly decorating a room where they meet in the evenings. Yet Steerpike's role is shattered before the romance is consummated. Flay has crept back into the castle and hides in a deserted section, watching secretly over the young Groans. His warning whisper, " 'Be careful, my lady'," halts Fuchsia outside the private room (*G*, p. 312) and Steerpike, when he finds her standing there in plain sight, pushes her inside with the exclamation " 'Fool' " (*G*, p. 313). Humiliated, Fuchsia withdraws from him: "She was shocked and resentful—but less resentful, for those first moments, than hurt. She had also become, without her knowing it, *Lady Fuchsia* (echoing Flay's warning). Her blood had risen in her—the blood of her Line" (*G*, p. 313). Although she can be fooled into missing sight of some things, she cannot doubt what she once has seen.

However, Fuchsia does agree to one further meeting, and Steerpike makes cold-blooded plans: he will seduce or rape her, holding the threat of exposure above her from then on. He realizes that he must act immediately. Yet he feels a terrible tension, apparently sourceless, but overwhelming. After consciously surveying every aspect of his plan, he still is impelled to fill what he perceives as a hole in his knowledge: "his brainwork was done. His plans were complete. And yet there was one loose end. Not in the logic of his brain, but in spite of it—a loose end that he wished to tuck away. What his brain had proved his eyes were witless of. It was his eyes that needed confirmation" (*G,* p. 328). The "one loose end" refers to the Twins, who have rebelled against Steerpike and whom he has left locked in their rooms to die. Actually, as the preceding quotation shows, the matter—the Twins' death—is connected with a non-rational part of Steerpike's character. The "confirmation" is important not to the mechanics of Steerpike's plans but to his sense of himself as all-knowing and all-powerful. He is not conscious of *why* he acts as he does, but the impulse is too powerful to resist: "Steerpike was aware . . . that he was behaving strangely. He could have stopped himself at any moment. But to have stopped himself would have been to have stopped a valve—to have bottled up something which would have clamoured for release . . . . He was watching himself, but only so that he should miss nothing. He was the vehicle through which the gods were working. The dim primordial gods of power and blood" (*G,* pp. 338-339). In the Twins' apartment, unaware that Flay, Titus and Prunesquallor have followed him, he releases his confined self and begins to dance and to "strut like a cockerel about the bodies of the women he had imprisoned, humiliated, and starved to death" (*G,* p. 339). After glorying in his defiance, Steerpike rests, emotionally satisfied but still consciously afraid of this newly-discovered part of himself: "In looking back and seeing himself strutting like a cock about their bodies, he realized that he had been close to lunacy. This was the first time that any such thought had entered his head, and to dismiss it he crowed like a cock. He was not afraid of strutting; he had known what he was doing; to prove it he would crow and crow again. Not that he wished to do so, but to prove that he could stop whenever he wanted, and start when he wished to, and be all the while in complete control of himself, for there was no madness in him" (*G,* pp. 340-341). The natural desire to escape the brutal life of a kitchen servant has, under the rigid control Steerpike has cultivated to circumvent Gormenghast's ritual, evolved into vicious, selfish hatred of everything around him. While Steerpike consciously has tried to save himself, that self has degenerated into something murderous and uncontrollable. So Steerpike turns back to business: "He was himself again, or perhaps he had ceased to be himself" (*G*, 341). He has chosen an attractive appearance—or appearances—to gain domination over everyone in Gormenghast. He has seen *himself* as an ice-cold, purely rational manipulator. But the emotions he has denied still exist, though in grotesque, distorted forms. They steadily have gathered force to escape Steerpike's conscious control.

Consequently when he realizes that he has been found out, Steerpike immediately discards his careful schemes and is half glad to be openly himself: "A red cloud filled his head. His body shuddered with a kind of lust ... for an unbridled evil. It was the glory of knowing himself to be pitted, openly, against the big battalions" (*G*, p. 343). Rushing from the room, Steerpike flees, "turning left and right like a wild creature as he made his way ever deeper into a nether empire" (*G*, p. 343). Finally driven out of his hiding place by the flood that engulfs Gormenghast, Steerpike is trapped by a search party led by Titus. His self-control almost completely gone, Steerpike scarcely can master himself enough to devise a new hiding place in the ivy matted on the castle wall:

> he began to experience again, but with even greater intensity those sensations that had affected him when, with the skeletons of the titled sisters at his feet, he had strutted about their relics as though in the grip of some primoridan [sic] power. This sensation was something so utterly alien to the frigid nature of his conscious brain that he had no means of understanding what was happening within himself at this deeper level, far less of warding off the urge to show himself....
> He no longer wanted to kill his foe in darkness and in silence. His lust was to stand naked upon the moonlit stage, with his arms stretched high, and his fingers spread, and with the warm fresh blood that soaked them sliding down his wrists, spiralling his arms and steaming in the cold night air—to suddenly drop his arms like talons to his breast and tear it open to expose a heart like a black vegetable—and then, upon the crest of self-exposure, and the sweet glory of wickedness, to create some gesture of supreme defiance, lewd and rare....
> There was nothing left, no, of the brain that would have scorned all this. The brilliant Steerpike had become a cloud of crimson (*G*, pp. 441-442).

Finally, as Titus drives at him through the ivy, Steerpike delays defending himself to utter a cry of defiance, and Titus' knife rips the life out of him (*G*, p. 443).

Steerpike *uses* Gormenghast's tradition for his own ends, but by conforming to that tradition he denies his individual personality a chance to grow freely. His death shows the futile, self-destructive attempt to seize control. Yet Steerpike excites grudging sympathy—at least—as well as horror, because he represents a submerged side of normal character. Despite his monstrous actions and more monstrous plans, he develops consistently with his first appearance as a young man trying to escape an intolerable future, in a situation where the rules can only repress people who wish to live in their own way, to satisfy themselves.

That description, of course, could apply to Titus as well. In fact though Steerpike and Titus become bitter enemies in the course of the story, they resemble each other very much in some ways. In the eyes of Gormenghast, heresy (echoing Satan's act of rebellion against Divine Law) is the ultimate sin. Both young men are either secretly or potentially guilty of this crime. Steerpike is specifically compared to Satan several times and Titus, too, indulges in rebellious "devilment" (*G*, pp. 16, 20). These comparisons between Steerpike and Satan increase the reader's horror of Steerpike, but they carefully stop short of full religious force. Thus the reader is shocked at Steerpike's *mode* of rebelling: however, Peake does not label rebellion itself as evil. Steerpike's rebellion is not so much against Gormenghast as against his prescribed place in the castle. Actually, his plan to improve his position unconsciously echoes the self-delusion of the men who built Gormenghast, imagining they could see life whole and master it. Beyond this, Steerpike's and Titus' attitudes differ, and thus so do the actions of which they are capable. Titus treats servants as convenient devices (*G*, p. 20): Steerpike, though, considers *all* people merely tools. Titus is not aware of his own shortsightedness, but Steerpike sees very clearly what his actions do to people. Titus wants to have power over himself, and he pays little attention to most people; Steerpike must control others to feed his hunger for power. Thus Steerpike turns inward, taking his pleasure in exercising absolute power over the Twins in their gloomy warren: "He had led them gradually, and by easy and cunning steps, from humiliation to humiliation, until the distorted satisfaction he experienced in this way had become little short of necessity to him" (*G*, p. 46). Titus turns outward, exploring the castle alone for his pure delight. Titus lives for himself. Steerpike lives against others.

Titus' development presents an alternative response to the tyranny of a tradition-bound, purposeless future. Titus feels this need dimly at the beginning of *Gormenghast*, but he is still unable to

articulate it clearly. As in *Titus Groan*, ritual tries to create love of
Gormenghast in Titus, but Titus is instinctively repelled by that
kind of life. Even as a boy, he wants at least to "pretend . . . to be
free" (*G,* p. 90).

Titus is attracted by the world outside Gormenghast, because
there he can escape the restrictions of his official role. When he does
find a secret way out of the castle, he experiences real solitude for the
first time. However, unfamiliar with this freedom from restraint,
Titus is uneasy: "now, what he had loved he loathed . . . . For it was
as though he were being drawn towards some dangerous place or
person, and that he had no power to hold himself back" (*G,* p. 120).
He does not know what to do with himself. But he catches sight of
another human figure, springing so freely through the forest that it
seems to be flying. He cannot believe that such a creature really can
exist, it is so close to his deepest longing (*G,* p. 121). Actually, it is
Keda's child, now called the Thing, who lives alone in the forest. As
in *Titus Groan*, Titus immediately responds to the kind of freedom
the Thing represents; an important part of his nature is in tune with
hers.

Yet, as with Steerpike, the two show differences as well as
similarities. Despite Titus' intuitive supernatural link to the Thing,
Peake is careful to describe the Thing *as* a thing, presented through
images suggesting the unthinking, nonhuman order of nature: "as
the light quickened the creature moved in its sleep. The eyes opened.
They were clear and green as sea stones and were set in a face that
was coloured and freckled like a robin's egg" (*G,* p. 161). By contrast,
Titus cannot simply reflect the world around him, he must think
about it (*G,* p. 169). Titus cannot repress his instincts—and does not
try very hard—but he is not overwhelmed by them. Instead, he tries
to understand what he feels and act on the basis of that
understanding.

Titus' problem is that, since he is a young boy, his powerful
feelings have little experience to support them. His picture of
himself naturally is confused. Moreover, his feelings seem to pull in
several directions. He wishes to be free of Gormenghast at the same
time he rejoices in possessing it. But he does not want Gormenghast
to possess *him*. He cannot accept the narrow role set up for him,
either as a matter of course or as a calculated maneuver. His instinct
of self-preservation is too strong to compromise. Thus he is repelled
by the whole mechanical ritual of Gormenghast (*G,* pp. 153-154), and
when Steerpike winks at him, Titus is sickened: "beyond his
knowledge, beyond his power of reason, a revulsion took hold of him
and he recoiled from that wink like flesh from the touch of a toad"

(*G,* p. 134). After accidentally insulting Steerpike, Titus refuses to apologize because he realizes that "he had cried 'shut-up' to the arch symbol of all the authority and repression which he loathed" (*G.*p. 276). He faints, but he does not submit. For Titus instinctively hates the power Steerpike serves and the devious compromise that gives him a grip on that power.

As a complement to his hatred of Steerpike, his attraction to the Thing pushes Titus toward maturity. His growth is not simple, though. Defiance of everything around him does not in itself help Titus find any new way to live. Separated from the Thing, after Steerpike is outlawed, Titus drifts. His emotions seem to lack object. He feels that all things are equally vulgar. Instead, in this mood of total rejection, he performs his ritual duties earnestly because they give his life some value, however flimsy. The Thing shakes him out of this fearful lethargy when she interrupts a castle ceremony to steal a carving that she desires. The violation of ritual stabs at the castle's heart—and Titus,"sick with excitement" (*G,* p. 359), feels a powerful emotion he had almost forgotten. He violates the ceremony himself, running after the Thing, drawn by "something more fundamental than tradition" (*G,* p. 362). He loves the Thing for what she represents: "it was that Gormenghast meant nothing to his [sic] switch of a girl!... She was freedom" (*G,* pp 365-366).

This section of *Gormenghast* troubles some critics who have difficulty figuring out what to make of the Thing.[6] Is she a character? Is she a symbol? What *is* she? In fact she can be both. Fantasy does give a writer exactly this opportunity to identify a character with an abstract principle. Two things must be accomplished, however, if the writer is to avoid sterile allegory. First, the action must be physically convincing. We have seen how Peake's gift for visual detail accomplishes this. Secondly, the action must ring true psychologically. Even if we cannot always account "realistically" for all aspects of a character's personality, we must be convinced of the emotional plausibility of what we see. In this case, Titus—unwillingly shaped by Gormenghast and its values— reaches out toward the Thing—unknowingly produced by free nature. Whatever made her what she is and whatever made her represent all she does to Titus, the real question is whether Peake can sustain our sense of vivid, surprising growth or whether he will let the story lapse into a neat, orderly puppet show.

Considering Peake's earlier description of Gormenghast's folly, the latter course clearly is closed to him. Yet he also recognizes the essential human need to find *some* place to stand amid the rush of chaotic events. The difficulty is that each individual must find his own place.

This is what Titus begins to discover. When he finds the Thing squatting in a cave and eating a freshly killed magpie, Titus glories in her freedom from any tradition, her animal originality. Yet he also discovers the limits of such total freeom when he tries to talk to her: "the first sound which Titus heard her utter bore no relation to human speech. Nor did the tone of it convey that he was being answered even in a language of her own. It was a sound, quite solitary and detached. It had no concern with communication.... So divorced was it, this nameless utterance from the recognized sounds of the human throat, that it left Titus in no doubt that she was incapable of civilized speech and not only this but that she had not understood a word he had said" (*G*, p. 374). The Thing's death by lightning, a moment later, confirms Titus' discovery that he must live without his dream of purely non-rational, instinctive freedom. The Thing is as free as a perfect animal, but Titus recognizes that he is a human being. At the same time, however, he does not fall back into negation. Rather, at seventeen, Titus puts childhood behind him: "He was himself.... He had learned that there were other ways of life from the ways of his great home .... He had emptied the bright goblet of romance .... The glass of it lay scattered on the floor. But with the beauty and ugliness, the ice and fire of it on his tongue and in his blood he could begin again" (*G*, p. 377).

The next necessary step in Titus' development is the public declaration of his independence from Gormenghast. During the flood, after he watches Steerpike steal his canoe, Titus rushes to the Countess with the news of Steerpike's new hiding place. But all the reasons Titus blurts out for hating Steerpike are personal: " 'He stole my boat! He hurt Fuchsia. He killed Flay. He frightened me. I do not care if it was rebellion against the Stones—most of it was theft, cruelty and murder .... He must be caught and slain. He killed Flay. He hurt my sister. He stole my boat. Isn't that enough? To hell with Gormenghast' " (*G*, p. 408).

Having begun to discover who he is and to verbalize that sense of self, Titus must test himself in action. Yet the motion still is not as clearly directed as it might appear. Leading the party that traps Steerpike, Titus tastes the sweetness of his *own* power to command others, to make them do as he wishes though he recognizes that such power is dangerous, "for as it grew, this bullying would taste ever sweeter and fiercer and the naked cry of freedom would become no more than a memory" (*G*, pp. 417-418).

At this time, Titus' thoughts revert to the Thing much more than the situation demands. He remembers her again as the trap draws tighter around Steerpike: "Two images kept floating before his eyes, one of a creature, slender and tameless; a creature who, defying him, defying Gormenghast, defying the tempest, was yet innocent as air or the lightning that killed her, and the other of a small empty room with his sister lying alone upon a stretcher, harrowingly human, her eyes closed [Fuchsia has drowned]. And nothing else mattered to him but that these two should be avenged— that he should strike" (*G*, p. 423).

Titus' blaming Fuchsia's death on Steerpike is not altogether unjust. It is Fuchsia's growing melancholia, following her discovery of Steerpike's evil, that leads her to stand poised at her window, though she actually falls into the water by accident. But Steerpike does not even know the Thing exists and certainly is not responsible for her death. The connection found by Titus exists at a pre-rational level, and actually is based on the similarity between the two young men. Both, on their separate levels, are trapped in an unyielding, unfeeling social order. They both are too alive to submit. Steerpike acts in a way that Titus cannot, by exploiting his feigned submission to gain power. But Titus is not immune to the temptation to possess Gormenghast. Even after the Thing's death, he is torn between accepting or rejecting his role as lord of Gormenghast. Just as Steerpike attracts as well as repels the reader, the course of action Steerpike represents must attract Titus even while it repels him.[7]

Ritual is one possible guide for Titus' life, and the adults around him have submitted to ritual in one degree or another. Looking at the people close to his own age, Titus can observe three alternative ways of life, models of selfhood. Steerpike is adept but two-faced and vicious; the Thing is healthily unrestrained but nonhuman; Fuchsia, although she seems to possess the greatest capacity for growth because of her clear insights, is too romantic to develop her understanding of what she sees and lacks an instinct of self-preservation. No individual offers a fully developed and attractive alternative to submission to the laws of Gormenghast. Titus must grow through and past these failed courses of action. He must learn what he can from them, then discard them. Only after they are dead to him (figuratively—or literally) can he find his own course. Thus Titus' thoughts link the Thing, Fuchsia and Steerpike—because he needs Steerpike's death in the same way he had needed the others' without admitting it to himself.

Just before he spies Steerpike in the ivy and dives at him, Titus' real desire is not simply revenge for the death of the object of his romantic imagination, or for the death of the sister who mixed romanticism and realism as a way of life. Rather, Titus has built a new maturity: "a kind of power climbed through him like sap. Not the power of Gormenghast, or the pride of lineage ... but vengeance and sudden death and the knowledge that he was not watching any more, but living at the core of drama" (*G*, p. 438). Thus the components of Titus' rage show that he has learned all he can by his fascination with the alien Thing, his sympathetic pity for Fuchsia, and his hatred for Steerpike. He no longer needs to delay in uncertainty. As he acts now against Steerpike, directing the searchers, he feels at once a focus for all of life and also "only himself."

And now, with Steerpike dead, Titus can act on his feeling that he has outgrown Gormenghast, and his hunger for a setting outside Gormenghast's categories. In so doing, he is not actually free, but is following "a law as old as the laws of his home. The law of flesh and blood. The law of longing. The law of change. The law of youth" (*G*, p. 452). Earlier, Peake has stressed Titus' membership in the human race and thus his being subject to needs and pressures more basic than the demands of Gormenghast's ritual. Actually, in Titus and all the other characters, passion is the root of every action. Emotion cannot be repressed indefinitely without it exploding, as in Steerpike's life, in behavior more aberrant than any open display could have been. Even directing emotion through accepted channels tends to warp the individual, making him fit only for a constricted life. Judging from the failure of the characters who deny themselves in sincere or feigned service to ritual, it appears that emotion should be allowed to develop freely, to take its rightful share of command of human actions with the intellect. Thus, as he struggles to discover himself, Titus may behave selfishly and meanly, viewed from the perspective of ritual. The reader may even find Titus as unsympathetic, at times, as he finds Steerpike. But according to Peake, Titus still is doing the only thing that can help him find meaningful freedom. He has thought and doubted long enough: now he must act according to his own feelings.

The kind of action Titus must take—and the kind of world in which he must be able to act—are sketched in the remaining two works in the series. Before turning to them, however, I should repeat that these first two novels, *Titus Groan* and *Gormenghast*, form a unit by themselves. At the end of *Gormenghast* the situation set up in *Titus Groan* has developed to a conclusion. It is not simply that many of the characters are dead: Titus has broken away from Gormenghast to find a new life. A phase of his growth is over; a dramatic movement is complete. These two books contain a richness of detail, a convincing grasp of psychology, and a depth of human concern that mark a great work. The vividness with which Gormenghast is described, the careful presentation of characters— and in particular of Titus' passionate groping toward a true sense of himself—all work with Peake's thorough presentation of his thesis concerning individual freedom versus tradition. I believe *Titus Groan* and *Gormenghast* form a unified, successful whole.

Peake's next work dealing with Titus, the novelette "Boy in Darkness," was commissioned by Peake's publishers for a collection of three original stories, *Sometime, Never*. Although "Boy in Darkness" could fit chronologically somewhere in the middle of *Gormenghast*, it represents a major step toward the world shown in *Titus Alone*. Apparently Peake was preparing himself to write another major novel to carry Titus forward into another stage of development.

In "Boy in Darkness," Titus is just fourteen years old, still imprisoned within the castle's ritual. He already knows that he hates "the eternal round of deadly symbolism,"[8] and on the night of his fourteenth birthday he instinctively seizes the chance to escape. His flight takes him into a nightmarish country outside the castle. There, captured by two grossly ugly, semi-human creatures, the Goat and the Hyena, Titus is carried toward their master, the Lamb—in the person of whom Peake simultaneously attacks religion and science.

The religious implications of the Lamb are first apparent. The Lamb lives alone, blind, in an underground apartment lit by candles and carpeted in blood-red (cf. Revelation 7:14, 12:11). His face is "angelically white" (cf. 1 Peter 1:19), and his hands move "in a strangely parsonic way" ("Boy," pp. 189-190). The Lamb is, of course, a traditional religious symbol of innocence and purity; Christ is described as "the Lamb of God" (John 1:29). In Peake's story, too, the Goat mumbles to himself that the Lamb " 'is the heart of life and love, and that is true because he *tells* us so' " ("Boy," p. 174). So the Goat and the Hyena treat the Lamb with religious awe, as they pray to him: "O thou by whom we live and breathe and are!' " ("Boy," p. 209; cf. Revelation, 5:13). Their awe is justified; though he did not create them in the first place, the Lamb *has* made them what they are. Specifically, the Lamb has changed the natures of all living things, shaping them to resemble the beasts they are most like spiritually. With the change they have died except for the Goat and the Hyena who have survived because of "their coarseness of soul and fibre" (Boy," p. 201). Most recent to die was the Lion, who "only an age ago, had collapsed in a mockery of power .... It was a great and terrible fall: yet it was merciful, for, under the macabre aegis of the dazzling Lamb, the one time king of beasts was brought to degradation" ("Boy," pp. 201-202). Thus the Lamb has ironically fulfilled an image from popular religion, by making the lion lie down with the lamb.[9] Now, as he surveys Titus, Lamb's hands flutter "like little white doves" ("Boy," p. 213), another symbol of spiritual virtue. While the boy sleeps, the Lamb waits, lusting to change his nature too, but with "his hands together, as though in prayer" ("Boy," p. 216).

The host of specifically religious suggestions and images, in a story that until now has been devoid of such concern, suggests very strongly that Peake is here referring to the Christian religion as a debasing influence.[10] Peake's treatment of Gormenghast's ritual shows that he dislikes any system of values imposed on the individual from outside, offering him nothing directly relevant for himself and encouraging him in whatever weakness he possesses. So, here, the Lamb can break down but not build; despite his worshipper's praise, he does not really understand how to keep his creatures alive. Still the Lamb glories in his power. True, in changing men he has destroyed them, denying them freedom to develop for themselves; to the Lamb, however, that is incidental to his own gratification.

In addition to religion, however, Peake attacks modern technology. However different faith in religion and faith in science appear, they can function in the same way for their believers. When religion is employed systematically to manipulate and nullify human beings, it functions as a science for the priests who operate it; by the same token, when science gives man the satisfaction of godlike control over human beings, it serves a religious purpose for him. The country beneath which the Lamb lives is littered with the waste and debris of science and industry. Underground, also, is a dead wilderness of metal: "there had been a time when these deserted solitudes were alive with hope, excitement and conjecture on how the world was to be changed. But that was far beyond the skyline. All that was left was a kind of shipwreck. A shipwreck of metal ... vistas of forgotten metal; moribund, stiff in a thousand attitudes of mortality; with not a rat, not a mouse; not a bat, not a spider. Only the Lamb" ("Boy," p. 190). The Lamb belongs in this setting. He, too, like those who worked in metal and stone thrives on change, though like that of the others it is a sterile, ego-directed change only. He hungers excitedly for more living things to alter according to his desires.

Like the ritualists in Gormenghast, the Lamb frees the faithful from the responsibility of being individual human beings. Many of

Peake's characters seem to desire no more. In *Gormenghast*, for example, Bellgrove the schoolmaster gives up the masterful role that had so impressed Irma Prunesquallor, because "there was no joy in will-power" (*G*, p. 302). It is easier to drift, to let decisions be made by other people, by momentary pressures and, above all, by ritual rules. In "Boy in Darkness," the Lamb represents the tempting and horrifying surrender of self, this time as part of a specifically religious ritual. And, of course, the Lamb hates human beings, and his purpose in changing them is to destroy them. His only real pleasure is in the destruction of another living will, as the final proof of his power.

Facing the Lamb, Titus saves himself by using his strength of personality and his intelligence. Symbolically, when he attacks the Lamb, Titus reveals religion's physical and intellectual hollowness: Titus' sword "split the [Lamb's] head into two pieces which fell down on either side. There was no blood, nor anything to be seen in the nature of a brain" ("Boy," p. 224). Titus evidently loses the memory of his experience, while returning to Gormenghast. Yet that experience may become part of him subconsciously, to give him strength for his later development.[11]

Titus Alone was written during a very difficult period for Peake. Describing his purpose, in a letter to his wife, Peake says he wishes "to canalize my chaos. To pour it out through the gutters of Gormenghast " (quoted in *World*, p. 107). But chaos was gaining on him. Maeve Gilmore, Peake's widow, describes his appalling nervous deterioration and the increasing difficulty he experienced in concentrating—and even in the physical activity of writing (*World*, p. 115).

In addition Peake faced a major test of his creative power in this final book, since Titus now must struggle toward greater maturity. As part of the escape from Gormenghast, Peake evidently had decided to let Titus find his way in what Gilmore calls "a world which was probably closer to this one [than Gormenghast] and yet alien" (*World*, p. 120). With his flight from Gormenghast, Titus has ceased to be a boy; to become a man he must find his way in a setting that adult readers can at least half-recognize, confronting a tradition that stems more directly from modern life.

The society into which Titus wanders is technologically advanced.[12] But its proud achievements are supported by the factories "where the scientists worked, like drones, to the glory of science and in praise of death" (*TA*, p. 159). This is both figuratively and literally true. Traditional religion does not appear in *Titus Alone*, for it has been replaced by faith in the development of technology, of the conscious intellect by itself. As Muzzlehatch comments on Titus' destroying a robot spy-device: " 'You have broken something quite hideously efficient. You have blasphemed against the spirit of the age' " (*TA*, p. 106). Like all who surrender themselves to this new faith, however, Cheeta's father is a distorted grotesque: "His presence was a kind of subtraction .... For he was *nothing*: a creature of solitary intellect, unaware of the fact that, humanly speaking, he was a kind of vacuum" (*TA*, pp. 184-185). When his factory is destroyed, he collapses with the cry, " 'It is all I had; my science, *all* that I had' " (*TA*, p. 217).

The idea of technological superiority is not potent enough to unify people as well as does Gormenghast's tradition. However, because faith in technology is based on the same impulse to escape from personal freedom and doubt by asserting an objective principle over the self (the assertion made over the same volatile mixture of thought and passion) the society resembles Gormenghast—a heap of fragments, thronged with grotesques. The society in *Titus Alone* is unlike Gormenghast, however, in several specific ways. The society contains unexplained lapses, incongruous pockets of confused, frustrated activity like the Under River, which corresponds to a contemporary ghetto. But because the society *is* less cohesive, its inhabitants must enforce unity more feverishly. While the Grey Scrubbers in *Titus Groan* looked alike, here not only the workers but the police, symbols of state authority, are "identical in every way" (*TA*, p. 29). Finally, the society of *Titus Alone* has less ability to sustain an appearance of health. Though Gormenghast is crumbling insensibly with age, Titus' new surroundings are wilfully festering; the noise made by the factory belonging to Cheeta's father is "an endless impalpable sound that, had it been translated into a world of odours, might have been likened to the smell of death: a kind of sweet decay" (*TA*, p. 167). This new society is more incoherent, more intolerant of deviation, and even more dangerous to Titus' spirit than Gormenhast.

He becomes aware of this danger only gradually. Primarily he is trying to cut loose from his past and become an independent person. Titus is aided toward maturity by Muzzlehatch, zoo-keeper and renegade. Muzzlehatch is like Titus in the richness of his vision and his love of the world. The way Muzzlehatch adapts things to fit his dreams, however, stems from his being so intensely alive. Even his car has acquired a personality, become almost a living thing (*TA*, p. 61). Unlike the Lamb, Muzzlehatch makes things *more*, rather than less than they are, because he can love the world's variety. Muzzlehatch helps Titus because he recognizes that the young man is like him in hating the regimented society—in fact, Muzzlehatch comments that Titus is " 'rather like a form of me' " (*TA*, p. 65).

Unlike Muzzlehatch, however, Titus barely can keep his sense of identity intact. He is unable to settle into a relationship with any of the people who help him, because he is afraid they can only help him to love in their ways. He does not yet know what his way is, but until he finds out he must maintain himself independent. Juno, for example, saves Titus from imprisonment by taking him into her custody. But Titus accepts her offer only out of weakness (*TA*, p. 88). For Juno intends, in the most generous way possible, to possess Titus and give him *her* sense of direction. Subconsciously recognizing this, he resolves to seduce her and thus "to bring the total of their relationship to a burning focus. To bring it all to an *end*" (*TA*, p. 91). And so he moves on, feeling a mixture of "shame and liberation" (*TA*, p. 102), to return to the search for an independent identity.

Early in the story, despite his desire for freedom, Titus still pictures himself as a lost fragment of Gormenghast. Followed by a floating, metal spy-sphere, Titus shatters the machine with the chunk of the Tower of Flints he has carried with him (*TA*, p. 102), but later realizes that he has lost all physical proof of his past (*TA*, p. 105). Muzzlehatch, however, advises him: " 'Get on with life. Eat it up .... What of the castle you talk about—that crepuscular myth? Would you return after so short a journey? No, you must go on. Juno is part of your journey. So am I. Wade on, Child' " (*TA*, p. 107).

Titus does begin to age, and to act, as he wades on into the Under River, the haven for criminals and outcasts. There he helps the Black Rose, pathetic slave of Veil, escape from her master. But Titus still is not able to love or be loved, though even he is repelled by his desire to flee from the Black Rose's need; " 'Grief can be boring.' Titus was immediately sickened by his own words. They tasted foul on the tongue" (*TA*, p. 139). Just so, Titus is forced to run away again from his gratitude to Muzzlehatch. He exclaims, to the man who has just saved him again, " 'I am too near you. I long to be alone. What shall I do?' " (*TA*, p. 143). Muzzlehatch replies. " ' The world is wide. Follow your instinct and get rid of us' " (*TA*, p. 144).

The next person Titus falls in with, however, is not to be cast off easily—or understanding enough to wish Titus well when he must leave her. She is Cheeta, whom Peake describes as a "modern" beauty, perfect in each detail but distorted as a whole (*TA*, p. 160). To Cheeta, who is so much a part of the modern world and its ritual, Titus is a mystery that she can neither solve nor dismiss. On his part, besides his usual reluctance to form an interdependent relationship with anyone else, Titus feels subtly repelled by Cheeta and disgusted by the factory her father owns (*TA*, p. 168). But Cheeta, feeling that she is being robbed of "something miraculous" when Titus decides to leave her (*TA*, p. 173), vows revenge.

In fact, the thing that makes Titus so mysterious to Cheeta is the very thing that makes her hate him—the independent identity that strengthened itself until Cheeta can see Titus in the same way that once *he* had seen citizens of the society: "she hated him. Hated his self-sufficiency" (*TA*, p. 102), True, Titus' extreme form of self-sufficiency is unappealing to Cheeta, to most readers, and even to Titus at least part of the time; however, it is necessary to him in this period of his growth. At this stage, his only satisfying relationship is with a village maiden, described as "a rosy, golden thing" (*TA*, p. 206). By keeping himself thus free of entanglements, while exploring experience, Titus gains understanding of the possibilities of experience and thus gains strength.

But although Titus is stronger, he does not *feel* secure yet. He always feels "the legions of Gormenghast" pressing close behind him, and he cries to the world around him, " 'Give me some proof of me!' " (*TA*, p. 195). Cheeta attacks him on this point, by ordering built a distorted replica of Gormenghast in order to humiliate Titus, or drive him insane by destroying his belief in himself. She plans well. Tricked into this setting, Titus is struck by "terror; not of Cheeta herself or of any human being, but of doubt. The doubt of his own existence" (*TA*, pp. 227-228).

Muzzlehatch arrives just in time to break the mood and save Titus once more. In doing all this Muzzlehatch represents more than a handy *deus ex machina*; he is exhibiting a facet of maturity that Titus has not yet attained. Titus has been so busy maintaining himself that he has found no time to develop relationships with others. As he reels under Cheeta's attack, though, he asks: "Why had he been so singled out? What had he done? Was the fact that he had never loved her for herself but only out of lust, was this so dire a thing?" (*TA*, p. 236). However defensively, Titus' questioning of himself suggests both an awareness of responsibility and a glimpse of personal failure. In the story's context, though, the question is difficult. Cheeta's hatred of Titus is perverted and vile; Titus' aloofness is a necessary phase of his development. But beyond the stage in which Titus finds himself, of self definition by unrestrained experience, Muzzlehatch has learned that he cannot live by himself. At the beginning of *Titus Alone*, he loves the animals in his zoo, but even then he finds that they are not enough: "he wanted something else. He wanted words" (*TA*, p. 95). After his zoo is destroyed by the police because he has helped Titus, Muzzlehatch first flees, broken in spirit, then returns because of a desire to revenge himself by destroying the factory belonging to Cheeta's father—and because of an urge to help Titus. Their relationship has become a kind of love and Muzzlehatch has come to realize that meaning comes not only from the self but from the relationship of the self to others.

Titus has not come that far yet, but he may be on the way. He is essentially like Muzzlehatch, and he has passed through this difficult period without becoming corrupt. Titus' restraint from human involvement is not viciousness, and it need not be a permanent condition. At the very end of the book, wandering again in wilderness, Titus realizes he is near Gormenghast. If he wishes, he can look at the castle again to reinforce his identity; he can even enter it and return to his inherited role. He refuses: "He had no longer any need for home, for he carried his Gormenghast within him. All that he sought was jostling within himself. He had grown up" (*TA*, pp. 262-263). He is at the end of a period of doubt and defensiveness, ready to begin self-assured exploration.

As it stands, *Titus Alone* is as unfinished as *Titus Groan* would be if it were considered by itself. I have analyzed what I take to be Peake's intent to make Titus' maintenance of himself the foundation for later human connections. The change has not yet been worked out fully in *Titus Alone*. Instead the book's short chapters and choppy writing further emphasize Titus' confusion. By this time, however, Peake was unable to develop his thoughts fully, and only notes survive for the fourth book of the series (*World*, p. 106).

Because Peake's illness probably affected the writing of *Titus Alone* and because the series is itself a developing and incomplete structure, it is difficult to evaluate Peake's books about Titus as a finished work. Perhaps a fairer question is whether or not the stories accurately represent man's sense of himself as an unfinished, growing being. I believe that they do. The Titus series is overwhelmingly concerned with Becoming, rather than with fallen man's unchangeable state of Being, and shows great faith in the individual's ability *to become* a stable, free individual. Peake offers no moral judgments of a young person's actions as he matures. For Peake, the weight of moral standards comes from their being part of a tradition, and any tradition lies outside the individual's potential and needs. Thus adherence to a morality impedes development of the whole self and denies real maturity. Titus' values are based on what works or fails for him, what pleases him or makes him feel shame. Man lives, Peake shows us, in a fantastic world, unfathomable by any mind; therefore, one cannot rely on outside teaching, but must throw himself headlong into life, transcending any limiting scheme. Titus lives through a series of vivid experiences, developing through them in a convincing manner. Titus grows beyond the limits of his tradition to become a freeminded, sympathetic man.

As a presentation of this idea, Peake's work is very impressive. In particular, his first novels—*Titus Groan* and *Gormenghast*— form a vivid and convincing unit. Even in their unfinished state, Peake's stories of Titus Groan deserve their popularity for their successfully humanistic conception of contemporary man. It is unfortunate that physical illness kept Peake from continuing his depiction of Titus' development. But there is joy and wonder in what he completed.

Notes

[1] *"Gormenghast," Time and Tide* 31 (Oct. 21, 1950), 1065.

[2] We face two major problems in setting up an analysis of the Titus stories. One concerns the overall form of Peake's work. *Titus Groan* (1946), *Gormenghast* (1950), and *Titus Alone* (1959), can be considered a trilogy, with "Boy in Darkness" (1956) an outlying fragment. Actually in commenting on the effects of the nervous disease that left Peake steadily less able to work or think connectedly, Peake's widow says the *Titus Alone* is only "the last book in what was called a trilogy, but which would never have ended if nature in her aggressive way had not taken possession of all that made him a unique person" (Maeve Gilmore, *A World Away: A Memoir of Mervyn Peake* [London: Victor Gollancz, 1970], p. 105; hereafter cited as *World*.) I intend to examine Peake's work in its natural units, rather than in divisions artificially imposed by his illness. *Titus Groan* and *Gormenghast* form one such unit. Not only did the writing of another novel, *Mr. Pye* (1953), intervene between *Gormenghast* and the two later works, but *Titus Groan* and *Gormenghast* form a whole by themselves. These first two novels stick closely to the same setting and center on the same characters and issues, *Gormenghast* actually beginning with a synopsis of the first novel. Years pass before Peake returns to Titus, in "Boy in Darkness" and *Titus Alone*, and both the setting of the story and the focus of Peake's concern have undergone striking changes.

Peake's illness is the source of the second problem. As his widow says above, illness impaired Peake's ability to develop the design of the Titus stories. In addition, Peake's handwriting deteriorated severely. Thus *Titus Alone* offers severe textual problems, the manuscript being extremely uncertain and semi-legible as well. Both published versions required editorial choice and guesswork (in addition to *World*, see John Batchelor, *Mervyn Peake: A Biographical and Critical Exploration* [London: Duckworth, 1974], pp. 114-123, for a description of how both published versions differ from Peake's manuscript; see also Langdon Jones' note on his labors in preparing the second edition of *Titus Alone* [London: Eyrie & Spottiswoode, 1970], pp. 7-8). Thereafter, this essay will use the second, fuller edition of *Titus Alone* as its text, though other texts will be the first edition.

[3] *Titus Groan* (London: Eyrie & Spottiswoode, 1946), p. 310.

[4] In *A New Romantic Anthology*, ed. Stefan Schimanski and Henry Treece (Norfolk: New Directions, 1949), p. 80. Hereafter referred to as "Romantic Novel."

[5] *Gormenghast* (London: Eyrie & Spottiswoode, 1950), pp. 77-78.

[6] In the study cited above, for example, John Batchelor first states that "the 'Thing' . . . is to be seen as the embodiment of the entire natural world. Her death creates a disharmony in the universe, which then mourns her with a flood which engulfs the castle" (p. 96), but later calls her "a false goddess who deserves death by thunderbolt, although this is also a pathetic, and therefore morally exalting death" (p. 99). The scene is especially perplexing when one remembers that the Thing is killed by a bolt of lightning—surely another "natural" force. Batchelor attributes this discontinuity to inconsistent characterization; "why," he asks, "should the spirit of nature slaughter a missel-thrush?" (p. 98). The answer must be that "the spirit of nature" can

do *anything*. Nature does not have to fit our sense of decorum. The desire for consistency—as is the desire for a pretty, literally denatured existence—is characteristic of Gormenghast, not of the world around it. And we have seen what hollow pretension and folly that desire leads to.

[7]C.N. Manlove also observes that Titus and Steerpike are very much alike (*Modern Fantasy: Five Studies* [Cambridge: Cambridge University Press, 1975, p. 246]); unfortunately Manlove uses this perception to question Titus' motives in rejecting Gormenghast. Manlove looks for clearly comprehensible purpose, not appreciating how Titus is trying to work his way through a tangle of contradictory desires. (In a later essay, Manlove attacks the characterization of Steerpike also, stating that his keeping the Twins alive so long is "without explanation" ["A World in Fragments: Peake and the Titus Books," *The Mervyn Peake Review*, Autumn, 1980, p. 12]. Again, Manlove wants to oversimplify, missing the implication that it is the very rigidity of Steerpike's self-control in public that forces him to keep someone hidden whom he can humiliate and manipulate.)

[8](London: Eyrie & Spottiswoode, 1956), p. 159.

[9]The image does not come directly from the Bible. There, in Isaiah 11:6, "The wolf ... shall dwell with the lamb, and the leopard shall lie down with the kid; and the calf and the young lion and the fatling together...." However, the notion of the lion and lamb, in particular, lying down together has become a part of popular Christian imagery all the way down to Christmas cards.

[10]Although Peake was the son of a Congregational medical missionary he did not participate in formal religion himself. Also Peake's widow refers to the problems they experienced in gaining her traditionally Catholic parents' permission to marry, and she quotes from a poem published in Peake's last collection of poetry: "How foreign to the spirit's early beauty/and to the amoral integrity of the mind/ And to all those whose reserve of living is lovely? Are the tired Creeds that can be so unkind" (*World*, p. 25).

[11]Edwin Morgan suggests as much in "The Walls of Gormenghast—An Introduction to the Novels of Mervyn Peake," *Chicago Review*, 14 (1960), 76.

[12]Some space exploration has been accomplished, a situation common to science fiction at the time Peake wrote (2nd ed. London: Eyrie & Spottiswoode, 1970), pp. 176-177.

Critical Mass:
The Science Fiction of Frederik Pohl*

David N. Samuelson

The problem of determining Frederik Pohl's rank among SF writers is not a simple one to resolve. As a satirist and thinker, he is at the top of American SF writers who are "fan-oriented," but as an artist, even as a technician, he often shows significant defects. Even the best of his fiction is sometimes marred by the intrusion of melodrama, sentimentality, unrationalized fantasy, and other features more or less calculated to appeal to an addicted audience. For the most part, his work seems to lack depth, density, an authentic personal voice, and a sense of style as anything more than a serviceable medium.[1] This makes it difficult to take him seriously as a major writer, addressing with authority matters of significance.

One reason for these "flaws," if such they are, is not far to seek. Pohl's intimate connection with commercial SF over so many years has no doubt limited him at times to what he thought his known audience was willing to accept. If it was narrow and provincial, so were his stories prior to 1952. When satire and social criticism were in, he still felt constrained to gild them with snappy patter, melodramatic plots, and irrelevant aliens. His Hugos as editor were won for a magazine committed largely to adventure stories and essentially lightweight material—*IF* or *Worlds of IF*— in which he once objected editorially to the pessimism and anarchy being brought to SF in the 1960s by the "New Wave."[2] Yet his own work later shows signs of his having accepted without hesitation the greater freedom of content and complexity of form brought to SF by the "New Wave" controversy, not to mention the broadened audience.

The reader who comes to Frederik Pohl through his short stories anthologized by others, his novels written alone or with Kornbluth or Lester del Rey, even through most of his short story collections, is bound to recognize a critical bent, out of harmony with the simple-minded optimism of most SF adventures. The obvious butts of his criticism are individual incompetents, power-grabbing manipulators, and such communal vices as war, waste, overbreeding, and the kind of gullibility that allows manipulators to

---

*This article has appeared in *S-F Studies,* 7(1980), 80-95, and is reprinted with permission of the author and editors.

prosper. Some of these gulls and failures, wheeler-dealers and baby makers must have come from experience, however broadened and universalized. Though not alone, SF readers are addicted to power fantasies, escapism and an ever-rising material standard of living. However indirectly, then, Pohl is taking aim on his own readers, as well as the masses they look down upon. Furthermore, by acknowledging the underside of SF dreams and even by telling a familiar tale better than others have done, he implicitly criticizes his own predecessors and peers.

Over the years, the audience for SF has grown, and part of it has even grown up. Pohl himself has outgrown his role as enforcer of just such rules as hampered his own talents. But the habits of 30-plus years can be hard to break. Even some of his "mature" works continue to rely on melodramatic action, unearned sentiment, thin characterization, and a rapid pace that disallows contemplative savoring of people, places, acts and consequences. Style and structure take on more importance for themselves, realistic detail and emotional intensity have increased, and the often facetious comedy of his earlier works has turned toward an almost tragic representation of the human condition. The "great work," however, still lies beyond his grasp.

To support these assertions adequately would take a book. In the space available, I can only discuss briefly a relatively few representative examples.[3] Excluding most of Pohl's pseudonymous and collaborative work, I shall concentrate on 1) the "consumer cycle" of the 1950s, 2) the four novels published under Pohl's name alone between 1956-1969, 3) the static sketches of the 1960s, and 4) the "mature" stories and novels of the 1970s. Though stressing to some extent the conflict between critical acuity and fictional vacuity, I will focus largely on the growth of the artist.

1. By the "consumer cycle," I refer to stories concentrating on advertising and public relations, issues of production and consumption, and matters of social and economic regulation. These comprise the "comic infernos" Amis singled out for praise in 1960. Inverting, modifying or transforming some element of society, they rarely draw a coherent picture of technical and temporal change.

Aside from the collaborations with Kornbluth, Pohl's most famous consumer story is probably "The Midas Plague" (1954). Positing a "utopian" economy of affluence, Pohl turns upside down the idea of conspicuous consumption: the "poor" are burdened by having to consume huge amounts of foods and products churned out by automated factories. The desultory and forgettable plot, involving a newly married couple from disparate classes, concludes with the "happy idea" (long since telegraphed to the reader) of short-circuiting the process by involving robots in consumption as well as production. Well aware that the premise (suggested by *Galaxy* editor Horace Gold) was untenable, Pohl didn't really try to shore up its believability.[4] Instead he turned it into a "tall tale" with logically extrapolated details and a rarely flagging faculty of comic invention. Complaints of the story's impossibility or lack of verisimilitude are beside the point, which was to expose and skewer the *naivete* (or duplicity) of the attitude (not limited to the 1950s) that affluence is a never-ending spiral, meanwhile softening the blow with comic exaggeration.

Only the second story to bear his exclusive byline, "The Midas Plague" marked (along with *The Space Merchants*) the emergence of Pohl as comic satirist. Frequently reprinted, sometimes as "serious" utopian speculation, it was popular enough in its time to inspire three sequels. "The Man Who Ate the World" (1956), "The Wizards of Pung's Corners" (1958) and "The Waging of the Peace" (1959) do not come up to the original, but each has its moments of comic brilliance, as does another broadly conceived satire on the commercialization of Christmas. In "Happy Birthday, Dear Jesus" (1956), however, the proffered cure is a love affair between the sales-worshipping narrator and a missionary's daughter, characters too simple and cliched to shoulder the burden.

More successful as stories are four which attack, grotesquely but with less zanniness, aspects of social control. "My Lady Greensleeves" (1957), ostensibly about a prison riot, examines the society of which that prison is a symptom. The riot fails because the white-collar thinkers and blue-collar workers can't get together to engineer a break-out. A discordant note is provided by the fortuitous presence of a Senator's daughter, pretty and innocent, available as a hostage. Rebelling against the exaggerated system of segregation by occupational specialization which is the real issue of the story, she has to be made to fear for her life, and to recognize the "good sense" of the system, which eliminates illogical biases based on color, religion or ethnic origin.

Govermental *over*control is rejected as one solution to wasted human resources in "Rafferty's Reasons" (1955). The title refers to inchoate causes of homicidal tendencies in a former "artist," retrained (brainwashed) to fill a niche society finds useful. Mind-numbed by his involuntary conditioning, Rafferty finally attacks a politician with a cigar butt, thinking it a knife. The underdog draws some sympathy, but he is too pathetic and monomaniacal to earn much of it. The politicians, however, are much more unsavory both as characters (caricatures) and on the grounds of their "principles."

They have eliminated unemployment, overproduction and economic depressions, but at the cost (lightly dismissed) of love, religion, free speech, free elections, even—as in the case of Rafferty—of anything more than a semblance of free will, except for themselves.

Without controls, however, overpopulation and/or ecotastrophe are likely, as in "The Census Takers" (1956) and "The Snowmen" (1959). The job of the census takers is to regulate and reduce population, by execution if necessary, which the protagonist-narrator, an efficient but unimaginative civil servant, carries out well and without compunction. The latter story postulates a rapid approach to the "heat death of the universe" through overuse of "heat pumps" (shorthand for any temperature-regulating device). The satire is obscured, however, rather than illuminated, by the presence in both stories of alien beings. They serve as sane viewpoints, but the reader might be trusted to develop the same on his or her own, and their presence blunts the social criticism by turning our attention from human folly to alien invasion.

Cliched responses to alien invasion are definitely germane to "The Children of the Night" (1964). During an uneasy armistice, the Arcturans want a base in an American small town, which requires voter approval of rezoning. The narrator is another negative hero, a high-pressure public relations man, who doesn't let misgivings about the morality of his work stand in the way of doing a job well. Manipulating the good, the bad, and the public at large, he wins the referendum for the Arcturans by uniting the electorate with the hated aliens in opposition to himself as an agent of disruption, a scapegoat. Style and structure and rapid pace are all-important to this story, but the moral is far from clearcut. Pohl exploits his reader's anticipated sympathy for vivisected children and a decent politician to make the narrator's work look bad, even though the result may be a gain in peace and communication between the races.

Manipulation need not be so overt or organized. Sedation, voluntarily chosen, can do the job, as two other stories of the 1950s point out. At first glance a space opera, "The Mapmakers" (1955) shows a spaceship crew suffering hallucinations, and without the services of their navigator in hyperspace. Blinded in an accident, he is heavily sedated by a solicitous medical staff, until he convinces them of the reason for his agitated condition. The technicians' complacency is upset by his "second sight," which can guide them home unerringly and offers a definitive solution to the problem of interstellar travel. Chaotic and voluntary "control" by tranquilizers is the subject of "What to Do Till the Analyst Comes" (1956). Before hallucinogens were in the public eye, though long after Huxley's "soma" and right after the furor over "Miltown," Pohl posited a "non-habit-forming" drug which banishes worry, simultaneously freeing society from accuracy, efficiency, productivity and safety. Only the narrator is well situated to tell the story; overdosed at the drug's inception, he is allergic to it, making him the last person left to worry about anything.

None of these stories bogs down in melodrama and sentimentality. Extrapolation leads to exaggeration, action threatens to boil over, and the reader's sympathies are openly manipulated. But the author usually pulls back from the edge of bathos or overaction, achieving an emotional tone closer to the sardonic, most evident in "The Children of Night" and "What to Do Till the Analyst Comes." "The Mapmakers" is almost pure wish-fulfillment, "My Lady Greensleeves" pushes its message too much, the overconsumption tetralogy is maybe a little too zany, and "Rafferty's Reasons" is almost too dispassionate. And science, for stories ostensibly of SF, is almost conspicuous by its absence; it is a prop at most, since the stories are concerned primarily with social change. Simple moral judgments are generally avoided; the issues are real, if taken beyond contemporary parameters; and the characters, for the most part, are believable, though thin, which can be blamed both on the shortness of the stories and the pointed edges of the satire. Less credible are the cardboard figures in "Rafferty's Reasons," and characters in tales so zany (the tetralogy) or miraculous ("The Mapmakers") as to make believability irrelevant.

Comic or serious, these stories display a consistent motif, one familiar in the satiric tradition, but also pointedly relevant to the situation of a clear-sighted individual writing in an escapist medium. This paranoid sense that only one person can see clearly in an insane world is carried to its logical extreme in "The Tunnel Under the World" (1955). Arguably Pohl's best short work, this may be the ultimate fictional statement against commercial manipulation. Structured as a horror story, but without Gothic trappings, the story reveals its menace gradually, as Pohl takes his hero and us through several mistaken constructions of reality before announcing the devastating truth, which justifies the apparent melodrama.

Disturbed by insultingly strident advertising techniques and some bewilderingly effective salesmanship, Guy Burckhardt discovers—seemingly by accident—that the day of his experiences is being repeated again and again. It is his efforts to find out what is really happening that lead to startling but seemingly nonsensical revelations and then to a horrifying discovery. He and all his fellow-citizens, victims of an industrial accident, have been preserved through a miracle of science to function through miniature manikins in a table-top model of their small town. As a trade-off for this involuntary half-life, they sacrifice the consciousness of the passage of time, which might alter their responses. They must live, over and over again, the day after the accident. The advertising gimmicks with which they story began are their reason for existence; the whole town is nothing but a controlled test market for an advertising research firm. And knowing the truth, Burckhardt is powerless to do anything about it.

The technical premise is hard to credit, especially within the time frame suggested by the characters' manners and mores, but the idea that advertisers would do such a thing if they could is not all far-fetched. Vance Packard's *The Hidden Persuaders* detailed practices then going on, which Pohl's own experience in the ad business could verify.[5] Burckhardt's nightmare of timelessness may be beyond their reach, but the advertisers' grasp is hardly exaggerated. Our contemporary fascination with designer labels worn on the outside of clothing, not to mention T-shirts and apparatus blatantly advertising other products, shows how we willingly enter into complicity with the hucksters, more today than ever.

"The Tunnel Under the World" works in part because of its continued relevance, but also because of the appropriateness of its horror conventions and the "mechanical" nature of its stereotyped characters. These might put off readers for whom the satire could be a valuable dose of medicine, but for the SF reader who chews up those features as his daily bread, the application of the story to him *as an SF reader* may not be apparent. The satire seems to be directed at those other guys, who are not aware of Madison Avenue shenanigans. But like the other stories of manipulation, "The Tunnel Under the World" has an uncomfortably close fit to the cottage industry of SF itself, more today than ever, as movie makers and producers of spin-offs from SF properties make millions of dollars off their "harmless" addiction.

Besides relating to its audience, Pohl's attack on manipulation parallels the task of the writer himself manipulating his characters. This was especially evident to Damon Knight, who asserted that Pohl's characters just didn't care (nor apparently should the reader).[6] The author as puppet master was too conspicuous to Knight, but the reason could be just the opposite from what Knight implied. Pohl was not disinterested, but passionately involved, if his life and his writing have anything in common. This is a man who, however naively and lightly, was active in the Communist Party for four years, and whose liberal conscience frequently shows through his writing, perhaps nowhere more explicitly than in his political primer for the 1972 election year.[7]

It may be that he didn't have the tools, the desire, or the "permission" of the SF field to let that caring show, except in fictional polemics which raised issues above characters, and pulp fiction conventions above both. No doubt it is also true as Pohl has said that, even in the 1950s, few people in SF were writing for the ages. Writing for a deadline, for grocery money, and for an audience with a dubious memory, they had to produce a story good enough to fill pages in a cheap monthly magazine, but not to withstand repeated and critical readings. The wonder is not that these stories have flaws, but that they stand up so well after a quarter of a century. Within the sharply limited selection considered here, Pohl's stories certainly come close to deserving Amis's high praise of the time, if your taste, like Amis's, runs to SF as a social criticism.

2. Besides short stories, however, Pohl was also writing novels in the 1950s, 7 with C.M. Kornbluth (3 were not SF), 3 with Jack Williamson ("juveniles") and one with Lester del Rey (under the pseudonym of Edson McCann).[8] He also wrote the first of seven novels on his own, *Slave Ship* (1956-57). This novel and the three which followed it in the 1960s show graphically the problems involved in trying to combine trenchant social criticism with conventional pulp storytelling techniques. Unable to believe fully in his characters or their actions, Pohl mixed romance and satire somewhat incongruously, and undercut both the seriousness of his topics and the sentimentality of his characters with comic, even slapstick effects. The problem may be seen, in a sense, as one of trying to find the right genre, or mode, for his observations, since he vacillates between comedy and melodrama while trying to score satirical points.

Slave Ship has pointed things to say about man's inhumanity to animals, not to mention his fellow man, and postulates a take-over of much of the world by a fanatical religious sect, the Caodai. There is a lot of funny "business," in the stage sense of the term, but the story depends so heavily on melodramatic derring-do and corny romance that the satire and comedy are only fitful. There are a cartoon Russian, a female James Bond whose "cover" is a striptease act, and a stock comic hero, bumbling but seemingly indestructible. There is a military draft taking women and children (down to eight years old), a new way of getting high (by popping disease germs and delayed-action antibiotics), and a scoring of "ultimate pacifists" who would kill for peace. But the hero's simple-minded attitude toward women and his mooning after his missing wife are obtrusive, and the machinations which get them both out of the Caodai prison camp are little short of miraculous. Furthermore, the senseless confrontation between two human ideologies, a direct analog to Cold War posturing of the 1950s, is subverted by the introduction near the end of the novel of a double-barrelled "impossibility." The undeclared war escalates into nuclear conflict because of an alien life form in the city, a life form whose existence was unsuspected until the end. And its deadly effect upon human beings is due to its attempt to communicate with those who have experienced controlled ESP (a notable exception is the hero, who survives being zapped not once, but twice). In the abstract, these threads connect. Communication means getting along with each other—aliens with humans, humans with animals, the West and the East—but the mixture of genres and the piling up of impossibilities is self-defeating.

Drunkard's Walk (1960) and *A Plague of Pythons* (1962-65) share this conflict between romantic and satiric conventions, and this blaming of human problems on artificial fantasies. *Drunkard's Walk* devastatingly burlesques some of the practices, if not the ideals, of the modern "multiversity," such as watered-down teaching methods, blinkered specialization, faculty-student relationships, and often irritable relationships between "town and gown." The academic "establishment" is an all-but-hereditary privileged class who live in their own little world, a high-rise city within a city, with little awareness of, let alone responsibility for, the well-being of the society which supports them.

Another bumbling, indestructible hero literally "weaves" his way through the action, finding drunkenness has survival value as he tries *not* to commit suicide, though repeatedly ordered to by a conspiracy of "immortals" with telepathic powers. The title ties together a number of threads: survival through inebriation, the hero's victimization by the villains, the random "Brownian movement" of molecules, and the eventual moral of the story, that the real immorality of "the immortals" is in their overall attempt to control human development. Like any utopian scheme, their manipulation is for the stability and well-being of some, disallowing the "random" factors which are the real sources of human progress. The lesson is a bit oversimplified, since even the educators in the novel are busy manipulating minds, and even *laissez-faire* government does not do away with controls, though it makes the hands on the controls less visible.

The hands are completely invisible at the start of *A Plague of Pythons*, but they turn out to be those of normal humans, after all, as Pohl exposes the roots of the power fantasy growing throughout these three books. "Possession" of human beings is made possible this time, not through aliens, mutants or inborn extra-sensory abilities, but merely (!) through a single "impossible" invention, introduced near the beginning. With this as the only explicit violation of probability, the author is playing the game by the rules. Of a piece with critiques of less direct manipulation, this "possession" fantasy appears also in "The Day the Icicle Works Closed" (1959) and "We Purchased People" (1974). As a metaphor, it is less effective for the complexities of actual social control mechanisms than it is for auctorial omnipotence and usually sadistic wish-fulfillment. The extrapolation and its consequences here are rigorously worked out, and followed to a logical conclusion. Pohl makes only a couple of tentative detours in the direction of sentimental romance conventions and resolutely refuses to negate the story's implications with an arbitrary happy ending.

Early scenes have comic potential, before we know the causes of possession. This gallows humor turns quickly into horrific fascination with the potential god-like evil of the secret weapon, which is worn as a coronet by the ruling "Execs." Chandler's lease on life is extended by his being an electronics engineer who can perform useful tasks for the rulers. Though the morality of his work disturbs him—the Execs' willful toying with people is horrific—survival one day at a time and the faintest of hopes keep him going. Thanks to a friendly woman Exec, Chandler even gets to wear a coronet himself. He is tempted to join the charmed circle, if only to avenge their victims. He gets his revenge, but not until he is shocked out of complacency by a sadistic "love scene" in which the lady Exec wantonly kills the people in whose bodies they are making love. Even then, he cannot resist the temptation to maintain the power for himself alone.

The familiar moral is Lord Acton's: "Power tends to corrupt; absolute power corrupts absolutely." In order to survive, the hero is willing to change sides at the drop of a body. The real obstacle to this story's achieving its tragic potentiality, however, is its fast pace and melodramatic treatment, which deprive everyone of human dignity. In a sense, they do not have enough character for their submission to the lust of power to matter very much.

In *The Age of the Pussyfoot* (1965-69), Pohl all but abandons the gimmicks of previous novels in favor of straight-line extrapolation of social and technological trends. He also commits himself wholeheartedly to comedy, for the first time since *The Space Merchants* and the overconsumption tetralogy—with striking results. This time the bumbling and indestructibility of his hero have reasonable foundations. His saving the world despite himself, in confrontation with even more inept enemy aliens and human Luddites, is even believable, given the comic context.

In his "first" life, Charles Forrester had been a volunteer fireman (as Pohl once was—the occupation also has metaphorical significance). When he died in a fire (having been drunk on the job), his outfit's insurance paid for his cryogenic freezing, as a "corpsicle" awaiting medical advances that would restore him. A stranger in this strange land, he is perfectly consistent with his past life in repeatedly running afoul of the future's customs, laws and mores, because he refuses to learn anything about them in advance. A "fan" of science (like Pohl himself), he is ignorantly content to marvel at and take for granted technological marvels, without considering how to use them properly, let alone how they are paid for. An average man of the mid-20th century, he is brilliantly representative of our half-educated naivete and our addiction to "crisis management," not reacting to things until they happen, letting history make us instead of making history.

A little more visible this time, because we are being asked to take the extrapolations seriously rather than the story, is Pohl's kidding of the conventions of SF.[9] Because of an imagined slight, for example, a Martian (human) with a "German" (thin-air-induced) accent hunts Forrester down in a one-sided, legal "duelling" situation, hoping that Forrester's insurance will be insufficient to pay for the expensive operation that could restore his life. Then again, a Sirian (alien) prisoner hires Charles (who goes into it blindly) to tell him trivia of history, the strategic value of which (unknown to Charles) is that it will help him to understand human psychology. The only people with whom Charles seems remotely on a par are a couple of children, whose education via their computer-teacher-environment is fast outstripping him, and a fellow-derelict (when he falls through the poverty level) from whom he learns basic survival techniques among the "Forgotten Men."

This game-playing adds icing to the cake, but does not deter the reader from being entertained on the primary level, or grasping the story's relevance to our time. Pohl has used the techniques of extrapolation to expose, even to diagnose, a "utopia with warts," a society more sensible than ours, and significantly advanced, but which is no more sure of what it wants or where it is going.

Cryogenics has given its inhabitants more lives than a cat, but it has paradoxically made them more timid than in our society. Other serious extrapolations exploited, often for comic effect, include continued advances in education, electronics, social welfare and space travel. Should the reader find this all too fantastic, moreover, Pohl justifies his forecasts in an "Author's Note" at the end (*Slave Ship* has one also) and a "Foreword" referring the reader to the appendix. Given the futurological fun on which the book is centered, this works out fine, the end result being a book both clever and penetrating, just short of a masterpiece as a comic SF novel.

3. Through the 1960s, Pohl was also experimenting with "sketches" in which the story proper hardly interferes at all with the satire or speculation.[10] Displaying a verbal economy surpassing his previous efforts, they are essentially static, crammed with information rather than action. Four of them feature aliens, but not as the melodramatic menaces of hoary tradition. The first of these, "The Martian Stargazers" (1962), comments obliquely on our history and conceit, explaining through speculative Martian star lore why they killed themselves long before men landed there. "Earth 18" (1964) uses the Martians as the butt of racist jokes, irrelevant to a Florida hotel-keeper, but worth their weight in gold to his black bellman. And "Speed Trap" (1967) implies alien involvement in a suspected conspiracy to use travel, conferences and administration to keep real research from being done.

The best of these, "Day Million" (1966), is a self-proclaimed love-story imagining really altered people and conditions in the future (the millionth day, A.D.). Genetic engineering and social change have modified the meaning of gender, the forms human bodies can take, and the immediacy and exclusiveness of a love relationship. Without actually telling us a "story," the narrator presents us with two "genetic males" who "marry" by obtaining electronic replicas of each other to use for that era's version of a "full" love relationship. The jolting shift of perspective common to many Pohl stories occurs not once but several times in this story, as contemporary terminology proves inadequate, even misleading, for describing the future. The richness of this verbal experience may be marred for some readers by the narrator's direct address, even browbeating them into taking historical change into account when they look past tomorrow. The overall effect, however, is contemplation of, not recoil from, the supposedly outrageous circumstances, and vindication of the claim that this is indeed a "love story."[11]

"Day Million" and *The Age of the Pussyfoot* suggest the maturing of Pohl and his greater control of fictional techniques during the 1960s. Editing as many as four magazines at once, he was living through a change in social conditions which, along with more important things, made all kinds of SF seem vaguely respectable, and both allowed and expected it to be all things to all people. Changes were also happening in SF, if not most overtly displayed in his magazines, as the "New Wave" writers in England and their American counterparts rebelled against the old editorial formulas.

Long considered an apostle of doom, Pohl reversed his field slightly late in the decade, calling in an editorial for more hopeful and constructive stories in SF.[12] Backing this call with at least limited action, he printed in *Galaxy* and *IF*, as other SF magazines did also, paid advertisements for and against the American presence in Vietnam, signed by other SF professionals, and announced a contest to seek feasible solutions to this problem then ripping apart the fabric of American society.[13] But the magazines soon were sold, and he resigned as editor, entering a stage of depression in which he claims even living lost its appeal.

4. Reborn in the 1970s, he began re-examining the past, present and future.[14] From that introspection came a series of autobiographical reconstructions, at least four retrospective anthologies, and something new in his writing.[15] No longer tied to the editor's chair, and allowed, perhaps impelled, to write what he pleased, he surprised Pohl-watchers with some of the best writing of his career. Not simply comic infernos, these are coherent works of speculation and extrapolation tied to reasonably "hard" science, something almost completely lacking in his previous fiction. Pohl regards science as a great "spectator sport." It can reveal vistas inaccessible elsewhere, supply constraints or limits to work within or against, and lend authentic or authentic-sounding details to a narrative.[16] But though science may have an inside track to the "truth," or at least a close approximation, it is not a panacea; as Guy Burckhardt found out in "The Tunnel Under the World," the truth may not set you free, but rather define the boundaries of your prison.

Ecological consciousness has long been apparent in Pohl's work; over-population and exhaustion of resources play a role in his major and minor fictions. These newer stories seem even more clearly to be rooted in such matters and the problems of social control arising out of them, what the Stanford Research Institute has designated the "World Macroproblem."[17] Rather than simply bemoaning the crisis, Pohl's stories propose solutions. The solutions may still be fantasies, but they do not settle for aliens, ESP, or unlimited resources pulled out of a hat. Pulp conventions are subdued; he depends less on sentiment and more on emotional commitment, less on melodrama and more on plausible action. Satire is still present, but it seems more integrated into the fabric of the moral fable. The satire is still directed at human vice and folly, at insane or inhumane social arrangements, especially at our apparent incapacity to undertake coordinated activity to prevent or alleviate foreseeable disasters. Most of SF is indirectly indicted in these stories by taking easy ways out, simply crying "j'accuse" or resorting to magic formulas.

Formally, these stories are more complex, with interwoven viewpoints, narrators of questionable reliability, denser characterizations, radiating images, and an iron control of tone. Though every one of them has something resembling a "happy ending," they all apporoach the condition of tragedy. In "The Gold at the Starbow's End" (1972), for example, we have a "noble experiment" overseen by a science advisor to the President (vaguely similar to Henry Kissinger), in which ten healthy, sensible, disciplined and mathematically educated young people are sent in a starship to a nonexistent Centauran planet, in the hope that ten years' concentrated thinking will have unexpected results. It does. The adventurers develop new languages, arts and sciences, transcending contemporary scientific paradigms; they also develop hostility toward those whom they discover to have hoaxed them.

The story develops fairly slowly, however, as the narrative alternates between scenes at home and messages from space, which sets the stage for the destruction sent back by the "new, improved" species. The "final solution" engineered by the supposed subjects of the experiments makes for entertaining reading but uncomfortable reflection on our present way of doing things.

A more conventional adventure story is "The Merchants of Venus" (1972), which centers on the successful quest of a tour-guide and prospector to make a big strike in an undiscovered tunnel of the Heechee, an ancient alien civilization which once honeycombed the planet. This is the hellish Venus of contemporary scientific knowledge, and only the existence of the Heechee tunnels makes it possible for man to settle there, while the hope of scavenging useful artifacts makes it more or less desirable. The society is built up in the tradition of cutthroat capitalism, people preying on tourists and servicing each other, with the dangers somewhat obviated by high-powered medicine, provided you have lots of money. More prized than money is "Full Medical" insurance that covers you for anything short of resurrection of the dead (and maybe even that). The hero's health and wealth are both in bad shape when the story begins, and they get worse as he takes his tourist-employers out to the planet's surface. They turn on him, and time starts running out, but we know from the traditions of adventure fictions that he will snatch victory from the jaws of defeat. The real interest, however, is in the carefully worked out physical and social background, including the disastrous ecological-population situation implied on Earth which makes Venus even slightly attractive.

"In the Problem Pit" (1973) is only minimal SF and an unusually positive speculation for Pohl, in which the bad guys (and innocent bystanders) don't have to be killed off to realize some utopian results. The premise is that at regular intervals, groups of citizens, some voluntary and some "drafted" to make representative samplings of the population, be brought together and isolated with professional facilitators in a marathon problem-solving session. These rotating "encounter groups," starting from their own personal problems, also engage those of their whole civilization. Like Pohl's "sketches" of the 1960s, this is an essentially static idea—which calls for character interactions within the closed environment. But the story turns on an apparently lost member of the group, a search party, and the rescue of an attempted suicide, utilizing sentimentality and melodrama to make conventionally exciting what might have been a very moving and meaningful story.

Easily the most negative of the recent works is "We Purchased People" (1974), a superior narrative treatment of several recurrent themes in Pohl's work. A love story with a sado-masochistic twist, it reminds us of the possible tragic consequences for individuals in certain "utopian" solutions to social problems. Wayne Golden and Carolyn Schoerner (symbolically named "beautiful people") are would-be lovers, star-crossed in a literal sense. Found guilty by human tribunals of heinous crimes (at least Wayne was), they have been sold to aliens, who exercise remote control to use them as agents for their business dealings on Earth. They rarely meet or see each other, except when one or the other is controlled, although they do have a few "stolen moments." When the aliens themselves finally decide to bring the two together, it is not for a happy ending. The aliens wish to experiment, to learn more about patterns of human sexual behavior.

That would be bad enough as an invasion of privacy, which is what Wayne and Carolyn both think it is, but an added complication makes this story definitely not for the squeamish. Having been introduced to Wayne as a frustrated lover, we only discover just why he is a "purchased person." A homicidal maniac, he got his kicks from young girls, not exactly sexually molesting them but "watching them die." Unaware of any reform of his personality, such as the reader seems to be privy to, the aliens control him according to the "sexual behavior which has been established as his norm." Given the story's premises, the result is sick, even outrageous, but predictable, even inevitable. Moreover, a simple moral judgment is once again impossible. Unlike the protagonist of "Rafferty's Reasons," Wayne had no reason to expect anything better (Carolyn's guilt is obscure, her end more pathetic). Like the earlier story, however, this one also raises the question of what price is appropriate for a society to pay for benefits received. If the politicians were suspect, what of the aliens who brought us progress as an afterthought, while buying up our primitive artworks and artifacts?

The same question is asked again, as part of the fabric of *Man Plus* (1976), a literarily self-conscious scenario for the first manned expedition to Mars, given technology just beyond that available today. The ostensible reason is to provide future security for the technological West (i.e., the U.S.) in case of nuclear conflict. Computer analysis shows the potentiality for conflict to be at a flashpoint, an assertion obliquely supported by the revelation of the venal and calculating side of practically everyone connected with the Mars project. The apparent major focus of the project, however, to make a human being fit the presently known Martian environment, at whatever cost to his humanity, is a smokescreen. Roger Torraway and any other cyborgs who may follow him will presumably have some role to play in planetary exploration. But from the standpoint of the mysterious narrator—finally revealed as the consciousness of our linked computers—he is only one of three redundant man-machine systems involved. The machines have given false data to the military political analysts, because their aim is to insure their own survival.

"Man Plus" means man plus machine. Though the title suggests a superman, Roger Torraway is more a monster on Earth. He may be a superman on Mars, in so far as his mechanical aids do not fail him. He is completely dependent upon machinery to breathe for him, to circulate his blood through what's left of his body, to program his reflexes, even to filter his sense perceptions. We are all subject to hallucinations, but Roger's have mechanical causes; he has to learn to see and hear all over again, and to logically suppress what he recognizes as due to the machines' misreading of emotional overtones. Also part of the expedition are two other significant characters. One is a botanist-priest, who agonizes over Roger's responsibility for his actions. Tricked up to look like his unfeeling wife is a nurse who had learned to care for him despite his being sexually "man-minus." The lesson they enforce is that, as Roger is unable to tell what's true and what isn't, so are we all, whatever our "loved ones" or our instruments say.

For all that it seems to go into the private lives of the characters, the story is thin, dwelling on technical details and soap opera reactions. That is to be blamed, presumably, on the mechanical narrator's inability to understand the complexity of human beings; regardless of the intent, however, the result is still flat. Yet that in itself helps the novel to raise questions about logical, moral and technological aspects of our efforts to get into space. By being a flat, and seemingly factual account, geared to political and technological realities, *Man Plus* may serve as a useful corrective—if not a purgative—to more simple-minded stories of the "conquest" of space.

Gateway occupies approximately the same fictional universe as "The Merchants of Venus." The title identifies an asteroid hollowed out by the Heechee to use as a space station, from which their faster-than-light ships were programmed some 500,000 years ago to travel to distant points in our galaxy. The story concerns the exploits, in bed and in space, of Robinette Broadhead, an anti-hero whose luck has made him both rich and neurotic. Roughly half the book is told in terms of encounters between him and his "mechanical" (electronic) psychiatrist, "Sigfrid the Shrink," as Broadhead tries, despite himself, to come to grips with experiences related in the alternating chapters. In his stint on Gateway, Broadhead relived in modified form some of the traumas of his childhood and youth. In Sigfrid's office, he must come to terms with his latent homosexuality, and his feelings of guilt at having "betrayed" first his mother, then his fiancee, and finally, on a Gateway expedition, both friends and lover(s?). Although he got back alive and received their shares of the reward as well as his own, he can not shut off that event as past, because it is still present—and not just in his memory. Possibly by accident—they might have survived by chance instead of him—they are trapped in a "Schwarzchild Discontinuity," the gravity well of a black hole. Because of the time dilation effect, they are still alive, and still dying, and will continue to, long after Broadhead has passed from the scene.

In emotional impact, *Gateway* goes far beyond Pohl's other novels (vying with "The Tunnel" and "We Purchased People"). In its exploration of characters' inner and outer lives, it goes beyond anything before, though they are circumscribed by being filtered through the consciousness of a man who doesn't really care about anyone else. Furthermore, even Broadhead's wallowing in self-pity is interpreted by a "mechanical" Freudian analysis, which fits his profile (he has chosen it), and apparently enables him to cure himself. But people do love and hate, they act desultorily and live through more boredom and trivia than high adventure, giving the book an air of realism beyond Pohl's previous work. Instead of sentimentality, there is honest sentiment: love and hate and studied indifference. Instead of melodrama, there are the risk of confrontation and some very real tragedies. Told in a more leisurely fashion, *Gateway* has a density of detail—aided by "sidebars"—i.e. interpolated pages of want ads, lectures, mission reports, etc.— unmatched in other Pohl fiction.

Gateway also works allegorically on a more intellectual level. The "cutting edge" of human exploration and initiative, it drains human and material resources which might otherwise be spent on trying to solve problems on our own in order to take blind chances in a cosmic shell game. The most that can be hoped for is Heechee garbage; many ships or crews don't come back in working order; the fuel is gradually running out; and there is no known way to control one's destination, except on a repeat journey. With little to guide them but superstition, the prospectors are strictly out for themselves, in what they think of as free enterprise, which is actually state capitalism, overseen by five jealous space-going governments. They gamble for recreation, they gamble their lives in their work, and the whole Earth civilization seems to be gambling its future on the spin of the galactic roulette wheel.

Given ships shaped like mushrooms (hallucinogenic?) that deny Einstein's ban on faster-than-light travel, it is perhaps only fitting that *Gateway* seems to contradict one of Einstein's favorite sayings, one more associated with indeterminacy and quantum mechanics: "God does not play dice with the Universe." If God doesn't, life does, and man does so more or less consciously. Life is not a game you can win, you can only extend your playing time until the inevitable loss. Every SF probe, every scientific investigation, every exercise in human curiosity is a gamble, which may or may not bring back diamonds—but the odds are with the house.

The Gateway asteroid is one more chance, fortuitously encountered, to extend the game for man, though it may be dangerous to put all our eggs in that basket, whether we call it science, fantasy or something else. You don't have to be a good person to make a temporary killing, and Broadhead and his fellow prospectors are no better than they have to be. If they are not a flattering cross-section of mankind, they are no worse, and no worse off than the people back on Earth, which Broadhead escaped in poverty (by winning a *lottery*) and returns to in wealth. Things are even worse than in the time of "The Merchants of Venus": the race between population and resources is being lost, and the cause is more or less the same as that behind his venture into space. Each person thinks that he can beat the odds, and if the results trickle down to the masses, so much the better for them, but it's not his concern.

Though this presumably is not a position Pohl would espouse, it is rather close to the advice given Broadhead by Sigfrid: to recognize that *he* is living, and living well, in the here and now. If we take Sigfrid's advice, we too should enjoy our good fortune while we have it—regardless of how others are living? regardless of future repercussions?—and get more in touch with ourselves. We should not be afraid to feel, and to recognize that the "bad" emotions are as important as the good. Listing them—"Guilt. Fear. Pain. Envy. The motivators. The modifiers."—Sigfrid comes close to suggesting that they define man, at least as a being in the process of becoming, for whom change can be for the better. This is about the only ray of hope in an otherwise bleak alternative future.

The conventionality of the advice, the "mechanical" (or "vulgar") Freudian analysis, and the arbitrariness of its divsion into alternating sections on the couch and on the asteroid—these may be relatively minor defects in a book of *Gateway*'s scope, perspective and density. Nevertheless, the novel cannot be considered the "great" work by which Pohl will be remembered.

5. The one, three and five-person spaceships of Gateway make colonization of an alien planet, assuming the biosphere were congenial, an impossible logistic problem, despite the ability to exceed the speed of light. In *Jem* (1979), Pohl's latest novel, the technological obstacles are surmountable, via tachyon drive (tachyons theoretically must always go faster than light), but at enormous cost. The cost may be not only a sizeable chunk out of the budgets of all three power blocs vying to colonize the new world, but also the virtual ruination of the home world, via war. Though begun with good intentions on the part of most of the colonists, the colonization itself becomes a continuation of the war on Earth, while the camps of all three blocs are themselves attacking and under attack from three intelligent species indigenous to the new world. Who ultimately wins is problematical, since astronomical conditions—periodic deadly flares from the sun, "Kung's Semi-Stellar Object"—eventually lead to a civilization with elements

from all six rival cultures.

Each of the six segments has some fascinating aspects to it, but the geometric precision of the conflict and the fit between the pieces is too pat to be convincing. The Fuel Bloc, the Food Bloc, and the People Bloc on Earth (known familiarly as the Greasies, the Fats and the Peeps) are a near-future extrapolation of conditions shaping now. Representatives of all three envision on Jem a chance to start anew, to do everything right, without having to bear the burden of past mistakes, their own or those of others. But the need, if they are to survive, to withstand each other, and to exploit the land and the natives, leads to a repetition with variations: *"plus ca change, plus c'est la meme chose."* Utopian dreams all go up in smoke, literally, from warfare, and the end result is an amalgamation capable of surviving Jem's non-terrestrial conditions—one which is peaceful and stable, but relatively complacent only a few generations later, unsure if it even wants to make/maintain contact with another human outpost in the vicinity of Alpha Centauri.

The exploited natives are not exactly American Indians in disguise, though they may function that way. All three races are distinctly alien to ours, in appearance, behavior and thinking patterns, and Pohl has done a good job of imagining them for us. The potential for interaction patterns may be great in a novel of exploration; but with survival at stake, the pattern here is one of warfare, not only between the natives, who kill and eat each other when possible, but also between man and alien, and of course between man and man. The only variations are temporary, as each human groups tries to make alliances, sometimes with one or another of the natives, sometimes with each other; but all of these fail, until simple conquest ends the fracas, leading to the more complicated arrangement with which the book concludes. Given the cost and the circumstances, it seems inevitable that only the most determined and powerful can command the launching of the expeditions, and the military mind takes over on Jem as well before too long. Peaceful coexistence is never really tried.

A weighty book, *Jem* once again shows the limitations of Pohl (or of SF), for all that it is a *tour de force*. If *Gateway* were not due a sequel, one could make a case for Pohl's last three novels as a trilogy, a critique of three spaceward proposals for escaping, rather than facing, the "World Macroproblem." Strongly argued, variably styled and structured, they make an impressive case for his intellect and his mastery of different approaches to the central subject of SF, embracing or confronting the unknown, the "alien." But each comes up short in some dimensions, even though they rise above most of the competition.

These stories and novels of the 1970s come closer than their predecessors to dealing openly with human emotions, as if Pohl were trying to act on the advice of his mechanical psychiatrist in *Gateway*. By all accounts an intellectual, cerebral person whose public attitude toward his personal and emotional life is somewhat evasive, Frederik Pohl has lived by his wits for 40 years, mostly in a marginal literary field. In his comic infernos, he castigated the very kind of manipulators and manipulees on whom he depended for a living, without showing much more real emotion than indignation. His sketches of the 1960s were even more dispassionate, while his first four novels seemed to avoid real feeling in favor of substitutes off the shelf. But in the 1970s, writing about what seems to matter most, and criticizing as much by example as by direct exposure within his work, he seems to have made an emotional breakthrough, which gives his latest fiction added power as well as dexterity.

There is no question that Pohl has matured as a person, grown as a writer, come close to a representative in SF terms of a tragic vision of life, without renouncing his roots, both in commercial writing, and in the mode of satire. But not all of the literary devices work in *Man Plus*, *Gateway* and *Jem*, nor has he ridded himself completely of what I consider an unfortunate reliance on pulp conventions and cliches. Whether he can tap more of his unconscious, incite more passion, progress beyond the confines of this still and incestuous field I cannot predict, nor can I be sure that he even wants to. SF has been good to Pohl, and he continues to return the favor. If he can get beyond this plateau, however, as he has risen past others, he may realize a mission his writings about SF seem to suggest he envisions for it.[18] Then his work will be not only a criticism of society, and of other SF, but also a serious and constructive criticism of life.

Notes

[1]See Pohl's comments on style in "On Velocity Exercises," in *Those Who Can*, ed. Robin Scott Wilson (New York: 1973), pp. 323-28.

[2]Frederik Pohl, "What Science Fiction Is," *Worlds of IF Science Fiction* combined with *Worlds of Tomorrow* (March 1968), p. 4.

[3]For an almost complete listing of Pohl's SF, see Mark Owings, "Frederik Pohl: Bibliography," *F&SF* (Sept. 1973), pp. 65-69. The stories I discuss here represent a fraction of this known canon, of which I have been able to locate and read all but three pieces. Longer explications of *Man Plus* and *Gateway* appear in the *Survey of Science Fiction Literature*, ed. Frank Magill, 5 vols. (Pasadena, Ca.: 1979), in which an earlier essay of mine on Pohl's short fiction also appears.

[4]"What the Author Has to Say About All This," in *The Best of Frederik Pohl* ed. Lester del Rey (New York: Taplinger, 1977), pp. 302-03.

[5]Pohl's story antedates *The Hidden Persuaders* (New York, 1957) by two years, but neither he nor Packard invented the phenomenon.

[6]Damon Knight, *In Search of Wonder* (Chicago, 1967), p. 194.

[7]Pohl, *Practical Politics 1972* (New York: Ballantine, 1972).

[8]Not listed in Owings' bibliography are *Undersea Fleet* (New York: Gnome Press, 1956), written with Williamson; *A Town is Drowning* (New York: Ballantine, 1955), *Presidential Year*

(New York: Ballantine, 1956), and *Sorority House*—cited as the work of "Jordan Park" in Pohl's introduction to *The Best of C.M. Kornbluth* (New York: Taplinger, 1977), p. 4—these last three titles all written with Kornbluth. See also Edson McCann, "Preferred Risk," in *Galaxy Science Fiction* (June-Sept. 1955). For del Rey's side of the collaboratory experience, see "Frederik Pohl: Frontiersman," *F&SF* (Sept. 1973), pp. 55-64.

[9]Though there is no room for extended discussion of the point here, much of Pohl's fiction can be seen as part of a continuing dialogue in SF, with Pohl responding to suggestions and ideas put forth by other writers in books and stories with which his own are more or less competing. See his "Ragged Claws," in *Hell's Cartographers*, ed. Brian W. Aldiss and Harry Harrison (London, 1976), pp. 152-53.

[10]See Pohl's *The Way The Future Was* (New York: Ballantine, 1978), p. 244.

[11]For Pohl's comments see "On Velocity Exercises" (n. 1).

[12]Pohl, "Sufficient Unto the Day" (editorial), *IF* (May 1969), p. 4.

[13]*Galaxy* (June 1968), pp. 4-11, and *IF* (Nov. 1968), pp. 4-8; Winners were announced in *Galaxy* (Nov. 1968), pp. 4-9; but the promised follow-up report never appeared.

[14]"Ragged Claws," *loc. cit.*, pp. 170-171.

[15]The anthologies are all collaborations: *Jupiter* (New York: Ballantine, 1973) and *Science Fiction: The Great Years*, vols. 1 and 2 (New York: Ace, 1973 and 1976)—with Carol Pohl; *Science Fiction of the Forties* (New York: Avon, 1978)—with Martin Harry Greenberg and Joseph Olander; and *Science Fiction: Contemporary Mythology. The SFRA-SFWA Anthology*—with Greenberg, Olander and Patricia Warrick, for which Pohl and Thomas Clareson provided prefaces and editorial assistance.

[16]"Ragged Claws," p. 159; and *The Way The Future Was*, pp. 176-80. See also Gregory Benford's observations on "Science and Science Fiction," in *Science Fiction: The Academic Awakening*, ed. Willis E. McNelly (New York: 1978), pp. 13-21.

[17]Although the problem is not new, the term "macroproblem" is useful. One location of it is in "Alternative Futures and Educational Policy," Research Memorandum EPRC [Educational Policy Research Center] 6747-6, SRI Project 6747 (Feb. 1970), p. 4. Pohl is, among other things, a card-carrying Futurist, a member of long standing in the World Future Society; and he lectures publicly on aspects of the future as well as on SF. See "Ragged Claws," p. 171.

[18]See *The Way the Future Was*, pp. 252-54.

C.S. Lewis: Mythmaker

Horton Presley

Born in Belfast, Ireland in 1898, Clive Staples Lewis lost his mother nine years later and spent much of his childhood alone with books. He showed an early talent for writing stories about animals, under the influence of Beatrix Potter.[1] He later was educated at several boys' schools, most of which he detested.

After a period of private study in Ireland, Lewis received a scholarship to University College, London in 1916. Shortly thereafter he volunteered for military service and entered the Army as a second lieutenant. After recovering from wounds received in the front lines he reentered Oxford where he received Firsts in both "honor moderations" and "greats," receiving his A.B. in 1923. He continued studying at Oxford, receiving his M.A. some years later. He began teaching philosophy at Oxford on a temporary appointment in 1924, receiving a permanent one the next year in English language and literature. He remained in that position until 1954, when, disappointed by Oxford faculty politics, he accepted the new Chair of Medieval and Renaissance Literature at Cambridge where he remained until his death in 1963, on the same day as the assassination of President Kennedy.

His scholarly output, while not prolific, is of first importance in his field. Among his works is the *Allegory of Love*, probably the best in the field concerning the Courtly Love tradition in literature. His *Preface to Paradise Lost* is a very important contribution to Milton scholarship. He also wrote volume three of *The Oxford History of English Literature—English Literature in the Sixteenth Century, Excluding Drama.*

These are works of responsible scholarship. Yet not everyone is happy with Mr. Lewis:

> C.S. Lewis, the Oxford don, the pious paradox-monger and audacious word-juggler, will surely meet his match one of these days and be subjected to a severe debunking operation.... He is asking for it. Oh, for a Huxley, or a Heine, or an Ingersoll, to expose his tricks and call his bluffs![2]

Why the furor? The scholarly don, not content to keep to his own knitting, dared to write on religious matters and, what is worse, to

127

write for the general public. He used his considerable wit to aim at what were considered sacrosanct targets: scientists, public educators, philosophers, state planners and even religious leaders. He even dared to give popularized lectures on Christianity to the RAF during WWII, repeating much of them on the BBC in a series of broadcasts. He was also producing a variety of religious books, some, like *The Problem of Pain* and *Miracles*, are strictly theological but others are highly imaginative works which brought him wide fame. In 1942 he published *The Screwtape Letters*, purporting to be instructive missives from an elder demon in Hell to his nephew on Earth, Wormwood, concerning the best means of foiling the Enemy. It may still be his most popular single volume. Then came *The Great Divorce* (1945), an allegory postulating that an excursion bus runs from Hell to Heaven; residents of the nether world can visit Heaven and even stay there, though they seldom, if ever, really want to.

Two events, both of which may be termed conversions, led Lewis to this divergence from scholarship as an end in itself. In 1916, quite by accident, Lewis picked up a used copy of George MacDonald's *Phantastes*. He writes, "A few hours later I knew that I had crossed a great frontier."[3] He claims, possibly with some exaggeration, never to have written a book in which he has not quoted from MacDonald.[4] Then in 1929 came another change. In his youth Lewis became quite disillusioned with Christianity to the point of considering himself an atheist. A lengthy process of philosophical investigation led him, unwillingly according to his autobiography (*Surprised by Joy*), to believe in a personal deity in 1929 and then to full belief in a quite literal Christianity in 1931.

There were other influences of course; Lewis was a voracious reader, the antithesis of the stereotyped scholar innocent of anything outside his specialty. He had read Jules Verne and was quite familiar with H.G. Wells. He knew of the popularity of science fiction in America and seems to have read some magazine SF in the thirties. A good friend of long standing was Professor J.R.R. Tolkien, Lewis claiming to have heard every word of *The Lord of the Rings* read to him while that most popular work was being written.[5] A reference in the preface to *That Hideous Strength*,[6] published in 1945, indicates that he knew at least some of the contents of *The Silmarillion* although it was not published until 1977, posthumously edited by Tolkien's son.

Lewis made use of all these sources of inspiration to produce a steady stream of creative SF and Fantasy from about 1938 on. To be considered more in detail in this study are works he himself considered to be primarily mythic. In 1938 he published the first of his space trilogy, *Out of the Silent Planet*, to be followed by *Perelandra* in 1943 and *That Hideous Strength* in 1945. His series of seven children's stories (a categorization he disliked since it implies sub-literary standards) began with *The Lion, the Witch and the Wardrobe* in 1950 and concluded with *The Last Battle* in 1956.

Out of the Silent Planet begins with the kidnapping of a Cambridge philologist named Ransom. Weston, a dedicated scientist who built a space ship, and Devine, the financier of the project, needed someone to take to Mars as a human sacrifice and Ransom blundered into their grasp. After reaching Mars, Ransom escapes, living for a time with the Hrossa, a furry race of poets. Later a bright being called an Eldila instructs the Hrossa to send Ransom to Meldilorn where he is to meet the planet's ruler. Ransom is helped on his way by the Sorns, tall spindly scientists of the planet, and at Meldilorn he meets the Pfifltriggi, frog-like master craftsmen. At the meeting with Oyarsa, the invisible ruler of Mars, Ransom again confronts Weston and Devine who have been forcibly brought. Having never really learned the language of Mars when there before, they had misunderstood Oyarsa's interest in Thulcandra (Earth) and mistakenly got the sacrifice idea. After a kind of judgment scene, the three humans are ordered back to Thulcandra. Upon arriving, Weston and Devine abandon the craft with the unconscious Ransom inside. He wakes and gets out just before the ship is "unbodied" by the mysterious power of the Oyarsa of Mars.

Perelandra begins with Ransom's transportation to Venus at the request of the Oyarsa of Mars though this time in a crystal casket-like box. He finds Venus to be a world largely of water with floating islands all over it. He meets Tinidril, a green woman who soon proves to be completely innocent in a veritable Garden of Eden. Weston appears again in his space ship, though, when Ransom meets him, drastically altered and seemingly possessed by something 'evil. It is soon apparent that Weston is the agent of Something which wants Tinidril to be tempted to transgress the commands of Maleldil not to stay overnight on the Fixed Land. After a series of three-sided debates between Weston, the Woman and Ransom, Tinidril leaves without adopting Weston's suggestions. Soon Ransom has to fight Weston, now completely demonic, in an elemental no-holds-barred battle; he smashes Weston's head with a rock and dumps the body in a fiery chasm. Later Ransom discovers a nasty wound in his heel. After a royal audience with Tinidril and Tor, her husband, Ransom is taken back to Thulcandra in the same crystal casket he came in.

That Hideous Strength centers around the fortunes of Mark and

Jane Studdock. Mark is a young, modern-thinking sociologist newly appointed to the faculty of Bracton College near Edgestow, England. His wife is a bright young girl who fully intends "soon" to complete her doctoral thesis on John Donne. Their marriage is not really working though neither seems to know why. Mark is flattered by the attentions of the important Lord Feverstone (Devine's new title) who encourages him to join forces with the N.I.C.E. (National Institute of Coordinated Experiments) which is going to establish a scientific complex with wide ramifications at a site near Edgestow in Bragdon Wood, presently owned by Bracton College. Mark leaves Jane alone for a few days while he goes to N.I.C.E. headquarters in London to learn more of what his duties might be.

While he is gone Jane has some terrifying dreams, only to discover that she has second sight and is seeing the future. She is contacted by a mysterious group headed by Dr. Ransom who need her abilities as they attempt to counter vicious forces which, it seems, also want her abilities. It turns out that the N.I.C.E. wants Mark only as a means of getting Jane. Jane joins Ransom's group and helps them find Merlin who has risen from his grave in Bragdon Wood. Together they rescue Mark from the N.I.C.E. which is attempting to brainwash him. In a final cataclysmic scene, the disembodied "head," which is the mouthpiece of the evil "macrobes," is destroyed and also the whole N.I.C.E.

While the trilogy was written in order, not so the Narnia series. Lewis first wrote *The Lion, The Witch and the Wardrobe* but as the series progressed he felt the necessity of going back to describe the creation of Narnia. This he does in volume six of the series which should be the first read. The series will be described in the order Lewis felt they should be read.

The Magician's Nephew is set in the late Victorian period in England when two children, Polly and Digory, set about exploring the passages off of an attic. They blunder into Digory's Uncle Andrew's forbidden study where he frightens them into using his magic rings. Being transported into a strange world, they find that the rings will take them to other worlds as well. In one they meet a wicked queen who causes them much difficulty. Finally, in an empty, dark, silent world they look around for a while then hear the beginning of exquisitely beautiful music. Light begins to dawn, then flowers, trees and animals begin to appear from the earth. The song, they determine, comes from a magnificent lion named Aslan. Later, after a brush with a witch who tempts him into taking magic fruit, Digory is given the fruit by Aslan who knows that he wants it so that it can help cure his mother. Aslan than sends them back to London.

In *The Lion, the Witch and the Wardrobe* four children are playing in a house in the country where they had been sent to escape the air raids of WWII. While playing hide-and-seek, Lucy stepped into a wardrobe and found herself in Narnia. Ultimately all the children get there and after many adventures with strange creatures, go to meet Aslan; all but Edmund, that is, who turned traitor and joined the White Witch. The other children and some beavers meet Aslan who has begun to counter the witch's magic (she kept Narnia in winter) and bring back spring. Aslan shows them Cair Paravel, the castle where the children will reign on four thrones with Peter, the oldest, as High King. Edmund has a change of heart and they finally rescue him but not before Aslan has agreed to be sacrificed according to the demands of ancient law, an event which takes place on the old Stone Table. Later the girls come back to the table only to find that Aslan is alive; all then go to the witch's castle and free all the prisoners she has turned to stone.

In *Prince Caspian* the four children are drawn by magic back into Narnia centuries after they had been there before (Narnia time, that is) only to find that a usurper has taken Narnia from Prince Caspian, its rightful ruler. With the aid of the Talking Beasts, dwarfs, fauns and other creatures, they defeat Miraz the Usurper and restore Caspian to the throne.

The *Voyage of the Dawn Treader* draws the children through a picture into the sea and from there on board a ship commanded by Prince Caspian. He is on a voyage to rescue seven lords of his father's kingdom whom Miraz had sent on a dangerous journey hoping to get rid of them. In the search and rescue mission they meet all sorts of creatures (such as the delightful one-footed Dufflepuds) and even touch on the shores of Aslan's eternal Kingdom at The Very End of the World.

The Silver Chair tells how Eustace and Jill escape first from a "modern" English school, Experiment House, into Narnia where they meet Aslan. He sends them on a quest to find a lost prince. They meet a Marshwiggle named Puddleglum who agrees to act as a guide. After many dangers, including almost being eaten by giants, they fall into a hole and find themselves in the Dark World ruled by a wicked queen. There they find the Prince whom the queen binds in a silver chair regularly as a magical means of causing him to forget his real ancestry. They release him from the chair and destroy the chair only to find that he is Prince Rilian, son of King Caspian the Tenth of Narnia. They bring about the ruin of the underworld realm and return Rilian to his throne. When they return to Earth they set some things straight at Experiment House.

The Horse and His Boy differs from the others in that the hero is a resident of Narnia, not a "Child of Adam or Eve" as the Earth children are always called. Shasta is a boy raised among the Calormen who live a long way south of Narnia. He always longs to go North, not knowing that in reality he is a Narnian. He escapes from his foster father by stealing a talking horse which, in turn, had been stolen from Narnia by a Tarkaan nobleman. After many close escapes they meet a young lady from Narnia, Aravis, who is also on a talking horse. Together they race north to warn the Narnians of a surprise invasian by the Calormen. Shasta proves valorous in the ensuing battle and helps defeat the invaders. At the end, the leader of the foe, Rabadash, is offered forgiveness by Aslan but, upon his contemptuous refusal, is turned into a donkey.

The Last Battle centers around the attempt of Shift, a Talking Ape, to get control of Narnia by using a rather simple-minded donkey named Puzzle. He dresses Puzzle in a lion's costume and persuades the residents that Aslan has returned and is now issuing orders to the country through, of course, his loyal servant Shift. Tirian, the last king of Narnia, and some of his followers become disturbed at the strange orders of "Aslan" and try to find him to determine the truth. They are captured and treated cruelly on the orders of Shift. Tirian cries out for the help of King Peter from the Other World who, along with the other children, are brought by magic (so they think) to Narnia again. Soon the real Aslan appears and in a great battle centering around a stable the Calormen whom Shift has brought in are defeated. Then even Old Narnia itself undergoes cataclysmic change in which it becomes a new and eternal one where all is beautiful. The children are overjoyed to meet their friends from many years past. After a while, they become afraid that they will have to leave Narnia again to go back to Earth, only to be gently told by Aslan that this time they had not come by magic. They had "died" as was the term on Earth. Now, "The dream is ended: this is the morning."

Lewis' ideas of the nature and function of literature seem, at first glance, to be unconnected with his own writing. In his *Preface to Paradise Lost*, he speaks of the necessary solemnity of great literature, but more in the Middle English understanding of the word *solempne*:

> This means something different, but not quite different, from modern English *solemn*. Like *solemn* it implies the opposite of what is familiar, free and easy, or ordinary. But unlike *solemn* it does not suggest gloom, oppression, or

austerity. The ball in the first act of *Romeo and Juliet* was a 'solemnity.' The feast at the beginning of *Gawain and the Green Knight* is very much of a solemnity. A great mass by Mozart or Beethoven is as much a solemnity in its hilarious *gloria* as in its poignant *crucifixus est.*[7]

Good literature, then, is something out of the ordinary, is enjoyable and has pomp without being pompous. To Lewis, it has narrative enjoyment that is evident on the first reading, but contains more that comes out in the second and subsequent readings. His liking for children's stories comes from the fact that children, far from being "throw-away" readers, demand that the same story be read to them again and again. He says, "Not till the curiosity, the sheer narrative lust, has been given its sop and laid asleep, are we at leisure to savor the real beauties."[8] In an interview with Kingsley Amis and Brian Aldiss Lewis himself refused to comment on a prominent SF novel on grounds that he had read it only once. He did not trust his own judgment until he had read a work two or three times.[9]

Even so, that "narrative lust," that story line, is very important to Lewis since he feels that any work should be as exciting and interesting as possible on the first reading. The fact that such works are often called "escapist" doesn't bother him at all. Tolkien once made the revealing remark to Lewis that the only people afraid of escape are jailers: people whom Lewis characterizes as those who wish to imprison us in the present with all of its nagging problems.[10] Also, the exciting story is important if a work is to reach a great number of people. Lewis' goal was that of encouraging "a better school of prose story in England: of story that can mediate imaginative life to the masses while not being contemptible to the few."[11]

More than story line is called for, however, and any disciple of Northrop Frye can speak of the various levels of meaning to be found in works that endure. Purtill notes at least three levels evident in *That Hideous Strength*, the account of Mark and Jane Studdock who drift apart both physically and emotionally. The surface level is the romantic question, will they get back together again? At the intermediate level Mark and Jane become "a parable of what happens when two people in a relationship begin to go different ways." Finally, the story documents the soul's journey and the choices it must make between good and evil.[12] Here is one of those references to *Phantastes* that Lewis claims abounds in his work. Tixier claims that "the *real* story in *Phantastes,* the *real* travels and adventures, have no other geography than that of the soul. The action takes place in what Anodos himself calls 'the deeper fairyland of the soul!' "[13] It is also Frye's Anagogic level, one he mentions as quite prominent in medieval literature which, in turn, is a mine to which Lewis very frequently turns for material. In *That Hideous Strength*, medieval Arthurian elements mix with modern romantic themes to provide the reader with all the depth he wishes to search for.

The overt didacticism in works such as *The Screwtape Letters* has led many to feel that Lewis has used his fiction merely as an excuse for more preaching. Even Lewis' close friend Tolkien thought that the Biblical elements in some of Lewis's works were too obvious.[14] It will be a surprise to many to know that Lewis never began his fiction works with some moral or lesson in mind. To Amis and Aldiss he stated categorically that he did not have a didactic purpose in mind when he first had the idea for *Perelandra*, a work so parallel to a Biblical story that it is usually thought of as initially intentional. He says:

> The starting point [of *Prelandra*] was my mental picture of the floating islands. The whole of the rest of my labors in a sense consisted of building up a world in which floating islands could exist. And then of course the story about an averted fall developed.

> *Aldiss*: But I am surprised that you put it this way round. I would have thought that you constructed *Perelandra* for the didactic purpose.

> *Lewis*: Yes, everyone thinks that. They are quite wrong.[15]

Likewise he recounts his intention concerning the writing of the Narnia series:

> Some people seem to think that I began by asking myself how I could say something about Christianity to children; then fixed on the fairy tale as an instrument; then collected information about child-psychology and decided what age group I'd write for; then drew up a list of basic Christian truths and hammered out 'allegories' to embody them. This is all pure moonshine. I couldn't write that way at all. Everything began with images; a faun carrying an umbrella, a queen on a sledge, a magnificent lion. At first there wasn't even anything Christian about them; that element pushed itself in of its own accord.[16]

"Of its own accord" certainly cannot be taken to mean that Lewis is claiming some sort of automatic writing. It is recognition of the fact that any author writes out of his own world view; he does not decide in advance what bias to take any more than a musician consciously determines which muscle to use in guiding a given finger on the piano. It comes from deeply embedded convictions and training. It takes little scholarly digging to determine that Hemingway finds the meaning of life right at the edge of death: hence his love of bullfighting. Pohl and Kornbluth wrote *The Space Merchants* in a manner that could easily be termed overtly didactic concerning the excesses of the advertising industry. Yet this was not their intention according to Fred Pohl. His comment at an SFRA meeting[17] was that he and Kornbluth holed up with a case of scotch and two typewriters and just had a lot of fun writing. To be sure, they had the background in the industry from which to write and (though I don't recall Fred saying it) may have had some reservations about advertising morality. The fact is that the story line came first; the attitude expressed just naturally grew from their experience. Purtill says:

> The key point here is one which goes very deep in Lewis' thinking. It is the idea that any real and unselfish devotion to an ideal outside oneself leads to God and away from evil, whereas any ideal, no matter how apparently noble, leads away from God and goodness if pursued for the wrong reasons or by the wrong means.[18]

This is what "pushes in" to all of Lewis's writing.

Lewis's choice of SF as a vehicle for his writing, particularly the Trilogy, comes from two main sources. First, he had read a great deal of early SF and often speaks of his debt to Wells and others. They excited his imagination though not particularly the science element as such (hence his lack of enthusiasm for Verne). Lewis is not a physical scientist in any sense of the word and is not impressed by extensive, imaginative gadgets. Second, he feels that the world of literature is sorely in need of a new source of unknown geography to populate. Our world is so well known that we no longer can speak of any corner of it and raise instantly exotic, exciting visions. As a result, we need places that the reporter or TV camera can't go. Even the moon is no longer a mysterious place since we have been there; hence his creation of an imaginative Mars and Narnia.

Yet in adopting SF for its expanded horizons Lewis does not accept the demand of some that therefore all science must be impeccably and seriously treated. Others agree. Bernard Wolfe says of SF:

...that science embraces all matters and that therefore any
sf work, which is about nothing but science or the superficialities
of science deftly skimmed off, is by definition about everything.
Sf is the nature of things about things, sometimes disguised as
people. A very different kind of fiction becomes necessary when
you're interested in people not reduced to things....[19]

Lewis makes some rudimentary attempt at giving an aura of
realism to Weston's space ship in *Out of the Silent Planet* (after all,
Weston was a physical scientist) but mentioned much later that he
felt even that sop to science to be unnecessary. He thought that for
his purposes the crystal casket in which Ransom journeys to
Perelandra was a better vehicle.[20] The fact that Weston's ship was
powered by solar radiation in no way indicates that Lewis was
trying to be predictive, as he seems to be: solar radiation is now
recognized as a possible source of space ship fuel. When asked about
this bit of prophecy Lewis claimed that his guess was pure mumbo
jumbo.[21] The same may probably be said for his "pragmatometer," a
kind of computer, in *That Hideous Strength*. It was a device needed
as a story aid: nothing more. He says that "pseudo-scientific
apparatus is to be taken simply as a 'machine' in the sense which
that word bore for the Neo-Classical Critics. The most superficial
appearance of plausibility—the merest sop to our critical intellect—
will do."[22]

To Lewis the essence of SF lies in three main approaches: first,
the play of pure intellect in works such as *Flatland*. They have no
ulterior motives other than those which give rise to wit or conceits.
Second, the creation of impossibilities as means to farce. When just
anything can happen, comic possibilities abound as in *Baron
Munchausen*. Again, no further intent beyond the comic. The last,
and one he tries to write, is the creation of the Marvellous as a means
of adding a new dimension to life. In this category he includes such
diverse works as *The Odyssey, The Faerie Queene,* MacDonald's
Phantastes, and some of Ray Bradbury's stories.[23] If not obvious
before this, Lewis is in the camp of those who prefer the term
"speculative fiction" to Science Fiction though I don't recall his
saying it in exactly those words.

Lewis's constant intent is that of creating such a different world
that we are easily able to adopt the customary "willing suspension
of disbelief" and step eagerly into a world governed by laws quite
different from our own. This, in itself, raises no eyebrows: Lewis
Carroll does it in *Alice* with classic grace. Lewis adds a twist—
uncomfortable to some—when he implies that he just may not be
talking about a fairy tale after all: what if that other world is the

only real one, and ours is just an illusion? In *The Dawn Treader* Caspian is astonished to find that the children come from a round world. He had thought that such places were just in fairy tales.[24] This concept could, of course, be just a somewhat trite reversal of ideas for a quick effect except for the increasingly obvious fact that throughout the *Narnia Chronicles* Narnia is symbolic of a *real* world, one which ultimately will prove to be the only eternal one. Lewis indicates as much when he makes a distinction between a myth about a dying and resurrected god such as Bacchus and the one about Christ. The former, while interesting, is just an imaginative creation while the myth of Christ is true.[25] It is this kind of polemic that breaks through much of his work and raises difficulties with some readers.

The question involves more than the simple agreement or disagreement with Lewis's theology. There is a tendency among some to consider SF off limits for religious ideas other than those used strictly as foils for other concepts—Dickson's Friendlies, who aren't, from the planet Harmony, which isn't, for instance. Lem completely rules out any serious reference to supernatural beings: "...for it is the premise of SF that anything shown shall in principle be interpretable empirically and rationally. In SF there can be no devils or demons—and the pattern of occurrences must be verisimilar."[26] If Lem is right and the supernatural is taboo in SF, then of course Lewis doesn't belong. Yet if the broader "speculative fiction" concept is valid and works such as *The Faerie Queene* and *Paradise Lost* qualify, then no work with an overt theological bias can be ruled out.

Lewis states a critical principle he himself follows: he refuses to evaluate works he himself can't stand. Since he dislikes detective stories he feels himself to be totally incapable of valid analysis of their literary qualities. A reviewer some time ago castigated the deCamp biography of Lovecraft on the same grounds: deCamp does not seem to like Lovecraft's work. Didacticism per se, or theology, of whatever stripe, is not a valid element for consideration in the acceptance or rejection of any work of art: so with Lewis's work.

More to the point is his ability to create a new mythology, an objective he clearly attempts to achieve. *Till We Have Faces* is subtitled *A Myth Retold.* To him, myth has been the vehicle of man's expression of his humanity for untold ages. He says, "...Myth in general is not merely misunderstood history...nor diabolical illusion...nor priestly lying...but at its best, a real though unfocussed gleam of divine truth falling on human imagination."[27] Miss Eleanor Hull says of the folklore of Britain:

> It is no museum of dead things: it is the source and was once the motive power of large departments of life, a history of the progress of knowledge in the world. It is no mere frivolous amusement, as many people think. It is part of that fable, full of deep meanings, which lies behind the universe.[28]

Northrop Frye says, "Myth is the imitation of actions near or at the conceivable limits of desire."[29] He distinguishes myth from realism: "...as realism is an art of implicit simile, myth is an art of implicit metaphoric identity."[30] If man were only a creature of physical nature, Lewis would not need larger comparisons: realism would suffice. But if reality is in fact greater than our senses, myth is the only vehicle by which its existence can be understood. Only when humanity has transcended time can those truths be seen directly: "Those who attain the glorious resurrection will see the dry bones clothed again with flesh, the fact and the myth remarried, the literal and the metaphorical rushing together."[31]

A literature which can convey such transcendental meanings has several characteristics according to Lewis, summarized by Oury:

> 1. It has a "value in itself" apart from any particular account of it; 2. It introduces us "to a permanent object of contemplation— more like a thing than a narration—which works upon us by its peculiar flavor or quality, rather as a smell or a chord does;" 3. It has a "simple narrative shape" a pattern of...movements [with] a profound relevance to our own life;" 4. It is "fantastic, grave, and awe-inspiring."[32]

Lewis' mythology, then, presents a highly imaginative, pleasurable experience that reaches truth by indirect means.

Lewis' choice of such a medium was quite natural, given his own background. Already mentioned is his wide acquaintance with medieval and classical literature, works which abound in mythic allusions and mythic styles. His first writing as a child abounded with stories of mythic worlds of talking animals. His writing or speaking on almost any subject is likely to be replete with analogies; for instance, he begins his theological treatise *Mere Christianity* with an analogy comparing Christianity as a whole to a medieval great hall and the individual denominations to small rooms leading off of the hall.[33] Almost all accounts of his conversation include a similar example of his mode of thinking. Mythology, being the most vivid and imaginative of writing styles, was natural for him to use. Walsh says, "Lewis, in his more imaginative books, does not profess to describe the specific realities of the Universe: he is merely creating a myth of the *sort* of things that might plausibly exist."[34] One may find a similarity between Lewis' use of Mars and that of Bradbury. Neither had any intention of presenting a picture of what might be found on the actual planet one day. Each was presenting on Mars what we might find in reality in ourselves.

Mythology, to Lewis, was a source of truth, and not only the mythic creations of Christian civilizations. He often indicates that stories of the ancient world may have had factual basis. In a short story he wrote he has reference to the factual verification that the Cretan labyrinth did indeed exist.[35] In *Perelandra*, Ransom muses to himself: "He remembered his old suspicion that what was myth in one world might always be fact in some other." Later he thinks, "Or were the old myths truer than the modern myths? Had there in truth been a time when satyrs danced in the Italian woods?"[36] The form of any representation could not, of course, be representational. On Malacandra Ransom found himself, Weston and Devine portrayed in stone by a *pfifltrigg*. When he saw the work Ransom was rather startled. "I expect it is like me as I look to your people." "No," said the pfiffltrigg. "I do not mean it to be too like. Too like and they will not believe it—those who are born after . . . it dawned upon Ransom that the odious figures were intended as an *idealization* of humanity."[37]

Religious concepts outside of Judeo-Christian thought also can have validity to Lewis. In *The Last Battle* a noble opponent of Aslan, Emeth of Tarkaan, is cordially received into eternal Narnia even though he came to old Narnia to destroy it, mistakenly serving the false god Tash. Aslan receives Emeth not because Tash and Aslan are one (as a false prophet had attempted to promote) but because all who truly seek to serve truth serve the True God whether they know him specifically or not![38]

Lewis finds mythic commonality in another well known literary theme—the quest. He sees in quests from Homer to the Arthurian Grail stories the expression of a deep-seated longing in the soul, one that the soul itself may not want. In fact, readers often treat adventure stories from Homer to modern times as nothing more than itchy feet for "faraway places" when they really express a deep longing for something their heroes feel compelled, unwillingly, to seek. Oedipus must live out his exile and finally find peace alone on the mountain. Because of love for his wife, Odysseus endures monumental trials; Aeneas has a divine mission to fulfill, and so on. Tolkien takes up the same thread when Frodo must carry the Ring of Power to his destruction; Lewis' Ransom must travel throughout the solar system at the behest of Maleldil. Tolkien's Sam Gamgee quietly notes that heroes seldom *really* want the role they are forced into:

> The brave things in the old tales and songs, Mr. Frodo: adventures, as I used to call them. I used to think that they were things the wonderful folk of the stories went out and looked for, because they wanted them... but that's not the way of it with the tales that really mattered .... Folk seem to have been just landed in them, usually—their paths were laid that way, as you put it.[39]

Lewis is not the first, of course, to use the quest theme as a mythic recreation of Christian truth: *Everyman* and *Pilgrim's Progress* are but two which come to mind. Another which significantly influenced Lewis was *Paradise Lost* to which Lewis wrote the preface referred to earlier. Margaret Hannay feels that an understanding of Lewis' criticism of Milton is essential to an understanding of his own treatment of the Edenic myth in *Perelandra*:

> It becomes clear that Lewis rejected those aspects of Milton's Edenic myth which he found distasteful—the magnificent Satan, the anthropomorphic deity, the undignified corporeality of the angels, the mistaken attempt to describe prelapsarian sexuality. Lewis praises the magnificence of Adam and Eve, striving to emulate Milton's achievement.[40]

Myth and meaning, form and reality, merge in Lewis' style. Truth in essence, far transcendent over mere fact, may better be conveyed by metaphor than by specifics. Lewis may not start with an idea of some truth to convey but it is directly connected to the shape his work takes. He says,

> In the Author's mind there bubbles up every now and then the material for a story. For me it invariably begins with mental pictures. This ferment leads to nothing unless it is accompanied with the longing for a Form: verse or prose, short story, novel, play or what not. When these two things click you have the Author's impulse complete. It is now a thing inside him pawing to get out.[41]

In the process of working out that form Lewis, no more or less than other authors, expresses his concept in terms of existence as he sees it. Shumaker says of the trilogy,

> The chief vehicle of meaning ... is sensory impressions which carry a metaphoric burden and add up, as a series, to myth. The qualities of mind that enabled Lewis to write dream allegories and allegorical fairy tales permitted him to show more meanings than he explained even in his quasi-realistic fiction....[42]

Religious truth is not the only subject matter treated in Lewis' work. In fact, he might have had fewer opponents had he confined himself to matters of faith. He also had comments to make regarding science and scientists, education and teachers. As with religion, he is not at all reluctant to take sides.

Anathema to Lewis are all who feel that education should not present truth objectively. In 1947 he wrote a little monograph called *The Abolition of Man* attacking the "self expression" then becoming popular in English schools. Two young schoolmasters had written an elementary text in which they denied objective reality to, say, a beautiful waterfall. According to them, if someone should call it 'sublime,' he is saying nothing about the object: just making a remark about his own feelings.[43] In his attack on such a philosophy Lewis establishes very clearly his own belief in the existence of a platonic reality 'beyond existence,' a reality he finds best explained by the Chinese Tao:

> It is the reality beyond all predicates, the abyss that was before the Creator Himself. It is Nature, it is the Way, the Road. It is the Way in which the universe goes on, the Way in which things everlastingly emerge, stilly and tranquilly, into space and time. It is also the Way which every man should treat in imitation of that cosmic and supercosmic progression, conforming all activities to that great examplar.[44]

To those holding such a philosophy, values are not relative and cannot be adequately taught if children are allowed to find things out for themselves. If allowed to drift, children—and adults—develop concepts, to be sure, but not those of any depth. *The Silver Chair* opens on a depressing scene of bullying which was taking place at "Experiment House," just such a misguided school.

> It was 'Co-educational,' a school for both boys and girls, what used to be called a 'mixed' school; some said it was not nearly so mixed as the minds of the people who ran it. These people had the idea that boys and girls should be allowed to do what they liked and unfortunately what ten or fifteen of the biggest boys and girls liked best was bullying the others.[45]

Later Eustace swears he is not fooling Jill about Narnia, but swears very cautiously: "I swear by—by everything. (When I was at school one would have said 'I swear by the Bible.' But Bibles were not encouraged at Experiment House.)"[46] It may be coincidence, but the superintendent of Experiment House is called "The Head," the same literal name given to the demonic, disembodied head which was the mouthpiece of the fallen "macrobes" who controlled the N.I.C.E. in *That Hideous Strength.*

Ineffectual education is not limited to children's education. Mark Studdock, around whom much of *That Hideous Strength* revolves, is an easy dupe of the N.I.C.E. precisely because his own education had provided him with no convictions.

> It must be remembered that in Mark's mind hardly one rag of noble thought, either Christian or Pagan, had a secure lodging. His education had been neither scientific nor classical—merely 'Modern.' The severities both of abstraction and of high human tradition had passed him by: and he had neither peasant shrewdness nor aristocratic honor to help him. He was a man of straw, a glib examinee in subjects that required no exact knowledge....[47]

Bracton College had come into the control of "progressive" elements who thought they were going to bring the school up to date. In fact, their very fuzziness about educational goals makes Curry and Busby (administrators at Bracton) easy to manipulate. Such education was so common in England that educated people had become easy marks; the repulsive Miss Hardcastle, chief of the secret police for the N.I.C.E. stated: "It's the educated reader who *can* be gulled ... the educated public, the people who read the highbrow weeklies, don't need reconditioning .... They'll believe anything."[48]

Even religious education comes in for Lewis' scorn. In *The Great Divorce* Lewis has George MacDonald, in Heaven, speaking of theologians who are so interested in theology that they ignore God. It is the process of thinking that is important, not the product.[49]

Lewis believes that truth exists. When education of whatever stripe becomes a game, when methodology triumphs over subject matter, when students are encouraged more to learn *about* someone rather than learn *from* him, truth gets lost in the shuffle.[50]

In all this the real crux of the issue is that such education produces people with no convictions: manipulators seeking power rather than substantive ideas that can make anyone better. Wither, the dupe of the N.I.C.E. who thought he was really in charge, had "passed from Hegel to Hume to Pragmatism through Logical Positivism and out at last into the complete void."[51] When truth was ignored in religion, it resulted in a Theocracy, to Lewis the most subject to abuse of any source of Power.[52]

Yet those with convictions were admired by Lewis whether they agree with him or not. MacPhee, the companion of Ransom at Logres in *That Hideous Strength*, doesn't believe all the nonsense that's going on around him, never throughout the novel ever believing that Maleldil really exists. Lewis avoids any shoddy "repentance" scene at the end when MacPhee takes his leave of Ransom, still unconvinced. MacPhee is to the end a person of integrity and for that is accorded Ransom's blessing.

Lewis' views of education do not stir much opposition, probably because almost all forms of education today are suspect. His attitude toward science, however, is another matter. Having been an admirer of Lewis for many years, I have been interested in the gradual change in critical appreciation (or lack of it) of him. I had some difficulty getting an advisor willing to let me do my M.A. thesis about his trilogy in 1951 because the works were not really good literature to some or poor science to others. It is only in recent years when definitions have largely been abandoned that Lewis has been admitted as a Science Fiction writer. Professor Haldane stated common objections to Lewis' science and Lewis summarizes them in his reply: "1) That my science is usually wrong; 2) that I traduce scientists; 3) that on my view, scientific planning 'can only lead to Hell'."[53]

The main thrust of Lewis' answer is that he does not attack science at all. (He is, in fact, an outstanding scientist in his own right—a philologist as was Ransom.) Since the watershed year of 1938 for sf and the advent of Social Science Fiction certain scholars other than those in the physical sciences can be termed scientists and can be allowed to use the scientific method. The search for truth by scientific means is nowhere traduced by Lewis. He strongly opposes *Scientism*, that perverted use of science which makes science an end in itself. One has but to review the absurdities of the scientific community's uproar over Velikovsky's theories to see scientism at its worst. Nor does one need to uphold Velikovsky to deplore the attitudes and actions of those dedicated scientists who would demolish anyone whose views differ from their own. In *That Hideous Strength* Lewis describes William Hingest as a physical chemist from Bracton College who is well known outside of England for his excellence as a scientist. He saw through the scheme of the N.I.C.E. and advised Mark to get out as he was: or thought he was.

He met with an "accident" on his way back to Edgestow. The N.I.C.E. was not about to let any scientist hold independent views.

Nor is Lewis attacking scientific planning as such. Most modern countries are engaged in scientific planning, to a considerable degree, and those plans are needed for the good of society. As Lewis clearly presents in *Screwtape,* demonic forces choose the avenue of attack which is most likely to be accepted because it is the least suspect. In modern times science is often so uncritically accepted that it can become a very useful tool for deception. Lewis says:

> Under modern conditions any effective invitation to Hell will certainly appear under the guise of scientific planning—as Hitler's regime in fact did. Every tyrant must begin by claiming to have what his victims respect and to give what they want![54]

Even superficial analysis of the leadership of the N.I.C.E. quickly shows that real scientists had nothing to do with its direction. Lewis himself points out that if he attacks anyone in the caricatures he draws it is officialdom, not scientists. If a specific discipline is attacked, it is philosophy: his own first teaching field.[55]

The philosophy promoted by false science is precisely the opposite of a humane approach to life. Beauty does not exist and man as an individual does not exist. Early in his career as a skeptical young college student Lewis had met a man who became his model for Weston and the apostate Mr. Straik. Lewis describes him as

> ...an old, dirty, gabbling, tragic, Irish parson who had long since lost his faith but retained his living. By the time I met him his only interest was the search for evidence of "human survival." On this he read and talked incessantly, and, having a highly critical mind, could never satisfy himself. What was especially shocking was that the ravenous desire for personal immortality co-existed in him with (apparently) a total indifference to all that could, on a sane view, make immortality desirable .... All he wanted was the assurance that something he could call "himself" would, on almost any terms, last longer than his bodily life.[56]

Weston, Ransom's antagonist in the first two books of the trilogy, seems to be a grand humanitarian until we find out what he is really after: and it has nothing to do with any individual. He says:

> ...small claims must give way to great. As far as we know,

> we are doing what has never been done in the history of man, perhaps never in the history of the universe.... You cannot be so small minded as to think that the rights or the life of an individual or of a million individuals are of the slightest importance in comparison with this.[57]

Ransom disagrees and Weston retorts, "It would be easier if your philosophy of life were not so insufferably narrow and individualistic."[58] Ransom puts his finger on Weston's real goal when he charges that Weston thinks he is "justified in doing anything—absolutely anything—here and now, on the off chance that some creatures or other descended from man as we know him may crawl about a few centuries longer in some part of the universe."[59] Weston, in rare agreement with Ransom, answers, "Yes—anything whatever."

In *Perelandra* the theme returns. When Weston lands, Ransom helps him unload the space ship and soon is handed this rhetoric:

> To do myself justice, I should make it clear that the false humanist ideal of knowledge as an end in itself never appealed to me. I always wanted to know in order to achieve utility.

Weston rambles on, finally intoning:

> The majestic spectacle of this blind, inarticulate purposiveness thrusting its way upward and ever upward in an endless unity of differentiated achievements toward an ever-increasing complexity of organisation, towards spontaneity and spirituality, swept away all my old conception of a duty to Man as such. Man in himself is nothing. The forward movement of Life—the growing spirituality—is everything.[60]

This idea clearly is not Weston's, though he may have thought so early in his career. In a pitiful scene near the end of *Perelandra* Weston himself, terrified, appeals to Ransom for help against the diabolical force that has captured his mind, but it is too late. The identical concept surfaces quickly in *That Hideous Strength* as the goals of the N.I.C.E. begin to emerge. Devine, now Lord Feverstone, is propagandizing sociologist Mark Studdock concerning the objectives of the organization. "Humanity is at the cross-roads .... If Science is really given a free hand it can now take over the human race and re-condition it: make man a really efficient animal." His persuasion works well, for Mark obediently answers, "Hang it all,— the preservation of the human race—it's a pretty rock-bottom obligation."[61] The program involves a broad range of activities:

> ...sterilization of the unfit, liquidation of backward races,
> .. selective breeding. Then real education [which] makes the
> patient what it wants infallibly: whatever he or his parents try
> to do about it. Of course, it'll have to be mainly psychological at
> first. But we'll get on to biochemical conditioning in the end and
> direct manipulation of the brain.[62]

Mark is appropriately impressed.

Nor does the N.I.C.E. stop with "reeducating" man. It also will revamp nature. Filostrato finds any type of natural growth repugnant. He prefers to wipe the planet clean of all vegetation, substituting scientific chemical processes for the functions nature currently provides. He would wipe out birds since their singing cannot be controlled, substituting "art" birds which can be switched off. This would also be more hygienic.[63]

Lewis's attack here is not against science but science turned back on itself to the point of abolishing even rationality:

> The physical sciences, good and innocent in themselves,
> had already, even in Ransom's own time, begun to be warped,
> had been subtly manoeuvred in a certain direction. Despair of
> objective truth had been increasingly insinuated into the
> scientists; indifference to it, and a concentration upon mere
> power, had been the result.

A bit later, "They believed no longer in a rational universe."[64]

Lewis' view, admittedly an extreme one, is no more of an attack on science than that seen in *Brave New World*. Indeed, he manages to avoid the cynical conclusion Huxley reaches, one that he later had to counter by writing *Brave New World Revisited*. The N.I.C.E. doesn't quite succeed. They lose Mark. While he is undergoing some further "education" by Frost, his mind turns back to "Jane and fried eggs and soap and sunlight and the rooks cawing at Cure Hardy and the thought that, somewhere outside, daylight was going on at that moment .... He was choosing a side: the Normal."[65]

In contrast to the N.I.C.E., Ransom works for forces which intend to restore Nature as it once was. Originally all the universe was of the same creation and shared communication. When Thulcandra (the Oyarsa of Earth) rebelled against Maleldil, he was confined to Earth,[66] he and his followers forbidden to go outside the orbit of the moon; angelic beings who remained faithful to Maleldil were not to go inside it. When Weston went to Mars he broke that barrier and allowed the entry to the sphere of Earth of other heavenly beings.[67] When that happens criteria of a renewed Nature appear. When Lewis himself goes to Ransom's house at the beginning of *Perelandra* he notices something peculiar about the eldil he meets—probably the Oyarsa of Mars. The faint, flame-like light seems to be vertical, but not a verticality in reference to Earth. Yet, rather than think that the Oyarsa was "tilted," Lewis got the uncomfortable feeling that it is our Earth that was tilted away from some celestial standard.[68] Jane Studdock had the same experience when she visited Ransom at St. Anne's. The entire room seemed to be tilted.

In a world governed by its creator, there is no war between any of the created. In the Narnia series animals of whatever variety have peace with one another and cooperate for the good of all unless some evil force gets temporary control of them. Such a concept could, of course, be just another typical animal story cliche, quite common in children's stories except that Lewis feels that such behavior is the way things really should be. When Jane first meets Ransom she sees a delightful scene where mice, in obedience to Ransom, come scurrying out to clean crumbs from the floor.[69] In *The Lion, the Witch and the Wardrobe* it is mice that cut the cords holding Aslan's body to the sacrificial table.[70] At the end of *That Hideous Strength*, when the macrobes are defeated, all of nature begins to frolic in a manner that scandalizes the skeptical MacPhee who claims that it is indecent. Ransom disagrees:

> Man is no longer isolated. We are now as we ought to be— between the angels who are our elder brothers and the beasts who are our jesters, servants and playfellows.[71]

The ultimate goal of nature, then, is a very real happiness for all of nature, an inner peace felt equally by the followers of Aslan and Maleldil. The symbolism Lewis uses strikingly shows this as he contrasts what is going on at St. Anne's with the N.I.C.E. or between Aslan's Narnia and Narnia when captured by the White Witch.

The Biblical base of these concepts has been mentioned. Even the imagery often is Biblical. Lewis' creation myth follows the account from Job chapter thirty-eight where creation was accompanied by the song of the morning stars as the sons of God shouted for joy. In *The Magician's Nephew* the creation also began with singing:

> It was very far away and Digory found it hard to decide from what direction it was coming .... It was so beautiful he could hardly bear it .... The voice was suddenly joined by other voices; more voices than you could possibly count .... One

moment there had been nothing but darkness; next moment a thousand, thousand points of light leaped out—single stars, constellations, and planets, brighter and bigger than any in our world.[72]

Lewis is also following his friend Tolkien here since in the *Silmarillion*, recently published but the concepts in it well known to Lewis since at least 1945, creation came from the singing of the Ainur.[73]

The Garden of Eden image in *Perelandra* has been discussed, but it appears elsewhere; for instance, in *The Magician's Nephew* Digory enters a beautiful garden only to be met by a witch who urges him to eat forbidden fruit. It is evident that she has climbed over the wall instead of entering by the gate as instructions on the gate directed. Here again, Lewis' debt is multiple. Parallels with *Pilgrim's Progress* and *Paradise Lost* are not accidental.[74]

Much of the animal imagery is biblical. Aslan as a lion comes from the representation of Christ as the Lion of the Tribe of Judah as recorded in Revelation 5:5. Then in *The Dawn Treader* the voyagers land on the shore of the Silver Sea and find a Lamb that invites them to have breakfast of fish, a combining of Christ as the Lamb of God with the story of the resurrected Christ preparing breakfast for his disciples in John 9:9-12.

Lewis' debt to Tolkien has been mentioned in several places so just a few more will suffice here. Lewis has Merlin become a remnant of old Numinor.[75] He also refers to a poem about Heaven and Hell eating into Merry Middle Earth which is, of course, the location of Tolkien's amazingly detailed world.[76]

The joys of source-hunting can be carried on at great length in Lewis' works. Lewis made use of many birth and rebirth myths from classical literature; he was saturated with medieval literature, both English and continental, and Arthurian materials in particular abound. He was well acquainted with philosophy and theology, both ancient and modern. His reading was far ranging and, as was the case with Milton, Lewis may not have always been aware of his allusions, some of it surfacing in the natural course of his creative composition.

The concept of an impersonal, mechanistic universe is quite common in SF, being seen in Simak,[77] in many of H.G. Wells' works, and others. Attitudes engendered from such views range from heroic facing the blackness to the nihilism of Harlan Ellison. Lewis, to the contrary, feels that something beatific is "out there," a something to be sought rather than feared:

We mortals, seen as the sciences see us and as we commonly see one another, are mere "appearances." But appearances of the Absolute. In so far as we really are at all (which isn't saying much) we have, so to speak, a root in the Absolute, which is the utter reality. And that is why we experience Joy: we yearn, rightly, for that unity which we can never reach except by ceasing to be the separate phenomenal beings called "we." Joy was not a deception. Its visitations were rather the moments of clearest consciousness we had, when we became aware of our fragmentary and phantasmal nature and ached for that impossible reunion which would annihilate us or that self-contradictory waking which would reveal, not that we had had, but that we *were* a dream.[78]

He recounts an experience with his wife just before she died:

Once very near the end I said, "if you can—if it is allowed— come to me when I too am on my death bed." "Allowed!" she said. "Heaven would have a job to hold me; and as for Hell, I'd break it into bits." She knew she was speaking a kind of mythological language with even an element of comedy in it. There was a twinkle as well as a tear in her eye. But there was no myth and no joke about the will, deeper than any feeling, that flashed through her.[79]

Lewis has, all his life, written myth with a twinkle as well as a tear in his eye because, like Robert Frost, he too "had a lover's quarrel with the world."

Notes

[1]Chad Walsh, *C.S. Lewis, Apostle to the Skeptics* (New York: Macmillan, 1949), p. 2.

[2]Victor Yarros, in an issue of *The American Freeman* quoted by Chad Walsh, p. ix.

[3]Roger Lancelyn Green and Walter Hooper, *C.S. Lewis A Biography* (New York: Harcourt Brace Jovanovich, 1974), p. 44.

[4]Ibid.

[5]Referred to by W.H. Lewis, *Letters of C.S. Lewis* (New York: Harcourt Brace and World, 1966), p. 14.

[6]Lewis, *That Hideous Strength* (New York: Collier, 1962), p. 7.

[7]Lewis, *A Preface to Paradise Lost* (New York: Oxford University Press, 1961), p. 17.

[8]Lewis, *Of Other Worlds, Essays and Stories*, Walter Hooper, ed. (New York: Harcourt Brace Jovanovich, 1966), p. 18.

[9]Ibid., p. 89.   [10]Ibid., p. 67.   [11]Ibid., p. 18.

[12]Richard Purtill, "That Hideous Strength: A Double Story," in *The Longing for a Form*, ed. Peter J. Schakel (Kent, Ohio: Kent State Univ. Press, 1977), p. 98.

[13]Elaine Tixier, "Imagination Baptized, or 'Holiness' in the Chronicles of Narnia," in *The Longing for a Form*, p. 139.

[14]Walter Hooper, "Narnia: The Author, The Critics and the Tale," in *The Longing for a Form*, p. 110.

[15]Lewis, *Of Other Worlds*, p. 87.

[16]Ibid., p. 36.

[17]Science Fiction Research Association, Evanston, Ill., June, 1977.

[18]Purtill, p. 96.

[19]Bernard Wolfe quoted in "Perception and Value in Science Fiction," *Extrapolation, 16 (May, 1975)*, 103.

[20]Lewis, *Of Other Worlds*, pp. 68-9.

[21]Ibid., p. 87.   [22]Ibid., p. 68.   [23]Ibid., p. 69ff.

[24]Lewis, *The Voyage of the Dawn Treader* (New York: Macmillan, Collier, 1970), p. 201.

[25]Lewis, quoted by Tixier, pp. 142-3.

[26]Stanislaw Lem, "On the Structural Analysis of Science Fiction," *Science-Fiction Studies*, 1 (Spring, 1973), 28.

[27]Lewis, *Miracles* (New York: Macmillan, 1947), p. 161n.

[28]Eleanor Hull, *Folklore of the British Isles* (London: Methuen, 1928), p. 2.

[29]Northrup Frye, *Anatomy of Criticism* (Princeton: Princeton Univ. Press, 1957), p. 136.

[30]Ibid.

[31]Lewis, *Miracles*, p. 192.

[32]Scott Oury, " 'The Thing Itself': C.S. Lewis and the Value of Something Other" in *Longing for a Form*, p. 11.

[33]Lewis, *Mere Christianity* (New York: Macmillan, 1952), p. xi.

[34]Walsh, p. 99.

[35]Lewis, *Of Other Worlds*, p. 122.

[36]Lewis, *Perelandra* (New York: Macmillan, Collier, 1962), p. 102.

[37]Lewis, *Out of the Silent Planet* (New York: Macmillan, Collier, 1962), p. 114.

[38]Lewis, *The Last Battle* (New York: Macmillan, Collier, 1979), p. 162ff.

[39]J.R.R. Tolkien, *The Two Towers* (New York: Ballantine, 1965), p. 407.

[40]Margaret P. Hannay, "A Preface to Perelandra," *The Longing for a Form*, p. 90.

[41]Lewis, *Of Other Worlds*, p. 35.

[42]Wayne Shumaker, "The Cosmic Trilogy of C.S. Lewis," in *The Longing for a Form*, p. 59.

[43]Lewis, *The Abolition of Man* (New York: Macmillan, 1947), p. 2.

[44]Ibid., p. 11. Paraphrasing *The Encyclopedia of Religion and Ethics*, vol. 10.

[45]Lewis, *The Silver Chair* (New York: Macmillan, Collier, 1970), p. 1.

[46]Ibid., p. 5.

[47]Lewis, *That Hideous Strength*, p. 185.

[48]Ibid., p. 100.

[49]Lewis, *The Great Divorce* (New York: Macmillan, 1952), p. 68.

[50]Louis I. Bredvold, "The Achievement of C.S. Lewis," reprint from *The Intercollegiate Review*, 4 (Jan.-March, 1968), n.p.

[51]Lewis, *That Hideous Strength*, p. 353.

[52]Lewis, *Of Other Worlds*, p. 81.

[53]Ibid., p. 75.   [54]Ibid., p. 80.   [55]Ibid., p. 78.

[56]Lewis, *Surprised by Joy* (London: Fontana Books, 1959), p. 162.

[57]Lewis, *Out of the Silent Planet*, p. 27.

[58]Ibid.   [59]Ibid.

[60]Lewis, *Perelandra*, pp. 89-91.

[61]Lewis, *That Hideous Strength*, pp. 40-41.

[62]Ibid., p. 42.   [63]Ibid., p. 172.   [64]Ibid., p. 203.   [65]Ibid., p. 299.

[66]This idea discussed by Lewis in his *Medieval and Renaissance Literature*, the idea coming from a 14th century French poem. p. 42.

[67]Lewis, *That Hideous Strength*, p. 294.

[68]Lewis, *Perelandra*, p. 18.

[69]Lewis, *That Hideous Strength*, p. 149.

[70]Lewis, *The Lion, The Witch and the Wardrobe* (New York: Macmillan, Collier, 1970), p. 156.

[71]Lewis, *That Hideous Strength*, p. 378.

[72]Lewis, *The Magician's Nephew* (New York: Macmillan, Collier, 1970), p. 98ff.

[73]J.R.R. Tolkien, *The Silmarillion* (Boston: Houghton Mifflin, 1977), p. 15ff.

[74]Lewis, *The Magician's Nephew*, p. 157ff.

[75]Lewis, *That Hideous Strength*, p. 265.

[76]Ibid., pp. 283-4.

[77]Thomas D. Clareson, "Clifford D. Simak: The Inhabited Universe," in *Voices of the Future*, Vol. 1 (Bowling Green, Ohio: Bowling Green Popular Press, 1976), 86.

[78]Lewis, *Surprised by Joy*, p. 177.

[79]N.W. Clerk (pseud. for C.S. Lewis), *A Grief Observed* (Greenwich, Ct.: The Seabury Press, 1963), p. 59.

Art and the Artist's Role in Delany's Works

Jane Weedman

Samuel R. Delany is something of an anomaly. He is a writers' writer who has earned back-to-back Nebulas, *Babel-17* (1966) and *The Einstein Intersection* (1967). Among enthusiasts—fans—there has never been a Delany "cult," and although he himself is an outstanding critic, his own works have provoked extremes of critical comment from his colleagues, both academic and popular. Finally, not until the success of *Dhalgren* (1975), now in its twelfth printing, did he achieve mass readership.

One notices at once that a number of common threads run through his novels, from *The Jewels of Aptor* (1962), written when the author was nineteen, through the massive *Dhalgren*. The same devices slide from novel to novel: the destruction of the Earth's civilization in a Great Fire; the presence of ruined cities, Telphar, Bellona, the City of New Hope. Images recur: green liquor in *The Jewels of Aptor, The Fall of the Towers* trilogy (1963-1965) and *Babel-17*; brass in *Nova* (1968), *Babel-17* and the short story "The Cage of Brass" (1968). Transported almost intact from *Babel-17* to *Nova* is a spaceport bar scene in which pilots wrestle to demonstrate their skills. In a sense each novel seems to add to what has been published previously so that one delights in finding and tracing his references to materials in and associated with other works. For example, at the beginning of *Babel-17* Delany quotes from a poem by Marilyn Hacker entitled *Prism and Lens*; the two major components of the Scorpions' optical chains in *Dhalgren* are prisms and lenses. This game could go on indefinitely—and significantly.

In Delany's early works are found the kernels of the subject which, as he matures, becomes central to his themes and to his style: the role of the artist in society and the process of that art. Art is not confined to literature in his works; he includes music, theater and painting as well as poetry and prose. Delany, by using these art forms, is able to discuss both the process of art and the qualities and purposes of artists in a culture.

The role which Delany defines for the artist is to observe, record or transmit and question paradigms in a society. He indicates that it is not the artist's duty to provide resolutions to problems, only to

151

provide order so that others may observe their situation and take their own actions. Delany, as an artist, applies this process to his own writings more successfully as he matures, particularly in his later works in which he uses open endings rather than resolutions.

In Delany's first novel, *The Jewels of Aptor*, the poet Geo is the central character, which makes it possible for Delany to use poetry for foreshadowing, for comment on the qualities of the artist, and to convey his theory of change rather than progress.

Delany uses the ritualistic verses to foreshadow the action of the novel:

> Freeze the drop in the hand
> and break the earth with singing.
> Hail the height of a man
> and also the height of a woman[1] (JA, p. 72).

This verse foreshadows Argo and Snake's escape through the singing congregation after stealing the jewel that controls minds. The similarity of the verses of Hama and Argo are also used to indicate to the characters and the readers the relationship between Argo and Hama.

Through the goddess Argo Delany comments on the qualities of the poet: "I need a poet, not a student. I need one who has suffered as he has .... How well do you know the workings of a man, how he manages to function? That is what you will sing of if your songs are to become great" (JA, pp. 112-113).

Initially Geo, the poet, incorrectly interprets the younger Argo's poem. It is only after he experiences the chaos of pain and terror and learns about the context in which the poem was written that he is able, with the help of its author, to interpret it correctly.

Delany does not yet combine the artist and criminal into one character but he does indicate a connection between them: "Why does a poet sing? Because he likes music; and because silence frightens him. Why does a thief steal? To get the goods from his victim; also to prove that his victim cannot get him" (JA, p. 131). But Delany does not yet recognize the similarity of their roles in society: to question the paradigms in that society.

Finally, Delany uses poetry to illustrate that change is inevitable in the individual and in society, but that change is not necessarily progress. Geo states: "Men change into animals .... I've changed too, I guess. Iimmi replies:

> "Change is neither merciful nor just.

They say Leonard of Vinci put his trust
in faulty paints: Christ's Supper turned to dust" (JA, p. 105).

Delany's questioning of the role of the artist appears as early as *The Fall of the Towers* trilogy. As Douglas Barbour [2] notes, Delany's connection between artist and criminal is also found in this work: both revolt against paradigms of the society. In *The Fall of the Towers*, Jon begins as a criminal not because he questions the values of his society but because of the circumstances in which he finds himself. However, because of his experiences after his initial criminal act, he does question those values and becomes an "intellectual criminal."[3] Although Jon is the central character of the trilogy, it is Vol Nonik who becomes the model of the artist/criminal who will appear repeatedly in Delany's works. Vol Nonik is a gang leader who is also a poet. When he falls in love with an artist, he disbands his gang and devotes himself to his poetry and to his wife. They decide to leave Toroman—the aristocratic society which he criticizes in his poems and which has issued orders for his arrest because of those criticisms. Vol's love and his art have become more important than his commitment to serve as questioning voice for his society. However, his wife is killed before they can escape and this is an injury from which he cannot recover. The pain drives him to create new poetry and here Delany discusses both what motivates the artist and what that motivation costs him: "... a poet is wounded into speech, and he examines these wounds, meticulously, to discover how to heal them.... ultimately his poem is the echoing, dual voice reporting the damage" (FT, p. 390). Delany also uses this section to connect the artist/criminal with insanity. It is important to note that Delany does not present Vol as insane. He only shows the artist as questioning his world's paradigms which results in his also questioning his own sanity since sanity is defined by one's adherence to a set of paradigms prescribed by society. Vol states: "I say I think my poems now are finer than anything I've ever done; I only hope that is the judgment of a ruined mind, with critical faculties shocked and fragmented on grief; because if they are great ... they cost too much!" (FT, p. 390).

Eventually the pain which Vol suffers becomes too great and he commits suicide. Vol has stated: "We are trapped in that bright moment where we learned our doom, but still we struggle, knowing, too, that freedom is imposed the very moment when the trap springs ... closed" (FT, p. 405). In his suicide, Vol differs from later artist/criminal figures. He chooses death. Delany states, through Akor's voice, that death is not freedom. Later characters will choose other worlds.

Delany sets up three things which must be completed before the way to defeat the Lord of the Flames can be discovered: Vol's poems, Clea's unified field theory of mathematics, and Rolth's historical interpretative theory of individual action. In the "Epilogue" Delany elucidates this problem and indicates its resolution. Vol is the symbol of what would happen if the war occurred. Each society would inflict such injury on itself that they would both destroy themselves:

> Beyond a certain amount of injury, life cannot exist. To desire as much destruction as a war would be such an injury. And if the injury is too great self-destruction may be necessary. Suicide is the safety valve for the sickness to dispose of itself (FT, pp. 409-410).

Juxtaposed with this statement is the scene of Vol dying in the radiation area.

Delany opens a way to discuss poetry by using the poet/criminal character Vol. Vol compares a mathematical theory concerning prime numbers to the structure of poetry:

> But between the Nth prime and the prime we arrive at there are always others lurking, scattered throughout the real numbers. Like the irregularities in a poem, the quirks in meaning and syntax and imagery that cage the violent, and the very beautiful (FT, p. 384).

Clea describes Vol's poems as clear and lucid and also notes that Vol "put wild and dispersed things into an order that came close to me" (FT, p. 384). This power to order is prominent in Delany's concept of the role of the artist. Additionally, Rolth's use of Vol in his historical theory research indicates another role of the artist in society: "What I wanted was a view of somebody definitely outside society—such as a brilliant mali leader who was an accurate enough observer to be a poet—to check my views against" (FT, p. 383).

Finally Delany addresses the reader and thereby analyzes the audience for which he writes, and by implication the audience for which he thinks artists should prepare their works:

> ... you write it to an ideal reader, one who will hear all the rhythmical subtleties, will respond to all the images, will reverberate to all the references, will even be able to catch you when you do something wrong;... I check and recheck my

historical theory for cultural, sexual, emotional bias, for that ideal man, who is ideally unbiased. To commit yourself to this concept doesn't mean that with your work you try to teach people how to be ideal. That's propaganda, and since most of the artists and scientists are pretty far from ideal themselves, they are more or less defeated at the start if they take that tack. It's rather to acknowledge that man, with all this chaos, even so, can be ideal, and to make your work worthy of him (FT, p. 398).

In Delany's next work, *The Ballad of Beta-2*, an anthropology student is assigned the task of researching the origins and meaning of a ballad generated by a group of Star Folk who survived a long flight from earth to the stars before quicker flights were available. The story is organized around Joneny's piecing together information from ship records and trial tapes to unravel the meaning of the ballad.

Delany acknowledges the problem of cultural ethnocentricity when one attempts to analyze products of another culture. Joneny almost misses the opportunity to discover the great gift left to his civilization by the Star Folk for two reasons. He considers, because of his cultural bias, his civilization superior to that of the Star Folk and their ballads as therefore unworthy of his attention. Secondly, he initially applies his own cultural meanings to the images and actions within the ballad, thereby disregarding the possibility that they may have different meanings in another culture. This discussion of ethnocentrism which weaves through the novel is the foundation upon which Delany later integrates multiple viewpoints.

Delany further discusses, by implication, the role of myth (of which the ballad is a part) in relation to history. What was conceived of as a ballad created by insane survivors of a catastrophe proves to be a factual historical account. Fortunately, Joneny is a good scholar and by previous definition an artist because he does overcome his cultural bias and begins to observe discrepancies in various versions of the ballad. It is only when he is willing to go to the source and accept things which make no sense to him within the strictures of his own culture that he begins to understand the meaning of the ballad. His rendition and interpretation of the ballad, based on other literary sources available to him at the Star Folk colony, not only tell him and his civilization about the actual happenings on the voyage but also uncover a group of half-humans who can travel through space and time devoid of artificial aids.

Delany continues to develop the theme of the artist/criminal in society in this novel. The One-Eyes are a group of people who go against the norm established by the ship's judicial systems. In order to protect the populace from a feeling of hopelessness on their long voyage, the ship's elders replaced the quest for knowledge with ritual. This usurping of power and decision from the populace results in the loss of the knowledge which is essential for their survival once they reach their destination. The One-Eyes will not accept the substitution of ritual for knowledge and leave the ships' cities to live in the bowels of the ships and so become criminals. They are artists in their transmission of knowledge and their questioning of the society's paradigms.

In *Empire Star* Delany is fulfilling one of his own imperatives for the artist: to question the paradigms of his society. This is accomplished through the relationship of the Llls to society which is an obvious discussion of the Blacks' position in our society. From a metafictional point of view it is interesting to observe that Delany chose to use multiple viewpoints within one character for the first time in the same work, which clearly points to his being a Black writer. As a Black man in the United States, Delany has experienced double consciousness. This psychological dichotomy is produced when an individual lives in a subculture such as the Black community whose survival depends on his awareness of the paradigms of a dominant culture such as the white or Western culture.

The viewpoints which Delany discusses are labeled simplex, complex and multiplex. A simplex point of view is defined as being able to perceive something from only one angle and therefore knowing only one part of it. A complex point of view enables the viewer to perceive more than one part at a time but less than the whole. A multiplex point of view allows the viewer to perceive the entire pattern from all angles. It is the multiplex or holistic viewpoint which is the most valuable to the artist in observing and recording his society.

After explaining in very simple terms the differences in these viewpoints, Delany demonstrates that it is necessary for Comet Jo to develop a multiplex viewpoint in order to understand and accomplish his mission of helping to free the Llls. Comet Jo is literally given his way of viewing the world by inserting Jewel (a multiplex being) into his eye, thereby gaining new sight. Jewel, the narrator of the story, is capable of presenting four points of view, which heralds *Dhalgren*.

Within *Empire Star* Delany continues his use of the artist character. The poet Ni Ty Lee is used to link together the experiences of the central characters and to expound on the time variances of their meetings. Delany also employs the poet character to continue his metafictional comments. In reaction to Comet Jo and Ni Ty Lee's conversation, Lump states:

> ... certain authors seem to have discovered all the things you have discovered, done all you've done .... Then you learn that lots of other people find the same things in the same writer, who have done none of the things you've done, and seen none of the things you've seen (ES, pp. 73-4).

Ni Ty Lee replies:

> I never do anything long enough to really get to know it—just long enough to identify it in a line or a sentence, then I'm on to something else. I think I'm afraid. And I write to make up for all the things I really can't do (ES, p. 74).

Besides these metafictional statements, Delany uses art in another way in *Empire Star*. He introduces music into his repertoire of arts. Delany uses music structurally and ironically to introduce the Llls and their plight when he has Ron and Comet Jo play their instruments (ocarina and guitar) for the Llls. This minor use of music as a performed art foreshadows the musician as artist in *The Einstein Intersection* and, to a lesser extent, Mouse in *Nova* and Lanya in *Dhalgren*.

Delany goes back to the artist/protagonist Geo of *Jewels of Aptor* for the model of his protagonist in *Babel-17*. Rydra Wong is a brilliant linguist and poet as well as a space captain. She is, in another identity, a saboteur and unconsciously works against her native Alliance society. The latter identity is hidden from her by the amnesia instilled by the language "Babel-17." Rydra has dual points of view, each trying to destroy the other.

The typical use of characters in science fiction, according to Mark Rose, is that "... the figures in the tale tend to be characterized principally by their ideological relationship to the quest. Put simply, characters are either for or against the quest: the 'good' or 'enlightened' assist it, the 'bad' or 'ignorant' obstruct it."[4] Delany twists this normal assignment. The two main characters in *Babel-17* are both for and against the mission. This is an excellent example of the expression of double consciousness. It is significant that a writer who, as a Black man, has experienced double consciousness was the first to incorporate this twist. And it follows one of Delany's writing mandates: "When I write I often try to say several things at the same time—from a regard for economy that sits contiguous with any concern for skillful expression."[5] Although other writers may know what double consciousness is, the Black writer has an advantage in having lived it. He has first-hand knowledge of the struggles and the triumphs of living and thinking in two diametrically opposed worlds, mastering both in order to survive physically and mentally.

Delany continues with his concern for the role of the artist in society in his discussion of the uses of language. One important use of language in the formulation of the novel is when Rydra analyzes the pattern of "Babel-17" in order to learn how it functions. Once she understands the language she uses its precepts to change it and thereby converts it from an Invader weapon to an Alliance weapon. This parallels what Delany has done, as have many other Black writers. They have mastered the language and turned it against its formulators in protest, one of the many facets of warfare. Indeed, the plot of the novel hinges on Rydra's assignment to find out what "Babel-17" is and incapacitate it. In order for her to find out how the language works, she must be cognizant of how her own language works.

Rydra thinks of words as symbols; she thinks of the differences in singular and plural; she thinks of the assigning of sex to all objects in some languages. Finally, she realizes the importance of names, the ability to define oneself as an individual as opposed to the impersonal use of a pronoun:

> My name is Rydra! An individual, a thing apart from its environment, and apart from all things in that environment; an individual was a type of thing for which symbols were inadequate, and so names were invented. I am invented. I am not a round warm blue room. I am someone in that room, I am— (B-17, p. 89).

The importance of the concept of self and the ability to define that self within the confines of a language is central to understanding the power of the language "Babel-17." When Rydra discovers that Butcher does not use the words "I" or "my" or any form to indicate himself, she discovers the key to "Babel-17" and thereby saves their world. As she tries to teach the concept of self to Butcher she discovers that without words which symbolize the concept of self, a person is malleable to the will of others since he/she can identify no self-interests.

Delany returns to the specific use of poetry which he began in *The Jewels of Aptor*. The discussion of poetry is complemented by the use of poems as epigrams and by their use within the text. Delany uses poetry in three ways in *Babel-17*. First, the poems of

Marilyn Hacker introduce each section of the novel. Secondly, the protagonist is a poet which allows Delany to discuss the function and the development of a poet. Finally, a poem written by Delany is used to demonstrate the ordering power of the language "Babel-17" and to initiate action in the prevention of Jebel's assassination.

Ms. Hacker's poems introduce setting, characters and themes in each section. These poems were not written specifically for the text and were previously published elsewhere. Delany selected these particular poems because they emphasize the paradigms which he, as artist, questions.

The fragment from *Prism and Lens* (B-17, p. 5) is retitled "Rydra Wong" and sets the scene and the mood of the Alliance society in the first section of the novel. The fragment emphasizes the hardship, the deprivation and the violence which inevitably occur in a society long at war. The ghetto scene of the poem parallels Alliance civilian life, hinting at the parallel which Delany develops between the Alliance culture and the Black culture. In the ghetto scene the priorities of the white culture (the street lights and the shipyard) are contrasted with the deprivation of the ghetto inhabitants (a crowd) and the violence in the streets ("a dark clot oozing on a chest"). The crowd cannot escape the ghetto: "They say the same crowd surges up the street/and surges down again." The "stragglers" who are trapped in the ghetto are contrasted with the "young sailors" who are escaping to their ships. The port, where some are trapped and some can escape, is described as "the hub of ambiguity."

In the first section of *Babel-17* we learn that the starport contains two groups: civilians who cannot leave the starport and transports who travel from planet to planet. Embargoes have limited food supplies and cannibalism has occurred several times. Science is used more to strengthen the war effort than to remedy living conditions. Rydra Wong, after whom the introductory poem is retitled, is the protagonist in the storyline and also functions as both civilian and transport. The juxtaposition of the poem and the first section demonstrates the parallel between today's society and the Alliance society of the future. Delany does not let the reader forget that he is writing about the present in a future tense.

Ver Dorco is an important character introduced in the second section and his name retitles this fragment: ". . . if words are paramount I am afraid that words/are all my hands have ever seen" (B-17, p. 50). The line means that words are important because they are symbols which allow us to think about them on an abstract level. Ver Dorco is head of the military science compound and, for him, science is supreme. Words, or language, are important to him when they symbolize material things or produce thoughts which, in turn, produce material things. Only the material things are real to Ver Dorco. Words are not used to communicate emotions or to relate to individuals. As his wife states to Rydra: "You come to us and immediately we start to learn things, things about you, and ultimately about ourselves" (B-17, p. 75). Ver Dorco's community uses all of their intelligence and creativity not to find out about themselves, but to design weapons of destruction. Therefore, the hands which can only touch and not see are Ver Dorco's only connection with words. The poem is a satire of their isolation from humanity and from self.

Two fragments precede section three (B-17, p. 88). Jebel Tarik is the character described in the first poem fragment and Rydra and Butcher are the subjects of the second. Jebel has rejected the confines of both worlds. He takes from each world what he needs, with or without (usually without) its permission. He is, foremost, a survivor: "Real, grimy and exiled, he eludes us." But his is a self-imposed exile. Society can neither control nor destroy him. He has not escaped his humanity: "... he has his own bad dreams, needs to work, gets drunk...." And he defies definition by others: "... maybe would not have chosen to be beautiful."

The second poem fragment is "... you have imposed upon me a treaty of silence" (B-17, p. 88). Butcher and Rydra have trouble communicating because neither knows that the other possesses a mutual language. The cause of Butcher's self-imposed silence is that he does not understand the concept of self. Rydra only knows half of herself because of the amnesiac effect of "Babel-17." The poem refers, then, to the treaty of silence between them, and the silence within themselves which "Babel-17" has inflicted. They are cut off from each other and from parts of themselves.

The poem fragment preceding part four foreshadows Butcher's discovery of selfhood (B-17, p. 144). He is symbolically born again as he sees behind the mask imposed by "Babel-17": "He ... turns, born, on the wet floor." The reference to "wires behind his eyes" parallels the technical, scientific use of language to subjugate the individual. The physical suffering depicted in the poem parallels Butcher's mental anguish as he forces himself to remember the agonies of his life. There is a parallel between the references to "twin" and the double consciousness which Butcher must confront once he goes through his self-discovery process. Both the references to "twin" and birth reflect the incident where Butcher attempts to save the infant's life. Butcher wants to raise the infant to be like himself in order to have someone with whom he can communicate.

On a superficial level the final poem, subtitled "Markus T'

Mwarba" (B-17, p. 149), depicts T'Mwarba's faith in Rydra and his wisdom in combining her instructions with his knowlege of psychology and technology in order to free Rydra and Butcher from the control of "Babel-17." But the final poem gives us more; it gives us the secret to freedom. According to Delany, that secret is the willingness to *change* what is and to *remember* the good and the bad of what has been. This works on two levels. Rydra and Butcher must be willing to change themselves, to assert their new-found identities. They must also remember what has happened to them and who they have been if they, as individuals, are to remain free from outside control. On the other level, society must be willing to change its emphasis from science to the individual, yet it must remember the devastation it has been through so it will not repeat the same mistakes.

Delany discusses the writing of poetry through Mocky's remarks toward Rydra: "Good poets tend to be practical and abhor mysticism" (B-17, p. 22). Here he is commenting on the need for a poet (or a writer) to have a clear concept of himself and of his subject matter in order to be effective. Delany also comments on the stages through which writers must progress to become craftsmen. Rydra states that she began writing poetry by listening to what other people tried to say:

> I go home and burnish it and polish it and weld it to a rhythmic frame, make the dull colors gleam, mute the garish artificiality to pastels, so it doesn't hurt any more: that's my poem. I know what they want to say, and I say it for them (B-17, p. 18).

This borrowing and imitating is the first stage that a writer goes through. Rydra realizes, as she progresses as a writer, that she must start writing her own thoughts instead of merely reshaping the thoughts of others:

> And now I have things to say that are all my own. They're not what other people have said before, put in an original way. And they're not just violent contradictions of what other people have said, which amounts to the same thing. They're new, and I'm scared to death (B-17, p. 28).

The comments on the development of a writer emphasize the relationship between the writer, his material and his society. Words are the symbols of thought. The poet puts these symbols into a special form which enhances their meaning for the reader through an increasing understanding of self-knowledge.

Delany does include one poem which he wrote. Rydra's purpose in composing a poem is to spur the assassin (Cord) into making his move too soon and thus exposing himself before he can complete his deed. As she recited the poem she

> ... tossed her words from the sling of her vibrant voice, so that they hung outside her, and she watched them and watched his watching: the rhythm which was barely intricate to most ears in the commons was to him painful because it was timed to the processes of his body, to jar and strike against them (B-17, p. 114).

The rhythm and the internal rhyme mesmerize Cord. The command, issued toward the end of the poem, is more powerful through incantation than it would have been through simple language. The combination of harsh consonants and the death images spoken in a strident cadence jangle the nerves of the would-be assassin. "... the personafix/inflicting false memories to make them blunder..." (B-17, p. 115) refers to the assassin's self-hypnosis which prevents him from remembering what he does. The power of "Babel-17" to destroy the concept of self is shown in the line: "you name yourself victim each time you fill/with swill the skull's cup lipping murder" (B-17, p. 115).

The poems which introduce each section of the book foreshadow the action, setting and characters which will appear. Through the poet Rydra, Delany discusses the necessity of self-knowledge for a writer. In Delany's poem he illustrates the power of "Babel-17" to destroy the individual while he also emphasizes the power of the language and the form of poetry for personal communication.

In *The Einstein Intersection* Delany again chooses an artist as protagonist, but this time the art is music. The performance of the art as well as the capabilities and motivations of the artist are more central to this novel than in *Babel-17*. The societies which the artist observes, the paradigms which he questions, and the effects of his art are the nucleus of this novel, for the theme and the plot are woven around them.

In *The Einstein Intersection* Delany uses the relationships of man to music to illustrate man's self-determining powers. The creation of music is used symbolically in this work to illustrate man's individuality. Conversely, the absence of music illustrates the suppression of individuality. The different functions of music in the tribal and technological societies in *The Einstein Intersection* will be discussed through Delany's use of theme, symbol, myth and description. Levi-Strauss' theory of music and Jung's definition of the collective unconscious will be summarized and applied as insights into different perspectives of the function and use of music in this novel. Also included will be Delany's use of the Orpheus myth to illustrate an historically primitive recognition of an innate relationship between man and music.

Delany invents two societies in *The Einstein Intersection* which inhabit the remnants of a highly technological world abandoned by its inhabitants. The ancestors of both societies came from another world. Some chose to populate the rural areas and formed tribal communities and some chose to populate the deserted cities. Those in the rural areas decided to begin afresh on the planet, developing their own culture. The city dwellers chose to relive the past in an attempt to find out why and how the previous culture destroyed itself.

In the urban technological society the people suffer from alienation of self which stems partially from the adoption of the culture of a dead past which is not their own. Their self-alienation is intensified by the very nature of their technological society. The scientifically imposed orderliness of their society produces a compact, efficient atmosphere which alienates the people from nature, from human compassion and ultimately from themselves. This artificial orderliness contrasts with the lack of order within the people's minds. Although the technological society is functional economically, and politically, and, in an abstract way, perhaps even socially, it does not function for the benefit of the individual. The people are not allowed to choose their sexual partners nor to determine when and with whom they will have children. They are trapped economically and therefore cannot freely choose to leave the society. The citizens feel incapable of controlling their own lives and may even have forgotten that such a possibility exists. In order to maintain their sanity and relieve their boredom, they live in a world of illusions created by Le Dove.

The inhabitants of the tribal society have not assumed another group's culture. Each person values himself and is valued by others as an individual. People are evaluated by their peers for their particular abilities to function within society as is demonstrated by the bestowing of the titles La, Lo and Le. Each person chooses his own work, friends, lovers and values. They decide when and with whom they will have children. Anyone is free to leave whenever he chooses. Part of the strength of their belief in themselves as individuals is structured upon their belief in the immortality of their souls as exemplified by Lobey's statement: "difference gave us a reality beyond dying" (EI, p. 53).

Difference is the key word in this novel for it designates the importance of the individual and his ability to make choices which affect his life, and to question the paradigms of his society. Lobey's difference is evident through his ability to create music. Difference is first commented upon by La Dire, wise woman of Lobey's village, as she speaks to Lobey: "You have seen it is dangerous to be so. It is also very important. I have tried to instruct you in a view of the world large enough to encompass the deeds you will do as well as their significance" (EI, p. 52). Difference in the tribal society is accepted and acknowledged as the expression of one's selfhood and abilities.

However, difference is not well accepted in the technological society. Certainly such citizens as Green-eye, Le Dove, Kid Death and Spider qualify as different, as extreme individualists who exert great power, but they are exceptions. Their leadership is required for the continuance of the community. The majority of the citizens, however, are not considered as individuals nor do they value such individuality. Pistol explains to Lobey:

> Difference is a private matter. Difference is the foundation of those buildings, the pilings beneath the docks, tangled in the roots of the trees. Half the place was built on it. The other half couldn't live without it. But to talk about it in public reveals you to be ill-mannered and vulgar (EI, p. 102).

The members of the technological society realize that difference cannot be explained in their scientific or their religious terms, and that necessarily makes it a matter which they prefer to ignore. Because they do not recognize the source of difference as individualism, they become subjugated to science and religion and cannot revive themselves as Lobey can. Once destroyed, they are dead both psychologically and literally.

In contrast, the tribal society is not consumed by the past or by technology. The citizens remain individuals with real needs which can be satisfied within their normal lives and within reality. The tribal society is therefore shown as functional and the technological society as nonfunctional in their abilities to provide what is needed for their citizens.

Therefore a conflict arises between these two societies. The alienation and lack of individualism in the technological society makes its leaders feel threatened by the tribal society, which is providing a better environment psychologically, if not economically, for its citizens. The tribal society is threatened by the technological society, which has determined to disrupt the tribal society by eliminating its most capable members. Kid Death comes from the technological society to kill those members of the tribal society who possess various observable abilities to control or change their environment. These individuals who are labeled as different have abilities which range from telepathic to telekinetic powers, through control over time and nature, to Lobey's power to establish pattern and order through his music.

Lobey, the Black protagonist, departs from his tribal society on a quest to restore safety to it. In order to accomplish this mission he must journey to and conquer the other society, not yet knowing, as he starts out, the meaning of the power of his music. Yet the protagonist not only conquers, he also contributes to the technological society, for he frees it from the religious and scientific requirements of the past so that it too can progress and find its own destiny.

Lobey's ability to reach into other people's minds and play the music he finds there is the source of his power in both societies. He is the transmitter, the creator. He takes the chaos of men's minds and imposes order, then gives it back to the listeners, leading them through the labyrinths of their own minds to their recognition of themselves. Levi-Strauss' theory of the relationship between myth and music lends insight to Lobey and his music. Levi-Strauss states:

> In both instances [myth and music] the same reversal of the relation between transmitter and receiver can be observed, since in the last resort the latter discovers its own meaning through the message from the former: music has its being in me, and I listen to myself through it.[6]

Prior to Lobey's journey, La Dire attempts to explain to Lobey who and what he is, but she has only fragments of the old Western myths and she sometimes assigns different interpretations to them. The great rock and the great roll, instead of merely a musical movement, is interpreted as philosophy: "the great rock and the great roll? That's all death and all life" (EI, p. 16). Ringo is presented as another Orpheus:

> You remember the Beatle Ringo left his love even though she treated him tender. He was the one Beatle who did not sing ... they returned, finally at one, with the great rock and the great roll ... In the older story Ringo was called Orpheus.... In this version Orpheus was the greatest singer, instead of the silent one (EI, p. 16).

The myth of Orpheus is used as a model for Lobey and as a

structural device in the novel. Instead of putting Cerberus to sleep with music as Orpheus did, Lobey uses music to make the minotaur turn to a position where Lobey can kill him. Lobey thus gains entrance to the underground tunnels to search for Friza, just as Orpheus gained entrance to the underworld to search for Eurydice. When Le Dove appears as Friza, she tells Lobey: "be careful ... do you want to look that closely?" (EI, p. 133). But Lobey refuses to be deceived by illusion. He recognizes that it is not Friza but merely an illusion of her created by Le Dove. At the same time he also sees the crucifixion of Green-eye through the music he hears: "It was the mourning song of the girl who shielded my eyes now, played for the garroted prince" (EI, p. 133). Orpheus also looked back and thereby lost Eurydice.

Like Orpheus, Lobey must make a choice between the past and the future, between illusion and reality. Through the deaths of Kid Death and Green-eye, Lobey frees the societies to change rather than attempt to continue to live within the myths of a long dead culture. And he accomplishes this through his music for it is he that plays the music which traps Kid Death so that Spider can kill him. But although the novel ends with music being the means of the destruction of Kid Death and the Christ-figure, Delany shows that whereas music can destroy, it can also revive or create, for Lobey learns that he can bring back those he kills: himself, Kid Death and Green-eye.

Lobey begins to understand music and its functions when La Dire tells him to play his music in order to properly mourn the death of his lover Friza. La Dire states: "All life is rhythm .... All death is rhythm suspended, a syncopation before life resumes" (EI, p. 17). This statement implies that life can be reinstigated, possibly through Lobey's music. Freud made this connection between music and death in his theory of animism in which he states that music is an expression of the soul, of an individual's life force, and the belief in the existence of souls is the result of an attempt to explain death.[7]

The relationship of life processes to rhythm and music is defined by Levi-Strauss in *The Raw and the Cooked*. He states that there are

> an equally infinite series of physically producible sounds, from which each musical system selects its scale. The second aspect of the continuum is internal and is situated in the psychophysiological time of the listener, the elements of which are very complex: they involve the periodicity of cerebral waves and the organic rhythms, the strength of the memory, and the power of the attention.[8]

This relationship between natural body rhythms and music illuminates the description of Lobey's playing:

> Notes came with only the meter of my own breathing, and from beneath that, there was the quickening of the muscles of my fingers and toes that began to cramp for the faster, closer dance of the heart's time. The mourning hymn began to quake (EI, p. 17).

Prior to Lobey's mourning, music was a plaything for him. Now he recognizes it not only as a medium for the expression of emotion but as an expansion of himself through which he relates to the living force of nature. As he experiences this totality, it gives him room to express the grief he had held in because he had found nothing large enough to encompass it. He thereby receives solace from the cycle of life and from the physical assertion of his own capabilities which leads him to discover their importance in the preservation of his sanity.

Lobey learns more about music when he saves the lizard from the carnivorous plants. The carnivorous flowers emit noises which depict that "the communication was fear and retreat. The music, though! Lord, the music!" (EI, p. 61). Here Delany demonstrates the universality of music, not just between men but also with plants and animals, as well as their common use of music to express emotion. This passage can be viewed as the linkage of music with Jung's theory of the collective unconscious expanded to include plants and animals. Jung's concept of the collective unconscious posits the existence of

> universal symbols and myths which are a function of the nature of the psyche itself; accordingly, they are produced by different people in different times and places, when the human situations they symbolize call them forth.... [Man] comes into the world equipped to structure and give meaning to the evidence of his senses.[9]

It is this ability to give "meaning to the evidence of his senses" which Lobey reaches for and withdraws from people's minds when he creates music. By creating order for them he reawakens their ability to create order.

When Lobey joins the herders, a nomadic group not part of Lobey's society and not entirely of the technological society, he meets Spider and Green-eye, and he learns about Kid Death. Spider functions as a mediator between the past and the present, making decisions as to what elements must be removed or added for the technological society to continue to function. It is he who eventually kills Kid Death with the help of Lobey. Spider is also the one who sends Lobey to Le Dove, thereby introducing his music to the society.

Lobey's first view of Kid Death is through the technology of television: "It wasn't a picture of a face. It was as if I was just looking at the particular dots of melody-hue that formed the face" (EI, p. 54). Artificial order is reflected as Kid Death's picture appears on the screen, merely a technological illusion. Kid Death is science, the science that discards humanity, that destroys anything which questions its methods, its supremacy, or its validity. Science offers control over humanity. Through his music Lobey offers patterns and order to the individual so that each can find himself in the chaos of his own mind and thereby make his own decisions. Kid Death's function in society is to eliminate those who would change the status quo.

When Lobey finally enters the city, part of his culture shock is that he hears music from millions of people instead of the few members of his village: "The millions' music melded to a hymn like when your ears ring and you're trying to sleep .... I kept losing myself while people jostled me" (EI, p. 111). This mass of impressions leads to confusion about his own identity. Whereas in the tribal society the music was individual to the person, in the city the music blends together, suggesting the constraints on individualism imposed by the technological society.

It is only after Lobey enters the city that Spider explains Kid Death's function in society and that Kid Death needs control over Lobey so that he can use Lobey's music:

> He needs order. He needs patterning, relation, the knowledge that comes when six notes predict a seventh, when three notes beat against one another and define a mode, a melody defines a scale. Music is the pure language of temporal and co-temporal relation. He knows nothing of this .... Kid Death can control ... but he cannot order (EI, p. 121).

Here Delany defines the relationship discussed by Levi-Strauss, the patterning of thought in music. But more than that, Delany draws on the relationship of music to society in the Black culture. He goes back to the function of music in African tribes where music was part of their rituals, part of their expression of their understanding of their world and an avenue to a state of mind where they could experience a oneness with the spirits they worshipped or feared.

Lobey plays music so that Spider can kill Kid Death. Spider tells Lobey: "As long as you make music, he can't use his mind for anything else!" (EI, p. 139). For Kid Death wants the ordering power of Lobey's music to help him control society and maintain the status quo by destroying those who are different. Lobey refuses to be part of this destruction and of the misuse of his power. Ironically Lobey misuses his own power in order to prevent its misuse on a larger scale. He plays the music fully knowing that Kid Death is helpless while under its influence, and as a result Spider can and does kill Kid Death.

When Lobey meets Le Dove he sees that her illusions compensate for the people's boredom and dissatisfaction which result from the uselessness and alienation they feel in their technological society. But these escapes must be paid for, resulting in a relentless circle of economic endeavors and a monotonous existence.

There is no music when Lobey enters the Pearl, which indicates that music is not one of the methods used by Le Dove. She asks Lobey to play, and the effect on the urban people is impelling: they began by tapping their fingers, and then as sound was "loosed through the room" they "beat their thighs and bellies to four melodies" (EI, p. 132). Through music Lobey draws them back to their beginnings, to their submerged needs masked by their society. He touches their collective unconscious which hungers for self-expression and assertion. Clearly music has been used in this society only as a backdrop, not as an emotionally impelling force to connect them with nature and their own needs. This sterile use of music is indicative of their emotional bankruptcy and parallels their sexual interchanges which are devoid of real emotion or commitment in contrast to the relationship between Friza and Lobey which was passionate as well as loving.

In the caged area under the dance floor, Lobey observes the mentally deranged people of this technological society. Unlike the cages of the Black tribal society, the white technological society's cages contain primarily schizophrenics. Their conflict between what their society offers and what they as individuals need had at one time been clear to them, but their inability to reconcile these two elements has driven them insane. This interpretation is substantiated by the effect that music has on them and PHAEDRA'S fear that Lobey can cure them with his music when she has failed.

PHAEDRA, the computer used by the technological society to care for the deranged inhabitants (the acronym derives from

Psychic Harmony Entanglements and Deranged Response Association) clings to her power. She rejects Lobey and his power to draw and create music on his knife blade: "Mother is in charge of everything down here. Don't you come playing your bloody knife around me" (EI, p. 135). PHAEDRA, ultimate symbol of the technological society, feels threatened now that the collective unconscious of her citizens has been awakened, for science will have to compete with individualism. Not only is PHAEDRA threatened by it, it is bewildering to her. She is not programmed to understand a humanistic approach to the care of her inmates. Her function, like Kid Death's, is to control, but unlike Kid Death she is only a highly sophisticated machine.

Lobey goes to the tree where Green-eye hangs and plays for him in an effort to persuade him to return Friza from the dead:

> I stood before the tree and played to him, pleading. I hung chords on a run of sevenths that begged his resolution. I began humbly, and the song emptied me till there was only the pit. I plunged. There was rage. It was mine, so I gave him that. There was love. That shrilled beneath the singing in the windows .... And nothing. I shrieked, as outrage broke. With the hilt in both hands, I plunged the point in his thigh, sank it to the wood (EI, p. 136).

Lobey begs this Christ-figure, and when he is rejected, he in turn rejects this mythological figure. Lobey uses the instrument of his begging to kill Green-eye.

Lobey kills this symbol of Western religion because it has shown that it cannot fulfill the needs of Lobey and his fellow beings, those who would go forward to carve a new destiny for their people rather than simply relive the past of another civilization. Although the Christian myth is set in motion by Green-eye's crucifixion, Lobey is the only one who can resurrect him and fulfill the myth. Lobey does not indicate that he intends to do this. The myth is changed because man, not God, decides Christ's fate.

Delany continues to explore multiple viewpoints in *The Einstein Intersection*. Whereas a Black American has double consciousness from an early age, Delany's protagonist does not have double consciousness until he enters the technological society so different from his tribal village. Even with the lizard herders, Lobey does not feel out of place, for there is still an affinity with nature, and the pattern of daily existence remains basically the same.

Delany illustrates how much more frustrating this double

consciousness is when it comes in young adulthood during the time when one tries to identify oneself. Lobey must identify himself in two societies, in two contexts, one of which is totally unfamiliar to him, while he is equally unfamiliar to it. Delany shows the anger and the aggression which result from the frustration of having a role, a definition, imposed upon an individual by a society which has little or no concept of that individual's background, experience, abilities or needs.

Lobey, as the angry Black protagonist, rejects the future projected for him and society. His rejection takes the form of the destruction of two of the institutions of the technological society: science and the Christian religion. Lobey finds both to be incompatible with his concepts of the world. It is significant that Lobey is able to accomplish this destruction through the power of his music which the technological society does not understand. Le Dove invited him to play, little realizing the revitalizing effect his music would have. But PHAEDRA understood its power, though not its source, and rejected it. PHAEDRA symbolizes technology, and in order to save science she turns Lobey toward Green-eye, the symbol of religion. Thus science sacrifices religion to maintain itself. But science has been weakened by the destruction of Kid Death, and is further weakened since Le Dove and the people have been exposed to music. The urban populace has become aware of their ability to exist as self-determining individuals which foreshadows the destruction of the technological power structure in that society.

In *Nova* Delany uses two artists, the musician and the novelist, as central characters. Although Mouse, who plays the syrynx, is an important character, it is not his music which makes him important as was the case with Lobey in *The Einstein Intersection*. Katin is the artist on whom Delany focuses. Katin constantly observes and takes notes in preparation for the novel he will write. At the end of Delany's work we find that the novel Katin plans to write is the novel we've just read. Delany will employ this technique again in *Tides of Lust* and *Dhalgren*. In *Empire Star,* Delany continued to use a kind of omniscient author, who, in the opening pages was identified as Jewel, capable of four viewponts. In *Nova* the story is again told by an omniscient author who is identified at the end as Katin. As in *Empire Star,* the narrator is primarily passive: he observes and records. On a superficial level the narrator tells the story of the conflict between Lorq Von Ray and Prince. But it is really Mouse's story that Katin tells, for the observations he records are primarily Mouse's.

Mouse is the artist who is capable of multiplex observation.

Katin is a complex character because he is capable of viewing different parts of the milieu, but Mouse sees the whole pattern. Mouse has acquired his multiplexity in the same way that Delany has. Mouse, like Lobey, is different. Mouse is a gypsy, a minority in the society, and as such he has known the pain and fear which prejudice inflicts, the aloneness of isolation and different perceptions and values, the hunger and deprivation of the alien orphan. Yet by close observation of all around him, Mouse learns how to survive. Delany uses Mouse to illustrate the negation of the cultural non-solidarity argument posed several times in the novel. The argument is that the societies of the world are crumbling because they no longer adhere to their original cultural imperatives since rapid travel and communications have imposed the cultures upon each other. Yet Mouse survives in any society because he chooses what he values from each culture and incorporates it into himself. Because of his multiplexic view, he is able to observe all elements and appropriately adapt to them for survival. On a more superficial level, Delany uses the character Lorq as an illustration of his argument against this theory. This is most obvious in the interchange between Lorq and Prince over their feud and its effects on their worlds:

> "Prince, what are you trying to do?"
> "Keep things as they are."
> "Stasis is death." (N, p. 180)

Delany incorporates his metafictional comments into Katin's discussion of why and how he'll write his novel. This quotation may give insight to Delany's formulation of *Dhalgren:*

> I haven't begun to think about the subject. I'm still making notes on the form.... On structure, the aesthetics of the whole business.... The novel was an art form. I have to invent it all over again before I can write one. The one I want to write, anyway.... Bear in mind that the novel—no matter how intimate, psychological, or subjective—is always a historical projection of its own time.... To make my book I must have an awareness of my time's conception of history (N, pp. 115-6).

Delany gives us additional insight to the important thematic elements of a novel and the role of art in society when Katin explains to Mouse:

> ...a great web that spreads across the galaxy, as far as you see? That's it. That's my theory. Each individual is a junction in that net, and the strands between are the cultural, the economic, the psychological threads that hold individual to individual. Any historical event is like a

ripple in the net.... It passes over and through the web, stretching or shrinking those cultural bonds that involve each man with each man. If the event is catastrophic enough, the bonds break. The net is torn for a while.... I want to catch the throw and scope of this web in my... my novel, Mouse. I want it to spread about the whole web. But I have to find that central subject, that great event which shakes history and makes the links strike and glitter for me (N, p. 155).

Katin and Mouse discuss the motivations and processes of creating art. Mouse asks Katin:

"Why are you writing this book?"
"Why do you play your syrynx? I'm sure it's for essentially the same reason."
"Only if I spent all that time just getting ready, I'd never play a thing; and that's a hint." (N, p. 159).

Katin elaborates on the differences between these two artists:

I could sit and watch you play for hours. But they're only momentary joys, Mouse. It's only when all one knows of life is abstracted and used as an underlining statement of significant patterning that you have what is both beautiful and permanent. Yes, there is an area of myself I haven't been able to tap for this work, one that flows and fountains in you, gushes from your fingers. But there's a large part of you that's playing to drown the sound of someone screaming in there (N, p. 160).

Finally, on the last page of the book, Delany uses the last conversation between Katin and Mouse, the two artists, to inform his readers who the narrator has been and to point the reader toward an interpretation of the novel as an allegorical Grail quest:

This last voyage of the *Roc*? I'm too aware of all the archetypical patterns it follows. I can see myself now, turning it into some allegorical Grail quest. That's the only way I could deal with it, hiding all sorts of mystic symbolism in it. Remember all those writers who died before they finished their Grail recountings?... The only way to protect myself from the jinx, I guess, would be to abandon it before I finish the last (N, p. 215),

And the novel ends with the last sentence incomplete.

In *Tides of Lust* Delany experiments with pornography which he incorporates into the many sexual scenes in his next novel, *Dhalgren*. The problems of sexual identification, superficially noted in *Tides of Lust*, become the subject matter of his more recent novel, *Triton*.

Tides of Lust is another metafictional novel in that the protagonist is both narrator and artist. Delany describes sexual acts with the same detail of observation that he has previously devoted to cultural relationships as well as art forms such as music. The work is a carefully constructed catalogue of bisexual and homosexual relationships including incest, bestiality, sadism and masochism, necrophilia, rape, and cannibalism. But this discussion of sex works as a metaphor for a discussion of the role of the artist/criminal in society.

One cannot, however, make the simple equation of Captain as criminal (despite his ship's cargo or his actions in port) and Proctor as artist (despite his fame), for Proctor is a pseudo-artist since he merely copies rather than creates and Captain is an artist, for he records his observation in his ship's log. The Captain and Proctor do share a common function in society: they, as outsiders, question the values of the society and thereby work as catalysts in the society. As Delany has stated: "An artist needs to write about things which he has done and which he has observed others experiencing in order to give his work the veracity and the distance so that it is not construed as simply self-therapy."[10] The reader should not assume, of course, that Delany has experienced everything that he writes about. That would degrade him to the level of Proctor, who merely copies, and deny Delany's imaginative and creative abilities. Yet the statement does illuminate this novel. Proctor finds that to survive he must destroy Katherine. Captain has no such need, for he can observe, participate and accept identities placed upon him (such as Proctor's assigning him the role of the devil) without submitting to their power, because he knows who and what he is—the artist. Katherine is the life force in all her perversities, her hungers and her powers. She is a symbol of all the things that range inside of ourselves as humans—unmasked. Without this knowledge, a writer merely copies; he presents no understanding—only a mirror image without the soul.

In his next novel, *Dahlgren*, Delany incorporates stylistic and thematic elements which he experimented with in his previous works. His holistic view of society, first introduced as multiple viewpoints in *Empire Star*, is in *Dahlgren* linked more strongly to theme. The sexual scenes of *Dahlgren* are extensions of *Tides of Lust*. Delany goes back to *The Fall of the Towers* for the artist/criminal concept, to *Babel-17* and *The Jewels of Aptor* for the poet as central character, to *The Einstein Intersection* for art as a motivating force in society, and to *Nova* for the novelist as narrator. The massive *Dahlgren* is the most complete metafictional statement of Delany's works.

In *Dahlgren* Delany presents what he called in *Nova* "that central subject, that great event which shakes history and makes the links strike and glitter for me" (N, p. 155). It is the moment in history following the assassination of Martin Luther King, Jr. when Blacks switched from non-violent to violent protest. In this work Delany demonstrates why this switch occurred, by illustrating the conflict between the American dream and reality for the Black American. Blacks, following the Christian precepts of non-violence advocated by King, believed that with time, patience and hard work they would achieve their goals—their American dream. The assassination showed them that what they believed was true was not real. They were forced to question the paradigms of their own movement as well as to reassess those of the American culture. Delany is not, however, addressing a problem solely restricted to Blacks. Events in our society or in our personal lives will force most of us at least occasionally to acknowledge a conflict between what we believe is true and what we observe as real.

The violence which erupts when a group recognizes their victimization and acts upon their questioning of their own and a dominant society's paradigms, is shown in the civil violence in the city of Bellona, which is destroyed from within both physically and socially. Bellona becomes a burnt-out city in which people must survive in a way different than they ever had before. Paul Fenster, who portrays a character similar to Martin Luther King, Jr., is assassinated by a man who feels so threatened by all society that he is not even sure that he killed Fenster. This white man, an army deserter, closely resembles James Earl Ray. He has found no place for himself in society and he strikes out against those he feels are beneath him. They must stay beneath him so that he can feel that he is superior to something which enhances his own self-image.

Despite the newspaper reporting, it is Fenster's assassination, not George's supposed rape of June, which precipitates the violence that destroys the metropolis of Bellona. George is representative of the desires of the Black Power movement of the sixties. He symbolizes their recognition that the Black man must regain his sexual, economic, political and social identity outside the identity imposed by the white society.

In *Dahlgren*, when Rev. Amy attempts to explain the phenomenon of the huge sun and the two moons, one of which has been named after George, the people reject her mythical explanations. Instead they choose a flesh and blood god, George, to believe in. They prefer to believe in one of themselves whom they can know and observe rather than accept the mystical which is unobservable. George is real and in this society the people have become aware that what they had conceived of as true simply does not apply in the world in which they find themselves living.

Nor is Calkins, the white liberal newspaperman, presented as a reliable source for a view of their city. He can be seen as a representative of our mass media which Delany attacks as hypocritical in its failure to acknowledge what is really happening in our time in our country. Calkins doesn't want to know, as is indicated by his refusal to read Kid's poems.

Notably it is Kid, a minority member himself, half Amerindian, half white, who observes and records what is really happening in the society. The society which he describes is not one of great social progress. The society has changed but not noticeably for the betterment of any group. The economics of Bellona, once founded on capitalism, has evolved into anarchy. Each person is left to his or her own devices to survive since there is apparently little transportation of goods into or out of the city and no one earns money. This results in people simply taking what they need. As Tak comments, most people find that they need surprisingly little.

The society which Kid describes includes a commune that lives in the park organizing numerous projects but seldom completing any; the Scorpions, a street gang which terrorizes the town to relieve their boredom because there is no meaningful or fulfilling work to do; people who still live in the Jackson ghetto; and middle class whites like the Richards who pretend that nothing has changed. There are no city services available.

Delany does not provide a resolution of the society's problems. He indicates that the society will continue to change by questioning what will happen when June finds George. However, he does not indicate how the society will change, only that a change will take place because two of the variables (June and George) will change, which will affect other variables (other citizens will react to June and George's actions). This is an indication of Delany's belief that societies change rather than progress.

Delany's examination of social paradigms is reinforced by his use of an apparently disoriented narrator, which creates the effect of multiple viewpoints. The reader at first doesn't know who the narrator is, nor does the narrator himself. He has periods of amnesia and little sense of chronological time, often telling about an incident twice and placing it in a different sequence of events each time. He suffers from topographical dislocations as well, seeing the sun rising in the wrong direction, describing the same bridge in varying locations.

There are various reasons suggested within the novel which could explain this unreliable narrator/protagonist. Kid could be an acid-head, his mind muddled by drugs—making perception of time, place and incident confused; he could be insane with the same result. Either condition could cause the physical attacks which Madame Brown calls anxiety attacks. Kid admits that he spent time in a mental hospital because of depression. Though superficially plausible, however, Delany seems to be using a more subtle cause for Kid's disorientation. By presenting the novel through the point of view of a multiple dyslexic with epilepsy, an individual whose brain works differently from what we suppose to be normal but not unintelligibly, Delany is able to take a fresh look at reality models.

Delany is himself a multiple dyslexic.[11] He has problems with right-left orientation, with visual reversal of letters and objects, with chronology of events, and with topographical disorientation. Although unable to remember the order of events, Delany is a keen observer of detail so that the incidents remain clear. All of these are symptoms similar to Kid's. Moreover, Delany has indicated that he purposefully created physical attacks resembling epilepsy prior to each of Kid's periods of amnesia.

Epilepsy has numerous effects depending on its location in the brain and its severity. It is not unusual for a person with epilepsy to have amnesia after a seizure. Not only will that person not remember the seizure, he may not remember what happens for minutes, hours or even days after the seizure, even though he will be capable of behaving "normally" during that period of time.

Kid exhibits left-right disorientation when he makes a wrong turn when leaving Tak's place and ends up on the other side of the street. Delany explains the effect of this type of dyslexia: "The whole tape of reality which he had been following had somehow overturned. It still continued; he still followed. But during some moment when he had blinked days had elapsed and everything right had shifted left: everything left was now right" (D, p. 432). This quote also indicates the time loss experienced by epileptics after a seizure. Two of many examples of sequence disorientation are the naming of months in the wrong order (D, p. 287) and more explicitly the narrator stating, "Rereading . . . I note the entries only ghost chronological order" (D, p. 759). Finally visual disorientation is shown by the reversal of letters in a word in Kid's journal: "This is the last full balnk [blank?] page left" (Delany's brackets, D, p. 759).

The epileptic interpretation is important in that it helps explain the long lapses of time that Kid doesn't remember and the physical actions which he cannot account for, such as suddenly having the orchid on his wrist without his remembering that he put it on. These periods of time cannot be accounted for as willful disrememberings, for, according to others, Kid's actions are very similar whether he remembers them or not. And these periods of amnesia also account for the four handwritings in the journal (D, p. 389). Since Kid is ambidextrous as noted on page one, the writings are different because he writes with his right and left hands when he is fully conscious of what he is doing, and writes in another manner with his right and left hands during periods of amnesia after a seizure.

More important than explaining Kid's behavior, however, the use of a dyslexic, epileptic narrator/protagonist allows Delany the opportunity to reveal the disorientation resulting from and involved in the problems which must be faced on a daily basis by minorities whose reality models differ from those of their dominant culture. It is also an attempt by Delany to break down the ethnocentricity and fear which we feel when our own reality models are questioned, when we perceive that there is a variance between what we have been taught is true and what we perceive is real.

Kid as criminal/artist/narrator presents a wholistic view of society which would not be possible through one viewpoint. And it would not be possible for Delany to explore the effects on the mind of a person who was experiencing the world from multiple viewpoints, nor to illustrate the effects of having multiple reality models at constant conflict with one another.

The multiple viewpoint technique which Delany chooses for this work is indicative of his concern for minority work. Kid writes in first and third person, often switching in mid-paragraph. A Black person suffers this same confusion: there I am in the white world, my actions defined by another culture, functioning as I must to survive. Somehow that imposed identity is partially removed from me. I have been taught that it is true, but I perceive that it is not real. I am different here within myself, but frequently in the white world, I am the only one who perceives that difference. I am the only one who agrees on the truth and reality of myself.

Delany's metafictional statements can be divided into two groups: those which explicate the novel *Dhalgren*, and those which discuss literature in general.

For most of the novel it is difficult for the reader to understand the identity of the narrator. This confusion over viewpoint is part of the disorienting effect which Delany creates to emphasize his theme.

Hints are given to the reader that Kid is the narrator in the opening chapter when a journal entry begins the same as the opening sentences of *Dhalgren* (pp. 1, 36), but neither the reader nor Kid knows for sure at this point that the author of the novel and of the journal are both Kid. Therefore the reader learns that the author of the journal is the narrator of the novel.

In section six Delany indicates that Kid is aware of the difficulties of writing dialogue which would not be an immediate concern of his as a poet: "(If I wrote her words down, Kid thought, what she's saying would vanish into something meaningless as the literal record of the sound June or George makes)" (D, p. 670). This is a metafictional statement in another sense because Kid is commenting on Lanya's statement which precedes this quote.

In an editor's note at the beginning of section seven, the journal is introduced as written by the author of *Brass Orchids*, establishing Kid as author of both the journal and a collection of poems. It is also in this section that Delany confirms that Kid has been the narrator of the text we're reading:

> Re-reading, I note the entries only ghost chronological order . . . .
> Sometimes I cannot tell who wrote what. That is upsetting. With some sections, I can remember the place and time I wrote them, but have no memory of the incidents described. Similarly, other sections refur [sic] to things I recall happening to me, but kne/o/w [sic] just as well I never wrote out. . . . Most annoying is when I recall an entry, go hunting through, and not find it [sic] find it or half of it not there. . .(D, p. 759).

There are many statements about literature in *Dhalgren*. Most of these metafictional statements are made through the characters of Newboy, Kid and Lanya.

Poetry is discussed in several contexts. Delany uses a novelist to comment on Kid's poetry, thereby commenting on one of the functions of poetry: ". . .watching your poems gain that effect showed me some of the reasons why my prose often doesn't. That condensed and clear descriptive insight is something I envy you. And you wield it as naturally as speech, turning it on this and that and the other . . ." (D, p. 671). Kid remarks that his poems are: ". . . not *descriptions* of anything. They're complex names" (D, p. 198). In a journal entry the relationship of viewpoint to poetry is discussed:

> Speech is always in excess of poetry as print is always inadequate for speech. A word sets images flying through the brain from which auguries we recall all extent and intention. I'm not a poet because I have nothing to give life to make it due, except my attention. And I don't know if my wounded sort is enough (D, pp. 783-4).

Delany comments on the process of writing when Kid comments

on the impossibility of totally retrieving an experience by writing it
down:

> Writing, he had not thought to retrieve any of it. But the prospect
> of publication had somehow convinced him magic was in
> process that would return to him, in *tacto* (not *memorium*), some
> of what the city had squandered. The conviction was now
> identified by its fraudulence, before the inadequate objects. But
> as it died ... he knew that it had been as real and unquestioned
> as any surround... (D, p. 558).

Through the narrator, Delany comments on the necessity of the
setting of Bellona for his novel: "There is no articulate resonance.
The common problem, I suppose, is to have more to say than
vocabulary and syntax can bear. That is why I am hunting in these
desiccated streets" (D, p. 84).

Newboy inundates Kid and the reader with his theories of the
process of writing. In his rather verbose monologue on pages 391
through 395, he defines two kinds of artists: one is committed to art;
the other, which he favors, is committed to life. Newboy also
rationalizes how his character traits of laziness, acrimoniousness
and lust for power make him a better poet. The thrust of these
statements is that the poet, to be effective, must value himself and
his relationships with his society.

Newboy describes the relationship between art and its audience
and questions its current relationship:

> The aesthetic equation .... The artist has some internal
> experience that produces a poem, a painting, a piece of music.
> Spectators submit themselves to the work, which generates an
> inner experience for them. But historically it's a very new, not to
> mention vulgar, idea that the spectator's experience should be
> identical to, or even have anything to do with, the artist's. The
> idea comes from an over-industrialized society which has
> learned to distrust magic— (D, p. 183).

In reference to the universality of art, Newboy questions Kid:
"have you hunkered down close to it, sighted through the lips of it
the juncture of your own humanity with that of the race?" (D, p. 288).
This is followed by a long description by Newboy of viewpoint,
illustrated by the labels of lens and prisms. Delany uses this method
of explaining to his readers the symbolic significance of the prisms
and lens so frequently mentioned in the Scorpions' chains. The lens
is described as a way of viewing things from a complex point of view.
The prism affords a multiplex point of view. Newboy speaks of the

wound which artists incur which never heals and claims that even without the complex and multiplex views of the world, the wound still would not heal, but "... that without it [the viewpoints] there plainly and starkly would have been nothing there; no, nothing at all" (D, p. 291).

Lanya describes three (self-perpetuating p. 50) systems—art, religion and psychiatry:

> All *three* of them promise you a sense of inner worth and meaning, and spend a lot of time telling you about the suffering you have to go through to achieve it. As soon as you get a problem in any one of them, the solution it gives is always to go deeper into the same system. They're all in a rather uneasy truce with one another in what's actually a mortal battle. Like all self-reinforcing systems. At best, each is trying to encompass the other two and define them as subgroups (D, p. 334).

The epigram, "You have confused the true and the real," indicates the paradigm which is questioned in *Dhalgren*. Kid, the narrator/criminal/artist, is the medium through which Delany discusses the role of the artist in society. Kid questions the reality models established by society. The struggle between what we believe is true and what we perceive as real is incorporated in the character Kid. Kid, as artist, observes and then records through his poems and journal. He questions his own sanity because of the differences between what he observes and what he has been taught is true. Through Kid, Delany urges the Wittgensteinian maxim that the metaphysical has only emotive force and that things must be observable to have meaning. The multiple viewpoints are an excellent example of the premise that style and content cannot be separated because the viewpoint influences the content of this novel and the content influences the viewpoint.

In *Triton* Bron is the central character, although it is the artist Spike who impels Bron's actions throughout the novel. Spike is a woman who writes, directs, produces and acts in mini-theater productions under a government grant. Her purpose is to awaken a person's self-recognition by use of a mild psychedelic and exposure to the beauty of a single unified moment of "verbal, spatial, and spiritual energy in resolution" (T, p. 88). She produces these brief dramas to make her audience question their own paradigms by contrasting that disorienting unified moment of beauty with themselves. Bron does experience that moment and he does question his paradigms: "It was as though, suddenly, I couldn't trust *any*thing" (T, p. 27). Unfortunately, instead of finding himself, Bron identifies with Spike. He tries to continue that moment of beauty by loving the one who produced it, rather than by valuing that part of himself which perceived it. When Spike rejects his love, he, in turn, rejects her rather than question himself. His decision to become a woman is based on his attempt to become a person whom Spike could love. What he never realizes is that a different sexual identity does not change all of him.

Bron is willing to change his sexual identity because he thinks it is easier to be a woman in his society. However, he is not willing to be truthful with himself. This is exemplified by his comments on lying to Audri. Bron constantly lied to himself before his sexual change, but he never recognized that he did. He is amazed that now that he is a woman he is lying to others. The fallacy of Bron's action is symbolized by the metalogics to which he subscribes. If Bron is P and all else is not P, then to find an equivalent for P is an impossibility. If P becomes something else, then the problem changes but it still does not afford a solution to the original problem. The problem with the metalogic approach is that it too rigidly adheres to cause and effect. That is, there is no consideration for the interactions of each part of the whole on each other. Each part is simultaneously cause and effect of each other part which is itself, simultaneously cause and effect on another, and so forth. Metalogically, Bron's decision to become a woman should have solved his problem. However, he failed to recognize that the variables, through interaction on each other, would change when he (P) changed himself.

Delany, as artist, questions many of the paradigms of our society in *Triton*: wars which kill civilians rather than soldiers— Vietnam; an economic system where citizens who need help are humiliated—our welfare system; and sexual persecution against women, bisexuals and homosexuals. Delany accomplishes this by contrasting Bron's society with that of earth's which has remained much as it is presently. The work is not a statement against homosexuality or bisexuality. It is a statement on the necessity of knowing one's self despite sexual identification, that one's sexual identity is not one's total identity.

Delany restricts his metafictional comments to the appendixes. In Appendix A, titled "From the Triton Journal: Work Notes and Omitted Pages," Delany discusses the "encounter between objects-that-are-words" and "processes-made-manifest-by-words" which he states are "as complex as the constantly dissolving interface between culture and language itself" (T, p. 334). He also discusses the metonymy of science fiction, pointing out that a metonomic analysis does not reveal the functions of science fiction. He states that because of the science element in sf, sentences are possible which have different meanings or which would have no meaning in mundane fiction, thus creating new possibilities of style for the writer:

> Because the added sentences in science fiction *are* primarily foreground sentences, the relationship between foreground and background in science fiction differs from that of mundane fiction. The deposition of weight between landscape and psychology shifts. The deployment of these new sentences within the traditional S-F frame of "the future" not only generates the obviously new panoply of possible fictional incidents; it generates as well an entirely new set of rhetorical stances: the future-views-the-present forms one axis against which these stances may be plotted; the alien-views-the-familiar forms the other (T, pp. 338-9).

Another metafictional comment included twice in this section is: "Everything in a science fiction novel should be mentioned at least twice (in at least two different contexts)" (T, p. 333).

Delany summarizes his preference for the genre of science fiction:

> I feel the science-fictional-enterprise is richer than the enterprise of mundane fiction. It is richer through its extended repertoire of sentences, its consequent greater range of possible incident, and through its more varied field of rhetorical and syntagmic organization (T, p. 340).

Appendix B, titled "Ashima Slade and the Harbin-Y Lectures: Some Informal Remarks toward the Modular Calculus, Part Two," appears to be either a section discarded from the novel or at least notes relating to the relationship of characters and motivation of the artist Spike. In this section Delany discusses a character, Slade, and his/her theories of modular calculus, which relate to art. Delany is also discussing his own theory of art. One fundamental of Slade's philosophy is:

> belief in the absolute distinction between the expression of "process/relation/operation" on the one hand and the expression of "matter/material/substance" on the other for rational clarity, as established by the contemporary episteme; as well as a belief in their absolute and indeserverable interface, in the real Universe .... This interface will remain **indeseverable** as long as time is irreversible. Indeed, we can

only model the elements on either side separably with those tools—memory, thought, language, art—by which we can also construct models of reversible time (T, p. 349).

Delany continues to discuss, through Slade, the relationships between the "psychologic, the logical and the political" (T, p. 357). The modular calculus theory is then applied to the five senses and the relationships between how the body receives the impressions from the objects (system B) and transmits them to the brain (system A). There are material models which can be tasted, touched or smelt. There are reflected-wave models of which sight is a primary example, and there are generated-wave models which can only be heard. Delany states that all three model types, once they reach the brain, become generated-wave models:

In other words, sound is the *modular form* of *all* information *within* the nervous system, itself, and that includes smell, taste, touch and sight. The poet Valery once said, "All art aspires to the condition of music." Yes, and so does everything else (T, p. 362).

From this discussion of models, Delany inserts: "Slade talks about the efficiency of multiple modeling systems, or parallel models, over linear, or series models" (T, p. 363). And it is evident that Delany uses multiple viewpoints in his works to create multiple models rather than linear models.

Finally, Delany describes the advantages of modular as opposed to nonmodular descriptions:

A modular description allows us reference routes back to the elements in the situation which is being modeled. A nonmodular description is nonmodular precisely because, complete or incomplete as it may be, it destroys those reference routes: it is, in effect, a cipher (T, pp. 368-9).

The emphasis on the role of the artist, metafictional comments, and the qualities of the artist in Delany's fiction has left little space for exploration of many aspects of importance: his poetic lyricism, his recurrent images and symbols, his use of myth and the quest motif. Several of these areas have already received critical attention, especially in reference to individual novels.[13] With the expansion of sf commentary, Delany's works will undoubtedly receive further critical attention.

Notes

[1] All references are to the paperback editions. In original publication order, the editions I cite and the abbreviations I use are as follows: *The Jewels of Aptor* (Ace, 1962), JA; *The Fall of the Towers* (Ace, 1970) FT; *The Ballad of Beta-2* (Ace, 1965) BB-2; *Empire Star* (Ace, 1966) ES; *Babel-17* (Ace, 1966) B-17; *The Einstein Intersection* (Ace, 1967) EI; *Nova* (Bantam, 1969) N; *Tides of Lust* (Lancer, 1973) TL; *Dhalgren* (Bantam, 1975) D; and *Triton* (Bantam, 1976) T.

[2] Douglas Barbour, "Multiplex Misdemeanors: The Figures of the Artist and the Criminal in Samuel R. Delany's SF Novels," in *Khatru 2* ed. Jeffrey D. Smith (Baltimore: Phantasmicon Press Publication No. 39, May 1975), pp. 21-24, 60.

[3] Barbour, p. 22.

[4] Mark Rose, ed., *Science Fiction* (Englewood Cliffs, N.J.: Prentice-Hall, 1976), p. 3.

[5] Samuel R. Delany, "About Five Thousand One Hundred and Seventy-Five Words," in Thomas D. Clareson, ed. *SF: The Other Side of Realism* (Bowling Green, Ohio: Bowling Green University Popular Press, 1971), p. 140.

[6] Claude Levi-Strauss, *The Raw and the Cooked* trans. J. and D. Weightman (New York: Harper & Row, 1969), pp. 17-8.

[7] Sigmund Freud, *Totem and Taboo* trans. A.A. Brill (New York: New Republic, 1927), p. 135.

[8] Levi-Strauss, p. 14.

[9] Edmund D. Cohen, *C.G. Jung and the Scientific Attitude* (New York: Philosophical Library, 1975), pp. 33-35.

[10] Personal interview with Delany, New York City, July 14, 1978.

[11] Ibid.   [12] Ibid.

[13] A partial bibliography includes:

Alterman, Peter S. "The Surreal Translations of Samuel R. Delany," in *Science Fiction Studies* 4 (March 1977): 25-34.

Barbour, Douglas, "Multiplex Misdemeanors: The Figures of the Artist and the Criminal in the Science Fiction Novels of Samuel R. Delany," in *Khatru*, No. 2, 1975, Ed. Jeffrey D. Smith, Baltimore, Md., pp. 21-4, 60.

Barbour, Douglas, "Samuel R. Delany and the Parts of Fiction," in *Khatru*, No. 5, 1976. Ed. Jeffrey D. Smith, Baltimore, Md. pp. 10-22.

Clareson, Thomas D., "Notes on 'Driftglass'," in *Spectrum of Worlds*, ed. Thomas D. Clareson, New York: Doubleday, 1972.

Gardiner, H. Jane. "Images of *The Waste Land* in Delany's *The Einstein Intersection*, in *Extrapolation* 18, May 1977: pp. 116-123.

Miesel, Sandra, "Samuel R. Delany's Use of Myth in *Nova*," in *Extrapolation*, 12 (May 1971):— pp. 86-93.

Samuelson, David. "New Wave, Old Ocean: A Comparative Study of Novels by Brunner and Delany," in *Extrapolation*, 15, (Dec. 1973), 75-96.

Naturalism, Aestheticism and Beyond: Tradition and Innovation in the Work of Thomas M. Disch

Thomas L. Wymer

In *The American Shore* Samuel Delany devoted a full book to the study of a single short story by Thomas Disch.[1] Although this proportion of criticism to a literary text may seem extreme, the fact remains that Disch is unusual among sf writers in the degree to which he rewards close reading. But the rewards are often mixed. John Clute calls Disch "perhaps the most respected, least trusted, most envied and least read of all modern sf writers of the first rank." Clute offers an impressive list of attributes to account for this conclusion: "his intellectual audacity, the distanced coldness of his sometimes mannerist narrative art, the arduous demands he makes upon the reader of genre sf, the austerity of the pleasures he affords and the fine cruelty of his wit."[2]

These are attributes which one would suppose would have attracted the attention of more serious readers and critics, especially the academics interested in sf, but Disch seems to have intimidated not only the readers of genre sf but academics as well. Aside from Delany's book, there are only the relatively short articles, largely laudatory, in the encyclopedias (see especially Clute's entry in *The Science Fiction Encyclopedia* and Erich Rupprecht's in *Dictionary of Literary Biography)*[3] and the introtions to the Gregg Press editions of *The Early Science Fiction of Thomas M. Disch, The Genocides* and *334.*[4] The pages of the major academic sf journals, *Extrapolation* and even *Science-Fiction Studies*, biased as it is toward the more intimidating of sf writers, are innocent of any but passing references to Disch.

Anyone attempting a study of Disch will find very quickly why there has been so little close study. What Clute calls his "distanced coldness," "the fine cruelty of his wit," points to pervasive irony and ambiguity, which are central to why he is the "least trusted" of major sf writers. One knows not quite where to have him. Like

186

Joyce's dramatic artist, he "remains within or behind or beyond or above his handiwork, invisible, refined out of existence, indifferent, paring his fingernails."[5] Such an artist does not necessarily defy analysis, but he certainly makes it difficult.

The richness and complexity of Disch's work, therefore, precludes any adequate study of the whole of his work, even the whole of his major works, except in a book-length study. For the purposes of this discussion, therefore, I will concentrate on two of Disch's novels, an early one, *The Puppies of Terra*, and a middle one, *Camp Concentration*, the second and fourth of his total of six sf novels to date. Others of his novels, expecially the first, *The Genocides*, and the third, *Echo Round His Bones*, will be briefly discussed along the way. In the process I hope to show that Disch has wedded sf to the strongest traditions of the mainstream of Western literature. Playing off of the assumptions and cliches of pulp sf, he portrays modern man in a vision shaped by that combination of Naturalism and aestheticism which has characterized modern fiction, together with the more contemporary tradition of fabulation, fiction which, as Robert Scholes describes it, "offers us a world clearly and radically discontinuous from the one we know, yet returns to confront that known world in some cognitive way."[6]

All these characteristics are apparent in Disch's first novel, *The Genocides* (1965). Playing off of the pulp tradition, it is an alien invasion story in which humans are exterminated like so many bugs by aliens of vast technological superiority who are using our earth for agricultural purposes: they have sown the entire land area of the planet with a plant that in a few years grows to a height of 600 feet, crowding out all flora and fauna in the process. Unlike the standard alien invasion story, humans neither come to an understanding with nor defeat the aliens. Unlike both the alien invasion story and the other variations of planet-wide catastrophe—nuclear war, ecological disaster or planetary collision—the last survivors do not emerge as the perpetuators of a chastened but stronger humanity. Unlike even the more ominous admonitory stories of nuclear or ecological catastrophe which portray human extermination in an effort to warn us of what we can yet change, Disch's story offers no suggestion that mankind could have survived by doing anything different. In short, Disch violates what had been a central tradition of pulp sf by presenting an ultimate problem that simply has no solution—notwithstanding Tom Godwin's classic, "The Cold Equations," which presents a much more limited problem without a solution.

As David Hartwell points out in his introduction to the Gregg edition of *Genocides*, this technique of presenting problems without solutions identified Disch to his first readers with the New Wave and writers like J.G. Ballard, and it roused the ire of sf traditionalists like Algys Budrys. In an early review Budrys disparaged the novel as a type of what he called "the inertial science-fiction novel,"[7] a type opposed to "the school" he approved, "science fiction which takes hope in science and in Man."[8]

But the novel is not simply a reaction to the sf tradition; it is a revival of Naturalism. With all the rigor of an experimental novel by Zola, Disch lays down his premises—the vast technological superiority, the agricultural purposes and the indifference to humanity of the aliens and the cast of ordinary middle American human beings struggling to survive as individuals and as a community in an impossible situation. With merciless honesty and an ironic sense of grinding inevitability, he works out the consequences of these givens as the community and most of its individuals disintegrate under the strain. The novel ends in the spring with symbols of rebirth ironically abounding and with the last survivors forming ironic painterly groups. The first is a man, woman and infant who form "a sort of Holy Family," although the woman is weeping and the infant is "futilely pulling at her dry breast." The last is a naked man and woman, "certainly ... Adam and Eve before the Fall," but in this case the two are not the first but the last human beings.

The Puppies of Terra is a novel with a somewhat complicated genesis. Its first version was a novella, "White Fang Goes Dingo," written in 1962 but not published until 1965 (in *Worlds of If*). By the following year Disch had expanded and published it as a novel (half of an Ace double) under the title supplied by an editor, *Mankind Under the Leash*. In subsequent editions Disch's preferred title, *The Puppies of Terra*, has been restored. But *Puppies* has generally been neglected in Disch criticism, partly because Disch himself, in the introduction to *One Hundred and Two H-Bombs* (1966), referred to the stories in that collection, which included the novella "White Fang Goes Dingo," as attempts at being "clown funny," not serious: "Stories that are intended to be funny are seldom intended, in the same breath, to be wholly serious. Of course, it can be done—Swift, Joyce, Genet have each proven that—and when it comes off, nothing, not even darkest tragedy, can be funnier. But *I* haven't tried it, not here, not yet."[9] John Clute seems to echo these words when he dismisses *Puppies* as Disch's "second (and rather minor) novel"[10] But Disch was speaking of the novella, not the novel, and the novel, I will try to show, comes rather closer to that ideal of the comically serious. Indeed its theme, a kind of portrait of the artist as a young dog, derives much from Joyce and the aesthetic tradition that shaped him.

The major thematic concerns of *Puppies* are announced in the last two lines of its extended title, written in the eighteenth century manner:

> Being a True and Faithful Account
> of the
> Great Upheavals of 2037;
> With Portraits of Many of the Principals Involved;
> as well as Reflections by the Author
> on the Nature of Art, Revolution & Theology[11]

The thematic concern of the novel most obvious to sf readers is the second in this list, "Revolution"; it is a novel about freedom, about revolt against the dominance of alien invaders, about the hero's choice between a comfortable slavery as the coddled pet of a vastly superior alien being and the life of a normal human being.

Puppies is almost as obviously a novel about theology. The alien Masters are godlike; their "substance" is neither matter nor energy; they are nearly omnipotent, nearly omniscient: "Like Jehova in his earlier, more anthropomorphic days, it was no problem for them to take over the management of Earth .... [They are] unaccountable. One could only accept them, reverence them, and hope for the best" (p. 213). And that best is the Leash, what White Fang can only describe as "their touch." Though what the Leash is remains a mystery, its effects are very like those of a mystical experience: "... the tides of knowledge that sweep through the mind; the sense of being in communion with the most transcendental forces, of being a spoke from the hub about which the universe is spinning; the total *certainty* that it affords; the ecstasy and the consuming love" (p. 213). Moreover, the experience of the Leash is "like the state of grace": "it came as a gift or not at all" (p. 214).

But if the order of the list in the extended title, "Reflections ... on the Nature of Art, Revolution & Theology," is of any importance, the novel is most especially about art. Indeed, the "kennels" in which human pets are bred are aesthetic paradises. The grounds may vary, from Shroeder Kennel on Earth, with its "acres of English landscape gardening and playing fields" spread around the central feature of "a reconstruction, perfect in every detail, of the

Cathedral of St. John the Divine in New York City" (p. 215), to Swan
Lake Kennel, a collection of "twelve smallish asteroids ... artfully
woven into a sort of celestial clockwork" among which the pets could
soar accompanied by ever changing music, "the single composition
of that composer which most suited our velocity, trajectory,
idiorythmic motion and mood" (p. 231). At the end of the novel,
Tennyson White, White Fang's father, considers writing his
memoirs, for which he has already picked the title, *The Esthetic
Revolution*. This title is doubly appropriate, since White, the leader
of the revolution, is himself a literary artist, while the Masters
constitute "a society that valued art above all things else" (p. 200); it
is a war of art against art. In the end the Masters are driven out by
the transmission of the brain waves of our aesthetically sensitive
hero, recorded while his senses were being deliberately assaulted by
every ugliness his friends could subject him to. In short, the aliens
are defeated by bad taste.

The aesthetic theme is carried out amid a virtuoso flood of
allusions to art, especially to the nineteenth century aesthetic
movement. Swan Lake Kennel, for example, aside from the obvious
allusion to Tchaikovsky, is described as exemplifying "the old
Romantic idea of a synthesis of the arts: the same that inspired
Wagner's Bayreuth or Diaghilev's *Ballets Russes*" (p. 232), or, we
might add, Coleridge's "Kubla Khan" or Tennyson's "The Palace of
Art"; the fact that the kennels are enclosed by "domes" might in
itself recall the "pleasure dome" in Coleridge's poem, the archetypal
Romantic aesthetic paradise. A major climax of the novel is an
escape from a prison in which the prisoners use a play production to
distract the guards. The play is a comic version of the story of
Salome, a figure enshrined, Disch reminds us, in "Matthew and
Mark and Wilde and Hoffmansthal—and in the Rita Hayworth
movie" (p. 295), and, we might add, in the poetry of Mallarme and
the paintings of Gustav Moreau, both of which inspired Huysmans
as well as Wilde. Salome is, in fact, the consummate *femme fatale* of
the aesthetic movement.

There are also minor themes in the novel dear to the aesthetic
tradition: incest (White Fang discovers that his mother's consort is
his own half brother), sadomasochism (White Fang's sometime
teacher, Roxanna Proust, is a masochist whom we first see in the
cathedral of Shroeder Kennel piously reading from a book that turns
out to be the fourth and most overtly sadomasochistic volume of *La
Recherche du Temps Perdu*), and attacks on Philistinism (the
Dingoes, the humans who are not pets either by their own choice or
because the Masters found them undesirable, are types of the

insensitive masses indifferent or opposed to art: "the groundlings, the Great Unwashed, the stinking rabble" [p. 294].)

But more important is the way Disch uses the aesthetic tradition to unite the major themes of revolution and theology. Freedom, both artistic and spiritual and sometimes political, is a central concern of the aesthetic tradition, often explored as Disch does in the context of a tempting aesthetic paradise that is also a prison. The archetypal aesthetic victim of this situation is the medieval knight Tannhauser, imprisoned in the Venusberg, the mountain of Venus. This story fascinated the likes of Swinburne, Wagner and Beardsley, and there is at least one overt reference to Wagner's *Tannhauser* in *Puppies*.

The issue of sexual freedom is an important dimension of the theme of freedom which further links the novel with Tannhauser, who is a slave to Venus' sexual allure, and with the aesthetic movement in general, preoccupied as it was with the conflict between sexual freedom and guilty fear of the body. Part of what makes the kennels a paradise is that pets are normally naked— unless some special occasion calls for costume—and they are encouraged to express themselves sexually as soon, as often and as freely as they desire. Moreover, White Fang, like Tannhauser, suffers temptation and guilt, for he loves his prison. Indeed, his separation from his Master's control is associated with a reenactment of the Fall as his wife, "Darling, Julie," plucks an apple and offers it to him.

Theological questions are likewise parts of the aesthetic tradition, most especially the use of religious images for purely aesthetic purposes. White Fang's mother leaves him with the aid of their Master, reproducing the religious event of the Assumption: "... wreathed in baroque spires of light like a Bernini Madonna, she ascended into the clear blue sky of October" (p. 216). Roxanna worships in the reproduction of St. John's Cathedral, reading from the gospel according to Proust (p. 215). This situation and Disch's play with the Leash recall the tendency in aestheticism to confuse, and often to replace, the religious experience with the aesthetic experience, indeed to think of art as the new religion which will replace the outmoded forms of traditional religions (cf. Matthew Arnold, Wallace Stevens, and many others). Moreover, in its attack on middle class values, aestheticism often reduces religious devotion to aesthetic affectation; in this regard Roxanna is a comic cousin of Flaubert's Madame Bovary.

Disch's elaborate play with the aesthetic tradition is not, however, simply a virtuoso performance; his purpose is to raise again in the context of sf some of the fundamental questions about literary art: the place of the purely aesthetic, the relation between art and society, the function of the artist.

Like early Victorian artists such as Tennyson and Browning, Disch clearly recognizes both the attractiveness and the ultimate insufficiency of the purely aesthetic life. White Fang thoroughly enjoys his life as a pet, loves his satin chains and might have remained a willing pet forever if it had not been for an accident: "a solar prominence of extraordinary intensity had erupted from the center of a sunspot cluster and knocked the Masters out of commission" (p. 259), a state of affairs that lasts for over a month. During this time White Fang, in company with his Darling, Julie, is gradually able to discover the advantages of being his own person: first there are satisfactions like providing for his family and playing Prometheus in his discovery of fire. His progress is delayed when he is captured by Dingoes trying to take advantage of his Masters' absence and launch a revolution; he thus discovers the ugliness, violence and irrationality of normal human life, a prospect that makes the Leash seem more attractive. But he escapes and finds himself masquerading as an inspecting officer in a Dingo prison camp where "liberated" pets are being kept. There he learns how ill prepared pets are for any but a totally dependent life. In a comic parody of a concentration camp, the ovens that White Fang thinks are used for extermination turn out to be used only for baking bread; the fewer than 120 guards are able to keep 13,000 pets confined not because the guards are so ruthlessly efficient but because the pets are so utterly helpless without their Masters; prisoners are nearly starving not because food is being withheld but because the prisoners themselves are unwilling to gather and prepare the abundant foods available in nearby abandoned farms.

Though pure aestheticism is thus exposed as impractical in the real world, it is also exposed as deficient in its own world. Though the Masters' domes are aesthetically pleasing, they are literally lacking in substance. White Fang discovers that one of the columns of St. John's Cathedral in Shroeder Kennel is "cool and tingly, reminding me that what here seemed to be stone was in fact much less substantial: an immensely strong force-field with a skin of matter only one molecule thick" (p. 217). Appropriately enough, therefore, architectural design is divorced from both structure and function: "It was this stagey method of construction (... though ... the stagecraft was consummate) that made 'architecture' a matter of indifference to the Masters. Under such conditions munificence was taken for granted, and taste became the sole consideration" (p. 217).

The effects of so narrow a view of beauty are apparent not only in the dissolution of all the Masters' constructions during their absence but in the literary "art" produced by the pets. Revealing his own want of taste, White Fang describes as noble "A Prayer of Investments," a poem composed by his brother; one of its three stanzas should illustrate its quality:

(Investment of the Ring)

Navy Blue Buttons
Soft black pus
Dark gold ochre
Blacky black black (p. 288)

Toward the end of the novel when White Fang speaks with his father, Tennyson White points out that the coming of the Masters has led to the near demise of art on Earth (p. 313), a fact that White Fang agrees is true of Dingoes but not of pets. Yet all we see of their productions reveals that both Masters and pets are really capable only in the performing arts, in dance and song, and little of their work is really original or creative: their best work—and here Disch's use of allusions can especially be seen as thematically functional—is highly derivative, indeed only imitations of past masters, and their great strength, like that of the intellectually and artistically arid stage of most of the nineteenth century, is spectacle, or, as we saw in St. John's Cathedral, "stagecraft." In fact, the only works of art we are led to really respect are by the rebel Tennyson White, works which provide some answers to those traditional questions, the function of art and its relation to society.

Tennyson White was an unusual puppy. Among the first of the pets, he was given an education which is compared to that of John Stuart Mill, and was raised by "one of the first truly great breeders" (p. 208). At the age of twenty he was discovered to have leukemia, a disease his Master could easily have cured, but in breeding circles "it was considered *unsporting* to tamper with basic genetic materials" (p. 208). While the Masters debated the issue in their version of a kennel club (they later decided to permit his cure), White was sent to an inferior hospital on Earth where, "haunted by the knowledge that his life or death was nothing but a sporting proposition to the Masters, he conceived of his great novel, *A Dog's Life*" (p. 209). Set in the nineteenth century and told from the point of view of a real dog, the novel was an allegory with the apparent effect of reconciling men and their Masters, making it "a point of pride to be a pet: to be

domesticated was self-evidently a superior state than to be wild"
(pp. 209-210). In fact, however, as White Fang learns later:

> His novel was a time-bomb disguised as an Easter egg and planted right
> in the middle of the Master's basket; it was a Trojan horse; it was a slow-
> working acid that nibbled at the minds of the pets—just a mild aesthetic
> tickle at first, then it worked in deeper, an abrasive that scarred them
> with guilt (p. 318).

In short, far from being a purely aesthetic production, *A Dog's LIfe*
was a subversive novel shaped to promulgate a thesis: "men, in the
last analysis, are not meant to be domestic animals" (p. 318).

The artistic ideal suggested here involves an element that will
be apparent in most of Disch's subsequent work, a social mission.
The references, however, to slow-working acid and a scarring
abrasive suggest that the mission is not to propagandize for a
particular answer but to write after the manner of modern
subversive literature, which Hazel Barnes, referring to Sartre,
describes in *The Literature of Possibility: A Study in Humanistic
Existentialism:*

> The function of literature, he claims, is to lead society to reflect upon
> itself. "Through literature, the collectivity turns to reflection and
> meditation; it acquires an unhappy consciousness, an unstable image of
> itself which it forever seeks to modify and improve." Thus the purpose of
> those writers whom Sartre approves is to change the world.[12]

Or as White Fang puts it, "Many authors have been accused of
corrupting youth and debasing the moral coinage of their times.
Probably none has ever set about so deliberately as Daddy" (p. 318).
Of course, "corrupting" and "debasing" are used ironically here, for
White's purpose was to undermine a corrupt social and moral
system.

And White does change the world, but in a way that reveals both
the power and limitations of art. First of all, the great mass of the
pets who read the novel misunderstood it:

> Those who stood the acid-test of that novel managed to escape to Earth
> and join the Dingoes .... Those who didn't (and sadly, these were by far
> the majority) stayed with the Masters and incorporated the monstrous
> satire of *A Dog's Life* into the fabric of their daily lives. They became
> dogs (p. 318).

In other words, like most of the great satirists, White suffered from
having his irony largely misread. His second novel, *The Life of Man*,
helped somewhat to correct this misconception. White Fang
describes its effect on him:

It begins with the same high and dry irony, the same subdued wit, but gradually—it's hard to say just when—the viewpoint shifts. Scenes from the first novel are repeated *verbatim*, but now its pleasantries have become horrors. Allegory gives way to a brutal, damning realism, and every word of it seemed an accusation aimed directly at me. (p. 317)

And its effect on most of its readers: "it showed the Dingoes what they were: an amorphous mass of discontent, without program or purpose; a race what had taken the fir,t step toward its own extinction" (p. 319).

But while most of the pets misread the first novel, most of the Dingoes, to whom the second novel was directed, didn't read it at all: "Only the more thoughtful read this second novel—and they didn't need to." The conclusion is inevitable: "Daddy gradually came to see that no amount of literature would spark the tinder of the Dingoes into a revolutionary firebrand" (p. 319). White, therefore, became a demagogue, invented a mythology and a religion built around electricity, wrote slogans and propaganda instead of poetry, and with the help of his son finally saved the world.

The conclusions we are to draw from this resolution about the place of art and the function of the artist are not made specific, although a number may be inferred both from the novel and from Disch's subsequent practice. First, although art has a social mission, that mission is clearly distinguished from politics. Whereas politics, even in a good cause, offers slogans, half-truths and outright lies in order to galvanize a disparate group into unified action, art tells—or at least aspires to telling—the truth, shows the Dingoes what they are, and speaks to the individual. Its function is limited, however, in part by its technique—the corrosive, subversive manner described by Sartre—in part by its effect—revealing the individual to himself—and in part by its audience—the thoughtful minority both willing and able to explore themselves. Such seems to have been Disch's practice in subsequent major works: *Echo Round His Bones* and *Camp Concentration*, novels of the late 1960s, exposed the major problems of the time, the cultural and intellectual patterns behind war; *334* and *On Wings of Song*, novels of the mid to late 1970s, explored in broader terms the cultural and social patterns that have been undermining the American dream.

But art functions also aesthetically. It is crucial to White Fang's development that he is able, finally, to have an aesthetic experience unaided by the Leash. And its occurrence is linked directly to the discovery of how to defeat the Masters.

Driven from a stadium by the repulsive sight of the senseless brutality of a boxing match, White Fang wanders alone into a park:

> A full moon shone overhead, like the echo of a thousand poems. All the Earthbound poets who had stolen the fire of their lyrics from that moon, age after age! It has passed them by, oblivious of histories, and it would pass me by in time. That's the way that things should be, I thought. The leaves should fall in autumn, snow in winter, grass springs up in spring, and the summer is brief.
> I knew then that I belonged to the Earth, and my spirit dilated with happiness. It wasn't quite the right time to be happy—but there it was. Julie and the moon were part of it, but it was also the frogs croaking, the poplars, the stadium; Daddy, cynical, aspiring, even defeated; partly too, it was Bruno and Roxanna, if only because they were so vital. These things melted into my memory of the farmhouse, and it seemed that I could smell the winy smell of apples rotting in the grass. (pp. 324-325)

This experience unites an understanding of change, embodied in images of the seasons, and an acceptance of the diversity of life, embodied in images ranging from the moon to frogs and rotten apples, combined in an aura of happiness and beauty. The fact that the experience is essentially aesthetic is confirmed by the appearance of White Fang's Master, who felt the young man's happiness and interpreted it as a call. White Fang, however, refuses the Leash and drives the Master away by continuing to concentrate on a frog, now being slowly devoured by a snake. This horrifying image, enhanced by a description of the beginning of the snake's digestive processes on the half-swallowed frog struggling vainly to escape, provides both a literal key to the ultimate defeat of the Masters and a symbolic key to what constitutes a proper aesthetic experience for Disch: it must be based on an inclusive and honest view of life, one that celebrates the whole of life. That which is traditionally considered ugly, far from being antithetical to art, in fact redeems it from triviality.

This view of the aesthetic and social functions of art seems consistent with the mainstream of modern fiction, with its combination, especially typfied by Joyce, of the traditions of Naturalism, with its rigorous honesty, its refusal to neglect the unpleasant truths of life, and of aestheticism, with its concern for beauty of language and structure. Certainly in his next two novels— *Echo Round His Bones* and *Camp Concentration*—most successfully in the second, Disch exhibits an effort, in the words of Stephen Daedalus, "to forge in the smithy of my soul the uncreated conscience of my race."[13] Important differences, however, apart from ultimate artistic greatness, whatever Disch's may be, remain between Disch and Joyce in the directions the efforts of each took. Disch seems to become more involved socially and less esoteric artistically. The greater social involvement apparent in the next two novels is also apparent in differences between the artists in Joyce's

Portrait and in Disch's *Puppies*. Whereas Stephen Daedalus moves from his father and from a restrictive, repressive, Philistine social community to the artistic freedom of exile, White Fang moves from an isolated and aimless aesthetic freedom into social involvement in becoming a key part of his father's revolution, a direction that seems to reflect Disch's own concerns. Moreover, Disch continues to write in a popular literary form, science fiction, although his approach to that form remains rigorously and uniquely his own.

Echo Round His Bones (1967) is a novel that has experienced even more neglect than *Puppies*. It appears in no Gregg Press edition; indeed although there have been two British editions[14], it has yet to be reprinted in America. Nevertheless it represents a significant achievement in its own right, while it begins to explore themes that will be central to *Camp Concentration*, themes concerning war, militarism, genocide and, more fundamental, man's alienation from his world. Indeed, Captain Nathan Hansard is described as being in conflict with the "Steel Womb," an instantaneous matter transmitter with some crucial side effects, "with the military establishment ... with society in general, ... with himself, [and with] the nature of reality itself."[15]

The conflict with reality develops questions which have been raised earlier. *The Genocides* ended with an explanation of the symbolic meaning of the journey the characters had made through the root system of the giant trees, "a long passage through the labyrinthine windings of their own, purely human evils." Upon emerging, however, they "were not aware of the all-pervading presence of the larger evil that lies without, which we call reality" (p. 141). In *The Genocides* that larger evil cannot be changed. In *Puppies*, however, Disch played in a comical-serious vein with an evil of external reality which the central characters do succeed in changing, and in doing so Disch sets up a question that reveals why he is in Scholes' terms a fabulator, why he writes in the genre of sf.

Disch writes out of the Naturalistic and aesthetic traditions we have described as typified in Joyce, yet he writes during the neoromantic period of the 1960s, a period of acute social consciousness and hope that the world could change, attitudes that Disch shares—or at least shared in the 1960s. Whereas for Joyce the union of Naturalism and aestheticism meant the effort to create beauty out of a rigorously honest depiction of reality, to transmute "the daily bread of experience into the radiant body of everliving life,"[16] Disch adds to this the effort to suggest models of what could be. Indeed, even Joyce, who is more of a romantic than many give him credit for being, suggested such a purpose in Stephen Daedalus: "How could he hit their conscience or how cast his shadow over the imaginations of their daughters, before their squires begat upon them, that they might breed a race less ignoble than their own?"[17] In exploring such a question, Disch explores in *Echo* the possibility dear to the sf tradition of a solution to the larger evil we call reality.

The problem to be solved is summed up in the Steel Womb, a central symbol of reality itself, both its limitations and its possibilities for change. The matter transmitter is first linked with a social and political dimension of reality by its having been expropriated by the government, especially the military, in order to be used to transport nuclear weapons and the personnel necessary to deploy and fire them. Rather than ensuring peace, however, America's exclusive possession of this device, providing the possibility of ending the cold war in victory, is too much of a temptation for the leaders in 1990. Our hero Captain Hansard is the courier carrying the orders to Mars base to fire its nuclear arms in six weeks time. The Steel Womb has another effect, however, which Hansard discovers when he is sent to Mars; for as he departs he discovers a second, a kind of shadow self, an "echo," still dwelling like a ghost on Earth within a second reality, a sub-level of being invisible to all except the echo selves of those who have likewise passed through the transmitter.

These features of the transmitter Disch exploits in interesting ways. On Mars both the original Hansard, Hansard Sub-One, Disch calls him, and his commanding officer General Pittman seem to be strangely affected, either by their passage through the transmitter or by their realization of the brutal and self-destructive reality that sent them to Mars. Pittman, an intellectual and poet, is overwhelmed by the destructive responsibility placed in his hands. He feels a numbing sense of soullessness, "As though of hemlock I had drunk," he thinks, remembering Keats' "Ode to a Nightingale." Indeed, reduced to ultimate nihilism he becomes more than "half in love with easeful death" as he contemplates the nuclear firing button: "Oh, I want to, I want to. I want to push it *now*" (p. 86). Hansard's reaction is similar, though not so extreme: he feels "as though ... he had lost some essential, if intangible, part of himself. A soul perhaps, though he didn't exactly believe he had one" (p. 109).

Back in the echo world on Earth, Bernard Panofsky Sub-Two, the echo of the inventor of the transmitter, justifies the suicides of several of his sub-two versions (for Panofsky Sub-One has passed through the transmitter many times, each time producing an echo self) on the grounds that he is without a soul, a mere epiphenomenon. In fact, however, Panofsky in all his versions epitomizes the effects of the modern world. Born in Poland in 1929, his youth was spent in Nazi labor camps. "Liberated" after the war, most of his middle years were spent behind the Iron Curtain until the late 1960s when he escaped to the West. When his invention was revealed in the early 1980s, he immediately became a prisoner again, this time of America for the sake of national security. With such a background, he has developed what he calls a concentration-camp philosophy: "it's best not to think too much about the future. Just try to get along from day to day" (p. 82); "one just tries to do the best one can, from day to day, without examining the ethical dilemma too closely" (p. 102). In short, the transmitter functions as a metaphor for the dehumanizing effects of the modern world, alienating individuals from their fellow men, dulling moral sensibility, blurring any sense of ethical responsibility.

The Steel Womb, however, also has several more creative effects. Hansard Sub-Two, who had been "this captain, the military man, the man of war" (p. 12), discovers in his ghostly form

> his perfect isolation and aloneness amid the throngs of that city..... He felt a hollowness at the core of his being; he felt a malaise; he felt curiously will-less, as though he had just discovered himself to be an automaton as, in a sense, he had. (p. 56)

Hansard discovers, in other words, the alienation he has been suffering from before without realizing it, and that begins a process of self-discovery, a new understanding of his relations with others which will culminate in marriage, and a new recognition of his moral responsibilities which will culminate in his saving the world. The latter change in Hansard is linked to his coming to terms with his guilt about having years before in Viet Nam incinerated with a flamethrower a four-year-old child. Before, he had dealt with this problem and other disturbing questions with "a policy of deliberate and selective amnesia" (p. 14), but as a result of his underworld experiences Hansard comes to realize, "It wasn't right," and more, "It *isn't* right," and finally that there is something he can do about it (p. 131). In doing so, he brings about even in Panofsky a rejection of the concentration-camp philosophy of merely enduring, surviving, not thinking beyond the day, hiding from, staving off reality; and he turns to a creative attempt to move the world to change. For Panofsky conceives of a way, which both Hansards carry out, of quite literally moving the world, transmitting Earth out from under its orbiting bombs to the opposite side of the sun, saving it from destruction and leaving behind a peaceful Earth Sub-Two, one made, Disch says, in the image of the changed and humanized Hansard Sub-Two.

The epithalamic conclusion is gloriously happy, perhaps a major reason why Clute devotes no more than a single sentence to it, dismissing *Echo* as "another minor work."[18] But the happy conclusion is described in strangely ironic terms: "Love bathes all landscapes in a softening light. It is only ourselves, at our greater distance, with our cooler view, who may feel a little sad to think that the world's loveliness will not always and everywhere bear too close examination" (p. 143). This observation seems to echo Panofsky's concentration-camp philosophy, the earlier Hansard's policy of selective amnesia, and other similar statements throughout the novel. General Pittman on Mars, for example, beginning to contemplate the morality of his impending involvement in genocide, observes, "Sometimes it is the wisest course to step back from too precise a knowledge of consequences" (p. 27). Later the narrator observes at greater length:

> At those rare moments when the skin of the world is peeled away and its substance laid bare before us, the world may assume either of two aspects—benign or malignant. There are those sublime, Wordsworthian moments when Nature appareds herself in celestial light; but there are other moments too, when, with the same trembling sensibility and the same incontrovertible sureness, we see that the fair surface of things— all flesh, these white and scentless blossoms, the rippled surface of the reflecting pool, even the proud sun itself—are but the whiting on the sepulchre within which ... it were best not to look. (p. 39)

In the context of a novel in which the central character does look, however, and acts and changes the world, the apparent advice not to look has an ironic effect. Indeed, back at the end of the novel, having told us not to look too closely at the world's loveliness, Disch goes on:

> However, even that is changing! Even the world will change now and become a better world, milder and mightier, and more humane. There will be power, and power to spare, to do all the things that were so hard to do till now. There will be no more boundaries, but everywhere freedom and unconstraint. There will be no more war. There will be room to move about in, places to go, destinies—all the universe, in fact. What a splendid world! What grand fun it would be to live there!
>
> But it is too late, for we are now quite at the end of *our* story. The rest belongs to them. (p. 143)

This passage illustrates, I think, something of why Clute calls Disch one of the "least trusted" of science fiction writers. He offers this idealized description of a better Earth, reminiscent in many ways of Shelley's *Prometheus Unbound*, then undercuts it with a clear metafictional reminder of its subjunctivity, that this is not our world but only a story. The effect is to leave us with an uneasy doubt: What is the function of such a fantasy? Is this one the product of a jaundiced satirist laughing at our follies, including our dreams of redemption, or of a romantic dreaming that a transformation, a metamorphosis of man into something more decent and humane is possible? The ambiguity is disturbing and, I think, deliberately designed for a subversive purpose, to turn us, in Sartre's words, "to reflection and meditation," to give us "an unhappy consciousness, an unstable image" of ourselves which we will seek "to modify and improve."

If there is any doubt about the subversive purpose of *Echo*, there is little doubt about that of *Camp Concentration* (1968). An external confirmation of that purpose is contained on the copyright page of the 1972 Avon edition. The line indicating the 1968 copyright by Disch which had been present in the 1971 Avon edition has been removed and replaced by one in the name of the American Civil Liberties Union. Apparently Disch transferred the rights to the book to the ACLU. This gesture is appropriate since the book extends the attack seen in the *Echo* on the kind of war culture America seemed to be turning into in the late 1960s.

Camp Concentration is first and most obviously an antiwar novel, but it also probes fundamental questions about science, about the kinds of people who pursue knowledge, and about religion. Moreover, it is an aesthetic *tour de force*, packed with allusions to such literary and philosophical figures as Thomas Aquinas, Dante, Marlowe, Shakespeare, Keats, Kafka, Dostoyevski, Joyce, Baudelaire, Rimbaud, Valery, Camus, Rilke, Mann and many others, all artfully woven into a frighteningly detailed and believable portrait of what American society was, and continues to be, on the edge of becoming. Indeed, attached as it is to a specific time, its allusiveness is part of what places it in the larger context of journeys into the darker recesses of the human imagination, and makes it, I believe, a novel overdue for recognition as a modern classic.

Written during the middle of Lyndon Johnson's last presidential term, when the Viet Nam War was just beginning to betray its worst horrors, Disch projects us an unspecified number of years into a future in which the war has continued and escalated. "President McNamara," no doubt Johnson's former Secretary of

Defense, has just decided to use " 'tactical' nuclear weapons"[19]; "there are parts of the country, the West Coast especially, where because of the germ warfare the handshake is no longer considered good form" (p. 28); and conscientious objectors, popularly known as "conchies," are imprisoned for resisting the war. As our conchie hero Louis Sacchetti (his last name is a portmanteau combination of Sacco and Vanzetti, identifying him as a type of the political prisoner) says, "Damn it, this war is *wrong*" (p. 12).

But it is not the war itself we look at or even the ordinary life of the nation at war. Instead, like Dostoyeski in *House of the Dead*, which Louie, who is also a poet, takes as the model for his first-person narrative, Disch looks at his society from the underworld of a prison. Though we begin in an ordinary prison, we soon move to a secret one (a very literal underworld since it is carved out beneath a mountain) where prisoners are being used in a privately sponsored but government sanctioned experiment to discover how to harness the genius-producing effects of the drug Pallidine. Disch's idea for the drug is inspired first by the speculations that genius and madness are closely related and that syphilis, which has in fact counted among its victims such invidividuals as Gaugin, Nietzshe and Hitler, may in fact induce genius. The idea is also inspired by Thomas Mann's *Doctor Faustus*, the story of a fictional musical genius, Adrian Leverkuhn, which explores the "disquieting share" that "the daemonic and irrational have" in the sphere of genius.[20] The connection with syphilis is also made in Mann's novel: Leverkuhn writes an extended description in his journal of an interview with the devil, implying that the musician's genius is the result both of having sold his soul and of having contracted the disease.[21] Building on these ideas, Disch posits the discovery of a syphilis-like bacillus which causes rapid and dramatic increase in intelligence. But also correspondingly more deadly than syphilis, a long-term degenerative disease, Pallidine kills in only nine months.

The connection with Mann's novel goes deeper than a reference to syphilis and genius. Narrated by Leverkuhn's closest friend, who writes during the last years of World War II, *Doctor Faustus*, first published in 1947, is permeated with a consciousness of what Germany had become in the sixty years since Leverkuhn's birth in 1885; this is a point introduced on the first page of the novel, together with an indication that it is being written from a metaphorical prison: the narrator hopes the book he is writing will "leave our beleagured European fortress and bring to those without some breath of the secrets of our prison-house." Moreover, Mann uses the disease as a metaphor for Germany's moral decay. In Leverkuhn's strange interview with the devil, which took place sometime around 1912, Mephistopheles, anticipating the ideas that will turn Germany into an unprecedented instrument of evil, argues

> that creative, genius-giving disease...is a thousand times dearer to life than plodding healthiness .... A whole host and generation of youth, receptive, sound to the core, flings itself on the work of the morbid genius, made genius by disease: admires it, praises it, exalts it, carries it away, assimilates it unto itself and makes it over to culture .... You will lead the way, you will strike up the march of the future, the lads will swear by your name, who thanks to your madness will no longer need to be mad. On your madness they will feed in health, and in them you will become healthy .... Not only will you break through the paralysing difficulties of the time—you will break through time itself, by which I mean the cultural epoch and its cult, and dare to be barbaric, twice barbaric indeed ....[22]

In a parallel manner, Disch portrays the underground effects of a corrupt American society, perhaps no more than thirty or forty years after the destruction of Nazi Germany, so enamored of scientific breakthrough and military power that it is ready to repeat the barbarisms of the recent past. The fact that experiments which condemn their subjects to death could be officially sanctioned is an indication of the sickness not only of the war society but of certain segments of the scientific community as well, and not just in the world of the novel. Indeed, revelations since the novel was published lend considerable credence to Disch's scientific, political and moral premises: the war would get far worse, the Ellsberg leak of the Pentagon papers would reveal systematic campaigns of misinformation about the war at the highest governmental levels, we would learn of fatal CIA experiments with hallucinogens on unknowing subjects, of cover-ups of gross negligence in experiments with nerve gases, of callous indifference to whole regiments of subjects in experiments with nuclear fallout, of a forty-year-long U.S. Public Health Service experiment with syphilitics, during the last twenty-five years of which a cure for syphilis was available and not administered. Indeed, Disch's metaphor is not only effective but accurate.

At first, however, those responsible seem to be more associated with the military than with science: the camp commander, retired General Humphrey Haast, and the camp psychologist, WAC officer Dr. Aimee Busk. Haast, somewhat famous for having conducted an abortive campaign on a Pacific island during World War II, a campaign he planned with the aid of astrology (p. 52), understands neither art nor science. His understanding of art is revealed in his request that Louie, whose ostensible purpose at the camp is to record his observations of the prisoners, not include any poetry in his journal: "You'll find an appreciative audience for poetry here. But in your journal you must try to make sense" (p. 22).

Science he understands no better. He is attracted, rather, to its magical qualities, like the possibilities, dear also to the sf tradition, of breakthrough. He expects to see the prisoners "break away from the old patterns of thought, blaze trails, *explore*" (p. 50). Like the Gnostics of old, he is enamored of secret knowledge, of mystery. As Louie puts it, "From his Army days Haast has preserved an unswervable faith in the efficacy of secrets: Knowledge is devalued whenever it becomes too generally known" (p. 52). He is therefore easy prey to the prisoners' plot of seeming to revive alchemy as the means of breakthrough while masking a deeper plot to take over the prison, which Louie and the reader do not discover till the novel's end. Haast is especially susceptible to the attraction of the alchemical quest for the elixer of life, for he is a man neurotically afraid of death, a trait revealed in what Louie calls his "fitness":

> I imagine Haast still does twenty push-ups in the morning and rides a few imaginary miles on his Exercycle. The wrinkly crust of his face is crisped to a tasty brown by a sun lamp. His sparse and graying hair is crew cut. He carries to an extreme the maniacal American credo that there is no death. (p. 23)

Haast typifies, therefore, elements not only of the military mind but of the American mind as well in his conception of science as a kind of magic and in his belief that all problems are essentially technological and that science can solve them all. Outside the novel these tendencies are evident in the manner in which generals' dream wishes for incredible capabilities in new tanks and air craft generate impractically complicated machinery and astronomical cost overruns. A more blatant example is the time when then Secretary of Defense McNamara, the real one, announced the beginning of deployment of an electronic "fence" completely around South Viet Nam, linked to artillery batteries and other instruments of death too secret to discuss, so that no living thing could cross the fence and live. What McNamara was dreaming of was, in fact, something right out of sf, a force field, and this connection reveals again an important element in much of Disch's satire on sf: He is aware of how modern sf reflects modern culture, how some of the worst tendencies of the literary subculture of sf—to see human problems as essentially technological and so solveable in technological terms—are dangerously pervasive ways of thinking in our culture as a whole. Indeed, it is Western culture's tendency to think in terms of mechanical and external solutions that produced the Nazi death camps, and the many connections between that attempt at a "final solution" and *Camp Concentration* set the stage for what will become a major theme of the last half of the novel, an examination of the nature of solutions themselves.

While Haast is a type who substitutes a bizarre imagination for intelligence, Dr. Busk is more solidly intellectual, although in ironically misleading ways. Her name, Aimee, suggests love, but she seems totally without compassion, mechanical—"crossing her legs, snick-snack" (p. 31). She functions first as the lying voice of the bureaucracy, describing the secret project as "an investigation of the learning process" prompted by a recognition of the "importance of education with respect to the national defense effort" (p. 32). Its purpose is "to exploit that most precious resource, the mind, as it has never been exploited before" (p. 33). Except for the disturbing word "exploit," the innocuousness of her language masks the fact that she lies egregiously. At this point, although we have observed symptoms of bad health in a few prisoners, neither Louie nor the reader knows that the prisoners, all infected with Pallidine, have only a few months or less to live (we won't discover this until a third of the way through the novel, p. 55). Nor do we know that Louie himself is not in fact merely an observer but was infected early in the novel (p. 15) when he and the reader were distracted by the news of the publication and favorable review of a book of his poetry (some may suspect earlier, but we won't learn for sure of his infection until nearly two-thirds of the way through the novel—p. 107). Busk, however, a knowing party to these lies, in her first interview with Louie appeals to his sense of truth: she asks him to "dispense with ... hypocrisy," to help her establish "an honest, if not altogether pleasant, relationship." "*Do* let us be candid, Mr. Sacchetti," she says as preface to her misleading explanation of the project (p. 31). Indeed, the only part of her conversation that reveals any candor is her revelation of how thoroughly the government knows Louie:

> We know you inside and out. Your schools, relatives, friends, what you've read, where you've been .... We know every girl you dated at Bard and afterward, and just how far you got with each .... We know, in considerable detail, just how much you've earned during the last fifteen years, and how you've spent it. Any time the government cares to, it can send you right back to Springfield on tax evasion charges. We have the records from your two years of psychotherapy. (p. 34)

Only a few years after *Camp Concentration* was first published, it would be revealed that such invasions of privacy and worse were standard ways of dealing with dissenters and not, as most people thought, the delusions of paranoids or the nightmares of dystopian sf writers.

Haast and Busk together epitomize those personalities, both silly and cruel, who, fostered and placed in power by a nation dominated by a war mentality, make of that whole nation a prison. But *Camp Concentration* takes us beyond the problems of any particular nation into deeper philosophical waters, into more universal kinds of sickness and prison. The vehicle for our passage into those deeper waters is the central action of the novel, the temptation of Louis Sacchetti.

Louie has just turned thirty-five years of age, "Nel mezzo del camin di nostra vita indeed," he writes, quoting the opening line of Dante's *Divine Comedy* and setting the tone for the infernal journey to follow. He is a scholar-poet, a Catholic who like Daedalus/Joyce has gone through a period of apostasy, "saying *Non serviam*," but who unlike Joyce is again a practicing Catholic, and a conchie: "I say *Non serviam* to Caesar rather than to God" (p. 14). His first tempter is himself, his own cynical alter ego, "my double, Louie II," a similar but more sophisticated vehicle for portraying internal conflict than the subscripted Hansards of *Echo Round His Bones*. Louie II was "in sole possession of my soul" during Sacchetti's period of apostasy twenty years before, and even now he appears for short periods of time like the morning early in the novel when Louie II appears in his shaving mirror and "mocked and raged and muddied the banner of faith, not to mention hope (already quite muddy these days), with his scurrilities" (p. 14).

Part of what Disch does is take the traditional sf theme of the conflict between science and religion and place it in a more broadly traditional context, both philosophically and literarily, with the aid of Louie's Catholic background and the allusions to Joyce. Like Daedalus, Louis is warned to "beware of intellectual pride," which he interprets, "Meaning, I have always supposed, beware of intellect." Louie's conflict, therefore, becomes one between faith and knowledge: "How to distinguish between righteousness and self-will? Between the two Louies? How, once committed [to faith], to stop *questioning*? (That is the question.)" (pp. 14-15).

A second level of temptation is Louie's struggle against his sense of the futility of his dissent:

> If persuasion were so easy a task, perhaps the few voices of righteousness might hope to have some effect. But it is a fact that not I nor anyone I've known on the Committee for a Unilateral Peace has ever

> convinced anyone of the folly and immorality of this war who was not at heart already of like mind, who needed no convincing but only our reassurance. (p. 17)

This is the same question that in a comic context faced Tennyson White in *The Puppies of Terra* and on a more serious level faced the artists and writers of 1930s Germany and 1960s America. Louie considers the choices:

> Abandon controversy that I may consecrate my talents exclusively to the Muses.
> And my soul, then, to the Devil?
> No, though opposition is a hopeless task, acquiescence would be worse. (p. 17)

Once transferred to the secret base, Camp Archimedes, Louie's temptation does not begin immediately. Haast reveals something of the national folly, but the general, too fatuous to offer any serious temptation, functions more as comic relief. Busk presents more serious problems, especially after Louie learns, appropriately enough right after the prisoners' production of Marlowe's *Faustus*, that the prisoners are all dying from an experimental drug. "Why that's the price all good men must pay for knowledge," says prisoner Mordecai Washington. "That's what comes of eating magic apples" (p. 54), words which link the experiment with the primal temptation. In an interview with Busk which follows, Louie is not moved by her initial justifications, which smack of public relations cliches: "Throughout its history, medical research has paid for its progress with the blood of martyrs" (p. 58). But she seems to hit a nerve when she analyzes the nature of genius and how Pallidine functions. She describes "what actually takes place *in the brain* at the moment that an Archimedes says, 'Eureka!' " as "a sort of breakdown—literally, the mind disintegrates, and the old, distinct categories are for a little while fluid and capable of re-formation" (p. 62), a process that Pallidine accelerates. The problem for Louie is her arguments, echoing those of the devil in Mann's *Doctor Faustus*, connecting genius and disease: "thought itself," she argues, "is a disease of the brain, a degenerative condition of matter"; creativity is "a disintegrative process"; "genius, like the clap, is a social disease, and we take action accordingly. We put all our geniuses in one kind or another of isolation ward, to escape being infected" (pp. 63-64). If this is indeed the case, the experiment is not only as barbarously inhumane, it is as useless as the experiments performed in Nazi death camps.

The degree to which Sacchetti is moved by these revelations is indicated by the fact that the next journal entry comes from the hand of Louis II, who argues that "there is nothing but an aching emptiness at the center of things," that "There is no God, there never was, and never will be, world without end, amen" (p. 65). Louie I, when he returns, has no answer except a lament—"Alone and unhoused, I lack grace: That is all that is the matter"—and a prayer—"O God, simplify these equations!" (p. 66). But sure enough, things get worse.

Louie's next major temptation comes in the person of Mordecai Washington, the unofficial leader of the prisoners and the originator of their alchemical project to produce the elixir of life. He is black, formerly a weak student and an anonymous highschool classmate of Louie, and in some ways a cruder Louie II: "Fuck faith, and fuck your epigrams" (p. 39). At their first meeting Mordecai is introduced as a temptor, but at this point he inspires only a mild doubt in Louie: "Perhaps the conservatives are right, perhaps free thought *is* dangerous" (p. 46). His primary effect is to strike Louie with a mixture of Keatsian/aesthetic and theological awe: "Like some watcher of the skies/ When a new planet swims into his ken. The morning star. Lucifer, prince of darkness. Tempter" (p. 46). His major temptation, however, does not occur until after the *Faustus* production—in which Mordecai appropriately enough plays Mephistopheles—and after Louie learns about the prisoners' impending deaths. As Louie struggles to come to terms with this revelation and Busk's arguments, Mordecai argues that everyone is "marked for extermination": "it isn't just Camp Archimedes. It's the whole universe. The whole goddamned universe is a fucking concentration camp" (p. 72). The Pope did not protest the Nazi's ovens, Mordecai says, because "Pius sensed that the deathcamps were the nearest approximation that mortal man has yet made to the Almighty's plan. God is Eichmann writ large" (pp. 78-79).

Mordecai, in other words, has developed another version of the concentration-camp philosophy we saw in *Echo*. Indeed, Mordecai is a domestic version of Panofsky; raised in the prisons of his race and his ignorance, he moved to the prison of the Army, thence to a literal prison for assualting an officer, and finally, volunteering for an experiment to get out of the brig, to Camp Archimedes. Rather than just getting by from day to day, however, Mordecai rejects the world: "I'm not *interested* in a universe in which I have to die .... I choose escape. I choose freedom." And his manner of escape is, "as Lucifer well knew ... by thumbing one's nose at ... the warden of this prison-universe" (p. 78) and by the Faustian means of seeking forbidden knowledge, his experiments to synthesize the elixir of life.

Those efforts seem to come to a disastrous conclusion on the evening of Mordecai's "magnum opus," a bizarre scene enacted on the still unstruck set of the *Faustus* production. In an elaborate pseudo-Eucharistic ritual adapted from alchemical writings, Haast, who must be the first to achieve immortality, and Mordecai, who is already near death from the degenerative effects of Palladine, both wired to a device ostensibly designed to accelerate the elixir's effect, drink the magic fluid. The device is turned on, and Mordecai, crying "Black! The blackness! All, all Black!" dies (p. 101).

The results are nearly as disastrous for Louie, who is sufficiently affected by Mordecai's death to suffer a relevatory dream that night. An obese Thomas Aquinas, in an obscene parody of the Eucharist and the Mad Hatter's tea party from *Alice*, is the vehicle by which Louie finally recognizes what he had been subconsciously aware of for some time but had refused to face: he is not at the camp merely as an observer but has himself been infected with the deadly spirochete. Having eaten of the magic apples, he is fallen. Part I of the novel ends with Louie realizing that he is not a Dante passing through this Inferno, he is one of the damned.

Since his infection, Louie has been showing signs of increasing intelligence, manifested especially in new poetic works he has produced. The night after the revelation that the prisoners are infected, he writes "The Hierodule," a poem in comparison to which "everything else I've done is dross" (p. 56). Only five days later he refers to this poem as "that recent thundergush of rodomontade" (p. 82), and, inspired "by Mordecai's blasphemies," he announces the beginning of "my own magnum opus," *Auschwitz: A Comedy*. This is completed only four days later, the morning of Mordecai's abortive experiment. A further stage of his development is manifest in the first few pages of Part II of the novel.

With Part II Louie abandons the dated journal format of Part I and shifts to a series of fragments separated only by asterisks. These fragments, covering pages 111-120, are a disjointed mixture illustrating a point Busk had made earlier about the danger of genius:

> And then think of what happens if genius *doesn't* reign itself in but insists on plunging ahead into the chaos of freest association. I'm thinking of that hero of you literateurs, James Joyce. I know any number of psychiatrists who could, in good conscience, have accepted *Finnegan Wakes* [sic] as the very imprimatur of madness .... (Disch's *sic*, p. 63)

Though no direct imitation of *Finnegans Wake*, Louie's fragments, material for an extended explication themselves, illustrate the blurring of that distinction between genius and madness, mixing images developed earlier in a bewildering virtuoso performance prefaced by an acknowledgment that what follows is lacking in Haast's demand for "factoricity" and by a brief justification: "My only excuse—that hell is murky" (p. 111). In answer to a more vigorous insistence on facts from Haast, Louie returns to a more intelligible style, rejecting, however, the journal format of dated entries—"Though my days are numbered, I will not abet their number" (p. 121).

With Mordecai now dead, Haast slipping into the background, and Busk having disappeared—we find out later she has gone AWOL—a new tempter emerges, a nuclear physicist named Skilliman, who represents an extreme even greater than Mordecai, of both the Faustian and the Mephistophelean. Working for the same corporation for which Haast is director of Research and Development, Skilliman managed to penetrate the security surrounding the Camp Archimedes project: "Once he understood the nature of the drug and had convinced himself of its effectiveness, he insisted on being injected with it himself" (p. 124). A charismatic figure in demonic perversion of Christ, he has brought with him twelve disciples, "former students or assistants, who have, quite willingly, volunteered for the Pallidine" (p. 125). Exhibiting the "Faustian urge to secure knowledge at any price" (p. 125), Skilliman's genuine genius is linked with Satanic qualities like a general dislike of people, a preference for scatalogical humor, a contempt for beauty, and a passion for destruction. In illustration of the latter, he says, "We must rid ourselves of the old pointillist notions of bombing—of individual, discrete 'bombs.' Rather we must strive now for a more generalized notion of *bombiness*, a sort of aura. I envision it as something like the sunrise" (p. 128). As Louie says, "He quests the grail of Armegeddon" (p. 135). Another project he envisions is "a sort of geologic bomb .... He wants to lift new mountain ranges from the earth. The Faustian urge is always toward the giddy heights" (p. 142).

Skilliman's temptation of Louie, however, is indirect and takes the medieval form of a psychomachia, a battle for the soul of one of Skilliman's disciples, Schipansky. Louie and Skilliman correspond to the contestants in the original *Psychomachia* by the fourth-century Christian Latin poet Prudentius, in which Christ and Satan contend for the soul of Man. Schipansky is a type of the scientist different from Skilliman, a seeker after knowledge not for power but for its own sake. His type is familiar especially to anyone who has attended a science and engineering college: "he has that look of perpetual adolescence so common to science swots: a scant gangling body, a pallid face, acne, hair just too long to be called crew cut, too short to lie flat" (pp. 145-146). The fact that this is also a battle for Louie's soul is suggested by Louie's recognition of himself in Schpansky: "I begin to wonder if I am limning Schipansky's features or my own. He comes to seem more and more a nightmare image of myself, or that aspect of Louis Sacchetti that Mordecai as long ago as our school days dubbed 'Donovan's Brain' " (p. 146).

But unlike Louie, Schipansky has an undeveloped moral imagination. When Shipansky tells Louie about his work on Skilliman's geologic bomb project, Louie touches, "ever so gently, on the possible moral implications of such researches . . . . Schipansky froze into near catatonia" (p. 142). But his curiosity is aroused, and he approaches Louie, who begins to prod his conscience: "What a career I missed," Louie muses, "in not becoming a Jesuit. Next to an out-and-out seduction, there is no game quite so absorbing at this of convert making" (p. 145). Indeed, in the context of a Jesuitical—i.e., intellectual—approach to conversion, Pallidine is an ally: "Like most of his contemporaries, S's attitude to history is one of peeved impatience. Its vast absurdities have no power as exempla. But it is difficult, especially with the gold of Pallidine in one's veins, to remain such a perfect ostrich as that" (p. 147).

But the limitations of an intellectual basis for conversion are made apparent when the psychomachia comes to a climax. Skilliman, learning of Schipansky's weakening, confronts him and Louie: "Skilliman took a seat, opposite me, with the contested soul between us" (p. 150). In a scornful monologue, Skilliman challenges Louie to "tell us about *values* and why we should buy some" (p. 151). Power and knowledge, he argues, are meaningless without love, which is itself no more than a biological phenomenon, and all three merge into their opposites, impotence, ignorance and hate. Indeed, impotence seems to sum up the universe and point to the one tangible value remaining, death:

> Not just your own individual and possibly insignificant death, but a death of universal dimensions. Oh, perhaps not the heat-death at the end of time—that would be asking too much—but a death that would advance that cause almost perceptibly.
> An end, Sacchetti, to the whole shitty human race. What do you say, my boy—will you buy that? (p. 154).

Skilliman expresses a desire much like that of the extreme nihilist in

Camus' *The Rebel*, who, wishing for death, is not satisfied with suicide or even murder, but must have genocide. The ultimate solution to the problem of being human is, after all, extermination. And the frightening thing, what Skilliman calls "the exciting thing,"

> is that it's altogether possible. It's possible to make weapons of absolutely god-like power. We can blow this little world apart the way we used to explode tomatoes with firecrackers. We only have to make the weapons and give them to our dear governments. They can be counted on to carry the ball from there.

To such an argument Louie has only silence for an answer, which impresses neither Schipansky nor himself. "But what reply might I have made?" he asks himself in all honesty. "Skilliman dared to say what we all dread may be so, and even Christ, finally, had no better argument for his Tempter than *Go Away!*" (p. 155).

Left alone, on the edge of despair himself, Louie picks up work on his latest project, a Museum of Facts, modeled after Ripley, which displays a set of newspaper clippings reporting unusual happenings: charismatic new religious leaders, unprecedented runs of luck at the gaming tables in Las Vegas, bewilderingly ingenious crimes, incredible achievements in sports. At the museum's opening it does not take the prisoners long to realize that Pallidine is at large. Dr. Aimee Busk, apparently having gotten herself infected in an unnatural relationship with Mordecai, escaped to infect the nation. Busk herself was a Lesbian, and it is not surprising that "the facts in my museum did show a preponderance of 'breakthroughs' in just those areas where homosexuality is thickest: the arts, sports, fashion, religion, and sex crimes" (p. 159).

It is a situation which, even Haast should realize, demands nothing less than a full, public revelation of the danger. But days pass, no hints appear in the media, and "a spectacular debacle" looms: "With 30 percent civilian casualties, an industrial society simply cannot *cohere.* . . . Consider the sheer disruptive force of so much undirected intelligence suddenly set loose . . . . it is exactly the people essential to stability who are likely to become infected" (pp. 160-161). Louie's despair deepens as his body's decay accelerates, rendering him blind, and he is haunted by the words of Thomas Nashe's "A Litany in Time of Plague."

But Schipansky is not lost, after all. If the intellectual approach could only undermine his complaisance, the ground for a more successful conversion was already present in him, an appreciation of the aesthetic as it is embodied in music. Schipansky is a lover of

music, especially the moderns, most especially the work of Olivier
Messiaen, generally considered the father of the French avant-
garde, one of whose earliest works, "Quartet for the End of Time,"
appropriately enough for Disch's novel, was written while he was a
prisoner of war in 1941 in Silesia. But it is not this work to which
Disch first alludes but to Messiaen's later (1964) *Et expecto
resurrectionen mortuorum* (p. 147), a work whose title anticipates
the novel's conclusion. Since Skilliman's satanic monologue
Schipansky has been wrestling with his conscience, and he returns
to Louie with three others of Skilliman's assistants and with an
explanation of what he has learned: "I kept telling myself I had to
find a *reason*. But [as Skilliman himself taught him and as Kant
argued long before] reasons always come in pairs—pro and contra,
thesis and antithesis, perfectly matched." The only answer—Kant
would call it transcendental—Schipansky describes as "a
completely irrational consideration." Listening to an aria from a
Richard Strauss opera, he thinks, "if only I could sing like that! I
suppose it's impossible, of course, considering my age and
everything. But I really wanted that .... And that must have been
what I'd been waiting for, because afterward there just didn't seem
to be a dilemma" (p. 165).

Schipansky's conversion, however, is not a Christian one. He
has undergone something like a modern existentialist's version of
Coleridge's Ancient Mariner blessing the water snakes. Caught in
an unpremeditated act of love and self-affirmation, he discovers the
ability to affirm life, the albatross of circular reasoning and
meaninglessness drops from his neck, and a sense of value in life
follows. And again, Disch's allusion is perfect: the Strauss opera is
Die Frau Ohne Schatten (1919), a story adapted from (and by) Hugo
von Hofmannstahl about death and resurrection and about a
"daughter of the spirits" who earns a human soul by a sacrificial act
performed in a subterranean vault. But it is not until the novel's
climactic and controversial conclusion that Louie undergoes his
own conversion.

Skilliman, outraged that Louie has now suborned six of his
disciples, together with Haas brings Louie up to the mountain-top
surface so that there in private he can convince Haast to kill Louie.
For Louie it is a renewing journey from rational abstraction, again
somewhat like the Ancient Mariner, back to nature:

> Air!
> And beneath my slippered feet not the Euclidean spareness of
> concrete but the unaccustomed and various-textured earth. I cannot say

> just what I did, whether I cried aloud, or if tears fell from my blind eyes, or how long I continued with my face pressed against the cold rock. I was beside myself. I felt such a degree of happiness as I had never felt in my life before: because this was the actual air and undoubted rock of the world from which, so many months before, I'd been removed. (p. 170)

With Haast's permission, Skilliman takes a guard's gun, faces Louie, then shoots not at him but at the stars; seven shots ring out, and with each, Louie says, "my happiness seemed to bound to a new dimension. *Alive!* I thought. *I am alive.*" With the seventh shot, we learn a moment later, Haast kills Skilliman. Appropriately enough Skilliman aimed, Haast says, "for Orion's belt," a constellation whose appearance is associated with the coming of spring. "You weren't, in the showdown," Haast explains, "a big enough target, Louie, for the considerable grandeur of his spite" (p. 172).

This situation and Louie's response are remarkably similar to and no doubt modeled on a major conversion experience undergone by Dostoyevski, his well-known mock execution. Condemned to death for revolutionary activities, Dostoyevski's sentence was commuted by the Czar to a number of years in prison, but the commutation arrived with special instructions that the prisoner was not to be informed until the last possible moment. He therefore went through the agony of his last night alive and was even marched before the firing squad before the commutation was read. His response was not, however, gratitude to the Czar but an intense sense of rebirth, an almost visionary perception of the world as though it were seen for the first time, and an ecstatic love of life in which it was delight merely to draw breath. And like Dostoyevski before him, Louie discovers that all questions of good and evil boil down to the affirmation or denial of life and that all value is based on the experience of loving life itself. Like Schipansky, however, and unlike Dostoyevski, Louie's conversion does not seem to take a Christian turn.

But Louie's life is not merely momentarily reprieved, and this is what has occasioned controversy. It turns out that the prisoners, under the guise of their alchemical researches, had in fact developed "a mind reciprocator," that Haast is in fact Mordecai, whose magnum opus was successful after all, achieving the exchange of his mind with Haast's, who died in Mordecai's body. Moreover, Louie, together with a guard who had been sadistically torturing him, is strapped into the machine before he realizes what is happening and is given in trade a healthy body. In Clute's words, this is "an sf ending which has been sharply criticized as a begging of the issues raised."[23] I would argue on the contrary that it is a brilliant ending that works on multiple levels.

Looked at in terms of plot, the ending offers that combination of surprise and honest inevitability we admire in the detective novel. The choice of point of view justifies the information withheld, while the conclusion is prepared for with numerous hints and foreshadowings artfully placed throughout the novel. Mordecai even wrote a novella, *Portrait of Pompanianus*, about a mad genius striken with syphilis, Flemish artist Hugo van der Goes, a type of both Mordecai and Louie, who dies and is resurrected by the devil, to whom he had sold his soul for "three years of supreme mastery as a painter" (p. 83).

Looked at thematically, the ending, rather than beg the issues the novel raises, fulfills them. Far from giving us simple or convenient answers, the "happy" ending is clouded by numerous ironies and ambiguities. When Louie was being strapped into the machine, he writes later, "I must by then have realized, if whisperingly, what was afoot, and I must hold myself to blame for the consequences" (p. 172). Louie's salvation is therefore mixed with guilt; he is still fallen, not so much redeemed as reprieved. His guilt is ironically intensified, moreover, by the fact that his seemingly saintly behavior in opposing Skilliman had inspired three prisoners before him who had more time to think about it, "to forgo 'resurrection'! Each chose to die his own death rather than condemn someone else to it" (p. 174). Though work procedes apace on a vaccine and "hope shines bravely" that disaster will be averted, there are no guarantees. In fact, part of Skilliman's argument is confirmed: the only ultimate solution to the problem of being human is extermination, for breakthrough at its best creates a new set of conditions in which the same agonizing questions of value and responsibility have to be faced anew. And in facing them, "There is terror too. Behind the mask of Haast/Mordecai's face lurks the dark knowledge of another, further-off future, of a height beyond the first rosy peaks, of a coldness and strangeness extreme as death" (p. 175). If disturbing shades of Mephistopheles remain in Mordecai, Louie's resemblance to Christ seems to disappear: "I exist without instincts, almost without images; and I no longer have an aim. I resemble nothing. The poison has had not two effects—genius and death—but one. Call it by which name you will" (p. 175).

What Disch has done thematically is combine the modern sf tradition with the philosophical and literary traditions of modernism. Unlike the antiscientific strain of humanists, he does not reject science and the quest for knowledge. Evil, rather, is in the Faustian urge to seek knowledge *at any price*, irresponsibly. As

Samuel Delany has said, the major concern of *Camp Composition*, and of sf in general, is "the human responsibility that comes with the acquisition of knowledge."[24] But Disch sees the responsibility in the broadest terms, terms that begin with Nietzsche. Liberated from traditional values and gods, truly modern man must face the terrible responsiblity of creating value. That is why at the end Louie resembles not so much Christ as Zarathustra. Add to this the twentieth-century vision of the prison-universe and the discovery of technologies that give man truly god-like power, and we can see how these ideas merge into Disch's central metaphors, the concentration camp and the prisoners' breakthrough. These are metaphors for modernity itself and for the discovery that the universe may in fact be a prison but that mankind *must* choose to be its wardens. Moreover, the spread of the disease beyond the camp emphasizes the need that this responsibility be widespread. The Faustian dimensions of knowledge, the irresponsible search for and application of it, are most likely to be manifest when it is secret, and if it is dangerous to make this knowledge available to all, the result can be no worse than when it was available only to the likes of Haast, Busk, Skilliman and their prisoners. The novel's end suggests clearly that the very survival of the human race depends on whether man has the intelligence to recognize and the courage to assume this responsibility. Disch concludes, therefore, not with a spectacular debacle but with questions and possibilities, presented in a tone both exhilarating and frightening, and summed up in Mordecai's closing words: "Much that is terrible we do not know. Much that is beautiful we shall still discover. Let's sail till we come to the edge."

Looked at in terms of structure, the ending is appropriate to a novel structurally comic, in the medieval or Dantean sense. We descend into hell and work our way out, but it is a modern, a secular, not a divine comedy. There is no "Paradiso," and Louie's image of "another, further-off future, of a height beyond the first rosy peaks," suggests that the top of the mountain containing Camp Archimedes, to which we climb with Louie, is at best the base of a long sequence of purgatorial mountains yet to be scaled.

This analyis of the conclusion to *Camp Concentration* has brought us inevitably to the major concerns of the whole novel and to the thesis of this study, Disch's success in uniting the literary traditions that have gone before him. In fact, by means of the mad artist in Mordecai's novella, Disch raises this question obliquely and suggests something of his own position at this stage of his development. For van der Goes also explores "the nature and purpose of art":

> Van der Goes' initial thesis is the one commonly held: that art should
> *mirror* reality. He cannot resolve how this may best be done—whether by
> the microscopic renderings and jewel-like tones of the Flemish school or
> by the Italianate mastery of space and plastic forms. Gradually,
> however, as he gains the promised mastery and achieves a synthesis of
> these two styles, his concern is no longer to mirror reality but (under the
> devil's instigation) to *compel* it. Art metamorphoses into magic. (p. 83)

Not only does this passage suggest the synthesis of styles we have
been describing in Disch—the union of Naturalism, aestheticism
and sf—it also suggests his concern for moving the world. Looked at
in these terms, even the sf device, the mind reciprocator, may be of
central symbolic importance: it represents, perhaps, art itself in
those romantic/modernist terms that idealize a "poetry of
experience,"[25] an art which communicates not merely thoughts and
feelings but the self and the experiential ground from which its ideas
and passions emerge. At its most successful this kind of art would
move the reader so deeply, transfer the artist's vision so fully, that it
would be to the reader as though he has changed minds with the
artist.

As I have argued elsewhere, sf can be seen as having
recapitulated within the last half century the last three hundred
years or so of cultural history.[26] This is a conclusion drawn from
looking at sf in terms of the history of ideas. A parallel kind of
conclusion can be drawn from looking at sf in terms of the history of
style. It has become commonplace in recent years to describe sf in
terms of its wedding of the traditions, and I would like to emphasize
the *stylistic* traditions, of realism and romance.[27] This is indeed an
accurate description of most sf, especially most sf until—with the
exception of an occasional maverick like David Lindsay—the 1960s.
But to say this is to suggest that most sf has dwelt stylistically in the
nineteenth century. Thus, J.G. Ballard, who has so often been
compared to Conrad anyway, exemplifies in sf the late nineteenth
century adaptation of the European symbolist tradition to fiction.
Similarly, Michael Moorcock turns the century stylistically for us by
wedding sf to a Wildean aestheticism. Disch takes us fully into the
twentieth century with his Joycean combination of Naturalism and
aestheticism, recast in sf forms, adapted to contemporary themes,
and merged with a later twentieth century social consciousness in
ways that preserve Joyce's ideal of the dramatic artist.

To point this out is not to suggest that such writers are mere
imitators, for each has placed his own indelible stamp on the
traditions he has exploited and each has contributed significantly
to the range of modern fiction generally and of sf in particular. Nor

are such comparisons meant to be limited to these three writers. Thomas Clareson, for instance, has pointed out the links in terms of Naturalism between Steinbeck, Farrel and Dos Passos on the one hand and certain works by Brunner, Silverberg and Herbert on the other.[28] And there are no doubt many more such links. Indeed, these relationships with earlier mainstream writers reveal the literary sophistication of today's best sf writers. I can think, for instance, of no exploration of the city of the future before Disch's *334* (1974) which can be compared as seriously, in terms of both style and contemporary significance, with the exploration of the modern city in Joyce's *Dubliners* or indeed in *Ulysses*. Nor should such comparisons be taken to limit such writers. Disch's latest novel, *On Wings of Song* (1979), has yet to suggest an apt comparison to me. There is certainly a great deal of work yet to be done on a writer as richly rewarding as Disch.

Notes

[1]Samuel Delany, *The American Shore: Meditations on a Tale of Science Fiction by Thomas M. Disch* (Elizabethtown, N.Y.: Dragon Press, 1978).

[2]John Clute, "Thomas M. Disch," in *The Science Fiction Encyclopedia*, ed. Peter Nicholls (Garden City, N.Y.: Doubleday, 1979), p. 174.

[3]Erich Rupprecht, "Thomas M. Disch," *Dictionary of Literary Biography*, vol. 8, *Twentieth Century American Science Fiction Writers*, eds. David Cowart and Thomas L. Wymer (Detroit: Gale Research, 1981), Part I, pp. 148-155.

[4]*The Early Fiction of Thomas M. Disch*, Introduction by Robert Thurston; *The Genocides*, Introduction by David G. Hartwell; *334*, Introduction by M. John Harrison (Boston: Gregg Press, 1977, 1978, 1976, respectively).

[5]James Joyce, *A Portrait of the Artist as a Young Man* (New York: Viking, 1968), p. 215.

[6]Robert Scholes, *Structural Fabulation: An Essay on Fiction of the Future* (Notre Dame and London: Univ. of Notre Dame Press, 1975), p. 29.

[7]*Galaxy*, Dec. 1966, p. 128.

[8]Ibid., p. 130.

[9]*The Early Science Fiction of Thomas M. Disch*, p. 3.

[10]Clute, p. 173.

[11]*The Puppies of Terra* in *The Early Science Fiction of Thomas M. Disch*, p. 197; all subsequent quotations from *Puppies* will be cited in text from this edition.

[12](Lincoln: Univ. of Nebraska Press, 1959), p. 13.

[13]Joyce, *Portrait*, p. 253.

[14](London: Hart-Davis, 1969; London: Panther, 1979).

[15]Thomas M. Disch, *Echo Round His Bones* (New York: Berkley, 1967), p. 12; all subsequent quotations from *Echo* will be cited in text from this edition.

[16]Joyce, *Portrait*, p. 221.

[17]Ibid., p. 238.

[18]Clute, p. 173.

[19]Thomas M. Disch, *Camp Concentration* (New York: Avon, 1971), p. 11; all subsequent quotations from *Camp Concentration* will be cited in text from this edition.

[20]Thomas Mann, *Doctor Faustus*, tr.H.T. Lowe-Porter (New York: Knopf, 1948), p. 4.

[21]Ibid.; the journal entry takes up the whole of Chapter XXV, pp. 221-250; see especially pp. 231 ff.

[22]Ibid., pp. 242-243.

[23]Clute, p. 173.

[24]Samuel R. Delany, *The Jewel-Hinged Jaw: Notes on the Language of Science Fiction* (Elizabethtown, N.Y.: Dragon Press, 1977), p. 200.

[25]See Robert A. Langbaum, *The Poetry of Experience* (New York: Random House, 1957).

[26]Thomas L. Wymer, "Perception and Value in Science Fiction," in *Many Futures, Many Worlds: Theme and Form in Science Fiction*, ed. Thomas D. Clareson (Kent, Ohio: Kent State University Press, 1977), pp. 1-13.

[27]See especially Thomas D. Clareson, "The Other Side of Realism," in *SF: The Other Side of Realism*, ed. Clareson (Bowling Green, Ohio: The Popular Press, 1971), pp. 1-28.

[28]Thomas D. Clareson, "Many Futures, Many Worlds," in *Many Futures, Many Worlds*, pp. 14-15.

Contributors

Thomas D. Clareson of The College of Wooster (Ohio) has edited *Extrapolation* since 1959. He has just completed *Robert Silverberg: A Primary and Secondary Bibliography* to be published in 1983 by G.K. Hall and *Robert Silverberg,* a monograph for Starmont House. He received the Pilgrim Award from SFRA in 1977.

Horton Presley, now with the English Department at Dalton Junior College (Ga.), has returned from an appointment at Hong Kong Baptist University. He was a founder of the MLA Seminar on Science Fiction.

Douglas Robillard, Department of English, University of New Haven, is editor of the journal *Essays in Arts and Sciences*. In 1981 he devoted a special issue to a Symposium on modern science fiction. He is currently working on a study of Murray Leinster.

David N. Samuelson, Department of English, University of California-Long Beach, has published extensively in the field of science fiction, including the first volumes of *Voices for the Future*. He is completing a bibliography of Arthur C. Clarke.

Joe Sanders, Department of Communications, Lakeland Community College, is an established reviewer of science fiction. Among his critical works is a study of Roger Zelazny.

Jane Weedman, Department of English, Texas Tech University, is perhaps best known for her recent study, *Samuel R. Delany,* published in 1982 by Starmont House.

Carol T. Williams is a member of the Department of Humanities, Roosevelt University, Chicago.

Gary K. Wolfe, Department of Humanities, Roosevelt University, Chicago has published widely in the field of science fiction criticism. His major work to date is *The Known and the Unknown: The Iconography of Science Fiction* (1979).

Thomas L. Wymer, Department of English, Bowling Green State University, has published widely in science fiction criticism. Most recently he co-edited the volume on *Twentieth Century American Science Fiction Writers* for the Dictionary of Literary Biography (1981) and wrote an article on Vonnegut for *The Mechanical God: Machines in Science Fiction* (1982).